## Praise for *Climate Cure*

"Weber's brilliant book offers a unique and integrated prescription for personal and global transformation in the face of the most threatening cataclysm humanity has ever faced. Read this book to heal your life and to become a deeply passionate and compassionate global citizen, what Weber poignantly calls 'becoming medicine for our times.'"

—Andrew Harvey, author of *Teachings of Rumi* and *The Hope*

"Weber addresses what climate change and other planet-saving books often fail to address: healing the world begins deep inside us. This guidebook offers sound psychological advice and spiritual inspiration for how to regenerate our planet from the inside out."

—David Richo, PhD, author of *When the Past is Present*

"For what is arguably the most critical issue facing sentient life everywhere, Weber presents a passionate, yet grounded portrayal of what it means to be a human being who has been gifted with a sacred home....Weber is a clear, thoughtful, and provocative thinker who takes on the issue of climate change from a place of depth and integral vision, at once psychologically sophisticated, emotionally mature, and spiritually inspiring. An important contribution to the modern call to balance the true urgency of our predicament with a poetic hope for the Earth and her creatures."

—Matt Licata, PhD, author of *The Path is Everywhere*
and *A Friend of the Breath*

"Climate Cure offers a feast of nutrients for soul enrichment and the energy-dense fuel required for driving the engine of sacred activism....Weber plants and cultivates a massive tree-like structure from which sprout tendrils and solid branches of insight that reveal our personal and cultural wounds. He then applies the healer's loving touch to restore wholeness on both the personal and planetary levels."

—Carolyn Baker, PhD, author of *Collapsing Consciously*

"Climate Cure contains a vital message—that inner activism is essential to regenerate not only ourselves but also the environment. Through beautiful prose and inspiring poems, Jack Adam Weber motivates us to health by using pain as an alchemical cauldron for change, teaching that this process is the fierce spirituality that 'knits us and the world back together.'"

—Dr. Michael Tierra, OMD, ND, author of *Planetary Herbology*, and Lesley Tierra, LAc, author of *Healing with the Herbs of Life*

"A passionately articulate call to a deeper life; a life of uncompromising ecological attunement not only outwardly but also inwardly."

—Robert Augustus Masters, PhD, author of *Transformation Through Intimacy*, *Spiritual Bypassing*, and *To Be a Man*

"We are experiencing massive change in the world that is frightening, confusing, and disorienting. Jack Adam Weber offers unique insights that help us all effectively address the impact of these changes as individuals and members of an interconnected planetary community. I highly recommend this book."

—Jed Diamond, PhD, author of *Stress Relief for Men*

"Climate Cure is a deeply thoughtful, reflective, compassionate, well-crafted message of optimism and hope for humanity in the face of planetary adversity and existential uncertainty. This is an important book!"

—Efrem Korngold, OMD, LAc, coauthor of *Between Heaven and Earth*

"Brilliant! An eloquent and raw look at our inner and outer worlds at this unprecedented time in human history."

—David Bruce Leonard, LAc, founder of Earth Medicine Institute

# CLIMATE
# CURE

## About the Author

Jack Adam Weber, L.Ac., is a Chinese medicine clinician with over twenty years of experience after having graduated valedictorian of his class in 2000. He is also a climate activist, organic farmer, and celebrated poet. Jack has authored hundreds of articles, thousands of poems, and several books. He is an advocate for embodied spirituality and writes extensively on the subjects of holistic medicine, emotional depth work, mind-body integration, and climate crisis, while encouraging his readers to think critically, feel deeply and act boldly. Jack also developed the Nourish Practice, a deeply restorative, somatic meditation practice that also serves as a guide for healing through the wounds of childhood. His work can be found at jackadamweber.com.

*Face climate change wholeheartedly
to act in ways that matter*

# CLIMATE
# CURE

Heal
Yourself
*to*
Heal
*the*
Planet

## JACK ADAM WEBER

Llewellyn Publications
Woodbury, Minnesota

FIRST EDITION
First Printing, 2020

Cover design by Shira Atakpu
Editing by Marjorie Otto and Lori Clelland
Interior art by the Llewellyn Art Department
Quoted excerpts used with permission from Dr. Daniel J. Siegel and Mind Your Brain, Inc. ©
    2020: *The Neurological Basis of Behavior, the Mind, the Brain and Human Relationships*

Llewellyn Publications is a registered trademark of Llewellyn Worldwide Ltd.

**Library of Congress Cataloging-in-Publication Data**
Names: Weber, Jack Adam, author.
Title: Climate cure : heal yourself to heal the planet / Jack Adam Weber.
Description: First edition. | Woodbury, Minnesota : Llewellyn Publications,
    [2020] | Includes bibliographical references. | Summary: "For all the
    bad news about climate change, there is a lack of wisdom for how to
    grapple with it. This book fills this void by showing how to emotionally
    cope and thrive through climate upheaval, face our climate predicament
    wholeheartedly, and become passionate and courageous enough to act in
    ways that matter"—Provided by publisher.
Identifiers: LCCN 2020023267 (print) | LCCN 2020023268 (ebook) | ISBN
    9780738764870 (paperback) | ISBN 9780738765129 (ebook)
Subjects: LCSH: Environmental psychology. | Climatic changes—Psychological
    aspects. | Environmental disasters—Psychological aspects. | Resilience
    (Personality trait) | Emotional intelligence. | Sustainable living.
Classification: LCC BF353 .W43 2020 (print) | LCC BF353 (ebook) | DDC
    155.9/15—dc23
LC record available at https://lccn.loc.gov/2020023267
LC ebook record available at https://lccn.loc.gov/2020023268

Llewellyn Publications
A Division of Llewellyn Worldwide Ltd.
2143 Wooddale Drive
Woodbury, MN 55125-2989
www.llewellyn.com

 Printed in the United States of America on recycled paper with soy-based ink

"We are capable of suffering with our world, and that is the true meaning of compassion. It enables us to recognize our profound interconnectedness with all beings. Don't ever apologize for crying for the trees burning in the Amazon or over the waters polluted from mines in the Rockies. Don't apologize for the sorrow, grief, and rage you feel. It is a measure of your humanity and your maturity. It is a measure of your open heart, and as your heart breaks open there will be room for the world to heal. That is what is happening as we see people honestly confronting the sorrows of our time. And it is an adaptive response."[1]

—JOANNA MACY

---

1. Macy, "The Greening of the Self," 174–175.

# Disclaimer

The material in this book is not intended as a substitute for professional psychological advice. Readers are advised to consult their personal psychological professionals regarding treatment. The publisher and the author assume no liability for any injuries caused to the reader that may result from the reader's use of the content contained herein.

# Contents

# Compendium of Exercises

**Chapter 1**

**Chapter 2**

**Chapter 3**

**Chapter 4**

**Chapter 5**

**Chapter 6**

# Acknowledgments

Many hearts and minds, invisible to you, have contributed to this book's completion, for which I am eternally grateful.

First and foremost, my deepest gratitude to Lori Clelland, the best editor I've ever worked with, who took this project to heart (not just to mind), worked overtime, generously and attentively carried on many a conversation with me about its contents and process, and who, nine out of ten times, improved my writing through her meticulous (and, at times, dangerous) editing. Caryn Starr-Gates contributed invaluable editing support in the early stages. Carol Vesecky's help with citations as well as Marjorie Otto's copyediting were both crucial at the end.

I wish to thank my mentors and colleagues, many authors themselves, who have added to my knowledge and wisdom over the decades and who have reviewed portions of the manuscript. I am especially grateful to the climate and transformational wisdom-writers who came before me and directly influenced this work, especially Carolyn Baker, Andrew Harvey, and David Richo, who have made invaluable contributions to help us all navigate the present and coming chaos.

I am indebted to my patients and sacred circle attendees who have shared their insights and heartaches that inform and enliven the comprehensive message of *Climate Cure*. I am indebted to the tireless and ever-generous climate scientist Matt Johnson, PhD, for indulging me in deep conversations while I researched and assembled the climate science in the appendix. And to my savvy and patient literary agent, Dana Newman, who believed in my writing and its cause.

I extend deep bows to climate activists the world over—especially those closest to me in our local Extinction Rebellion movement—for sacrificing their leisure time to disrupt our lethal status quo. And props to climate scientists everywhere who have risked their sanity and safety to save all we love.

From the most tender and ebullient place in my heart, I thank my nieces Olivia and Journey—and all youth around the world—for the love they inspire in me, inciting extra passion to try to make a difference for our future. Lastly, and perhaps most of all, I thank you, dear readers, for receiving this labor of love and helping to complete the circle; may it buoy you as I have been lifted up on the wisdom and graces of others.

Jack Adam Weber
Ojai, California
June 2, 2020

# FOREWORD

How do we really "fight" climate change? The answer is: We don't. According to Jack Adam Weber, the notion of "fighting" climate change is part of why it is so insistently in our faces at this moment in human history. Viewing our climate catastrophe as something we must fight is yet another manifestation of our woeful disconnection from Earth, from each other, and from ourselves—what Weber calls our "triangle of resilience relationships." This estrangement from what matters most to us is actually the root cause of why the potential extinction of all life on Earth is upon us.

Rather than view climate change as something we must fight, Weber invites us to consider that climate change is a self-created wound that is begging to be healed. It is not so much a menace descending from the ethers as it is a shadow arising from within us. It is therefore a wound that, if consciously worked with, can make us whole and benefit the world. This is what *Climate Cure* is about: our personal and collective wholeness directly translates to global integrity. If we focus only on the external healing of our planet, we miss the transformative psychological and spiritual rite of passage being offered by way of nature's desecration and destruction. But if we include all of ourselves into a holistic climate model of "interbeing," as described in the pages ahead, we are likely to make more sufficient and enduring change.

Specifically, Weber writes, "The lack of critical thinking and emotional wisdom that has hastened climate crisis are as unobvious to the naked eye as the cause-and-effect relationship between the greenhouse gas molecules in the atmosphere and the palpable and visible effects of storms, wildfires, droughts, and lethal heat waves. This book is dedicated to the unseen causes of climate crisis deep inside us and largely forgotten by our linear, outward-obsessed, and emotionally immature Western culture."

Humans tend to assume that healing our planet is as simple as instituting a number of climate agreements between nations which will deliver a series of global climate fixes. Therefore, we may be perplexed when the author shares: "If we are afraid of our grief and despair, we can't pay much attention to climate crisis. The capacity to bear unhappiness is crucial to climate cure." In other words, fear (and anxiety) can prevent us from facing our more vulnerable emotions like grief, which is why Weber includes two comprehensive chapters early on to help us masterfully navigate fear and anxiety so we can harvest their inherent wisdom and let go of the ways they cause us to unnecessarily suffer.

Who knew that healing our planet is so inextricably connected with healing ourselves? Serendipitously, because this book addresses how to navigate crisis generally, it is a treasure trove of wisdom for how to heal through many of the challenges surfacing in the midst of the COVID-19 pandemic.

Drawing from his training in Chinese medicine and experience with depth psychology, Weber deeply understands the necessity of tolerating paradox and experiencing that darkness and light are not opposites but different sides of the same coin. "Paradox," he says, "is another way of describing transformation, the cycle of death and rebirth."

The doorway to our transformation is through the emotions that arise most naturally in us as we view the devastating losses produced by climate catastrophe. In this vein, the author shares that grief is not an experience to be fixed or cured. It is not something we should try to "get over" or "get beyond," or even merely tolerate. In fact, grief, allowed by ourselves and supported by trusted others, heals the pain in our hearts and has the capacity to facilitate a bone-marrow connection with nature and the more-than-human world. For example, we abuse, neglect, and commodify animals because we are completely disconnected from our own animal being. We commodify nature so much because we ourselves have been commodified in a capitalist society. As the great naturalist and philosopher Thomas Berry notes, we have come to believe that nature is a collection of objects rather than a web of precious relationships.

As Weber makes unmistakably clear, our planetary predicament is a life-and-death proposition. He invites you to the sacred inner work and rebirth this crisis demands of us in order to experience the miracle of descending into our deepest humanity. Our work is not to *fight* climate change but to *surrender* to the transformation we have brought upon ourselves, and for our own good. "So, if you want a spiritual path," says Weber, "consider choosing the climate crisis, especially if you consider a broken-open heart a legitimate spiritual path. After all, without a habitable planet no other spiritual path is viable."

*Climate Cure* is a comprehensive emotional and spiritual support guide for all manner of troubling times. I urge you to not only read it, but to keep it handy as you would a favorite book of poems, so you may dip into it often and glean insight from its uncommon wisdom. Lastly, and perhaps most importantly, please make use of the many tools and practices Jack Adam Weber has carefully crafted so you can take full advantage of the myriad manifestations of global crisis as a spiritual teacher.

Carolyn Baker, PhD
Boulder, Colorado
April 10, 2020

---

## About Carolyn

Carolyn Baker, PhD, is a writer, speaker, and life coach whose teachings prepare audiences to navigate turbulent times associated with climate change and its effects.

# Introduction
## CARING ENOUGH

*To mobilize people, this has to become an emotional issue.*[2]
~DANIEL KAHNEMAN,
NOBEL PRIZE-WINNING PSYCHOLOGIST
COMMENTING ON CLIMATE CRISIS

In December of 2017 I evacuated Ojai, California, as smoke from the massive Thomas Fire rose above the mountains just outside of town. Five months later I evacuated from Kilauea's lava flow on the Big Island of Hawaii, which took my new handcrafted home and adjoining five-acre organic farm of eighteen years. Eventually, the lava covered my entire neighborhood and ecosystem under a mantle of black jagged rock.

I never imagined I would lose my home and habitat to natural disaster. It's still difficult to grasp at a visceral level. I know I lost everything, but my heart doesn't fully believe it. The lava taught me the strangest thing not only can but does happen at any moment. I suspect that similar disbelief—due to what is too overwhelming to imagine—also prevents many from grasping that climate crisis exists to the serious degree it does and the damage it portends to wreak in the future.

---

2. Mui, "3 Reasons There Might Be No Path to Success on Climate Change."

In effect, I have become a climate refugee,[3] an initiation I couldn't have fathomed when I began writing this book in 2014. In hindsight, I see writing it helped me prepare for the aftermath of fire—especially that monstrous, moving wall of lava that no one and nothing could stop. As a result, I'm an inkling closer to realizing what it's like to be a polar bear or an Australian spectacled flying fox, an orangutan or a dazzling scarlet-breasted fruiteater of the high Andes—all animals facing extinction due to climate change. And I feel closer to the millions of human climate refugees around the world fleeing unlivable conditions.

I've also let go of the expectation of living indefinitely in a place I enjoy, in a comfortable and standard home, with money in the bank. These luxuries, while helpful, don't comfort me as they once did. We are all now more nomadic and vulnerable than we realize or might prefer. We have been thrust, whether we notice it or not, closer to the edge of survival. More than ever, we can't know when we will be stripped of all for which we've worked so hard.

Experiencing these natural disasters firsthand has allowed me to psychologically "die" while still being alive. This has contributed more poignancy to my life, as did the years of emotional healing I had undertaken previously. As a result, I'm more earnestly in touch with what's most meaningful to me. This reckoning coincides with what many don't realize until they are on their deathbeds, after having worked too much and taken too little time to experience what matters most. This is but one of climate disruption's hard-won gifts when we allow ourselves to be initiated and transformed by it.

## Heart Matters

For all the bad news about climate change, there is a proportional dearth of wisdom for how to grapple with it. *Climate Cure* fills this void by showing how to emotionally cope and thrive through climate upheaval, passionately face

---

3. Sneed, "Get Ready for More Volcanic Eruptions as the Planet Warms." Climate change leads to increased volcanic activity; whether this was a factor in the 2018 Kilauea eruption is unknown. Regardless, it was a devastating climate event on par with a hurricane, flood, or wildfire. The lava flow's aftermath is arguably worse, as there can be no returning to my land or neighborhood in the foreseeable future. The roads are gone and my farm is now allegedly buried under at least a hundred feet of still-cooling volcanic rock.

our climate predicament wholeheartedly, and become caring and courageous enough to act in ways that matter enough to save our future.

While solutions to reduce fossil fuels abound, we have not changed enough to alter our fate.[4] Outer solutions remain only as effective as our passionate care to radically minimize, or "degrow," our personal lives so we (1) consume less, (2) free up time and energy to engage in regenerative acts, such as growing our own organic food and showing up to help one another, (3) demand top-down change from our governments, especially by joining a rebellion or strike movement, and (4) learn about climate crisis to support ourselves and others through it.

To effect any of these changes, we must pay attention and take climate crisis to heart, which means *feeling* it. This is why Nobel Prize-winning psychologist Dr. Daniel Kahneman says climate change must "become an emotional issue." To feel the many dimensions of the crisis—how it affects us, how to think about and talk to others about it, how to address and mobilize for it, and how to thrive and not go into denial—requires emotional intelligence and support. This is what *Climate Cure* is about.

## The Anatomy of Cure

Section I is an introduction to the origins of climate crisis in ourselves and its manifestation in the world. Here I introduce the resiliency tools for radical sanity needed to address the many challenges of climate breakdown. Section II explores dynamic emotional intelligence skills for working with and reaping the unique gifts contained within grief, anger, and fear, and concludes with a comprehensive chapter for managing eco-anxiety. These chapters set the groundwork for deep inner healing, skillfully engaging with climate breakdown, and building enduring resiliency. Sections III, IV, and V offer an in-depth look at the invaluable benefits of restoring what I call our three "triangle of resilience relationships" deeply healing ourselves, our connection with the

---

4. OXFAM International, "World's Richest 10 Percent Produce Half of Carbon Emissions While Poorest 3.5 Billion Account for Just a Tenth." Since the "world's richest 10 percent produce half of carbon emissions while the poorest 3.5 billion account for just a tenth," *we* and *us* throughout this writing refer primarily to those of us in industrialized and/or first-world countries, or to those who resonate with the message.

natural world, and community with one another—to both weather climate crisis and engage in its cure. The conclusion integrates the core messages of the book and summarizes how to address the roots of climate crisis from the inside out. Where further information on any topic is recommended, I include the prompt "Resource" followed by the Resource category, the category's number, the author's name, and the first word and any other key words from the citation in quotation marks. For example: (Resource 1: Rogers, "On Becoming"). The resources section is at the back of the book and contains a broad range of additional information and support.

The first appendix provides a unique synthesis of recent climate science themes to inform many of the recommendations and discussions offered in the main text. Thousands of hours of research went into this section, and the unabridged document is available online on my website (Resource 2: Weber, "The Science of Climate Crisis"). Even if you are well-informed about climate science, you might be surprised by some of the information provided. It's sure to enhance your understanding of our larger climate picture.

I've included carefully designed self-enrichment exercises at the end of every chapter to help you personalize the information provided throughout the book, to translate what you read into creating a better life for yourself and the world around you. In-text exercises also appear in the chapters pertaining to your inner work.

## Personal and Planetary Transformation

As a holistic physician and organic farmer, I consider the health of the environment and how we treat it as important for our well-being as what we eat and how we exercise. What we sink into the ground eventually seeps from our pores; the world we poison eventually sickens us. Earth itself is my patient, and the patient of each one of us, whether we acknowledge it or not. Climate activism, and all other forms of creating justice, are our most potent forms of medicine to effect climate cure.

We must all consider becoming climate activists to create a livable future. After researching the climate science for this book, the most sane and heartfelt response I could conceive was to found a chapter of the global protest movement Extinction Rebellion in my own city. Simultaneously, I took down the shingle at my Chinese medicine practice in the spring of 2019 and now dedicate myself full time to climate activism. This includes leading climate change support groups, giving talks, protesting, engaging in regeneration projects, and testifying for climate action at local government hearings, as well as continuing to write climate-rich prose and poetry.

Please consider that 75 percent of the battle to be climate aware and to take meaningful climate action occurs between our deep hearts and our first steps in the world. In other words, it's primarily an inside job. You are therefore not going to find many suggestions for outward climate mitigation strategies in these pages. Instead, I share with you how to inwardly liberate and impassion yourself to take commonsense actions. The heart of this inner work is emotional healing, what I also refer to as "inner activism," which has likely waited your whole life to engage. Climate crisis catalyzes this healing journey within us. In addition, reconnecting with the natural world and one another is paramount. We have an opportunity for comprehensive healing as we create a new Earth-centric and technologically wise iteration of our humanity.

The belief that climate crisis is separate from us perpetuates the myth that we have to fight against or combat it. While we must mitigate its effects, our efforts are more successful when they stem from our love of the natural world, ourselves, and one another. War terms do double harm: they distance us from being deeply accountable for climate disruption and they demonize nature and make it our enemy. Conversely, when we view climate crisis as an extension of our collective imbalances, we can better address both its root (largely inner) and branch (largely outer) causes.

We are climate crisis because we have caused it. And the roots of our polluting emissions are deeper than what meets the eye. Climate cure, like the crisis itself, functions as a reciprocal dynamic, an inner-outer continuum, reflecting our degree of symbiosis with the natural world. When we heal ourselves, we can better heal the planet. Similarly, the more we rehabilitate the natural world, the more we benefit in return.

We can understand climate chaos as a guru, a consummate healer in disguise. Climate cure is most robust when we engage intimately with the crisis and allow it to teach and change us, rather than merely focus on how to eradicate it. Viewing climate crisis as a relationship begging for our intimate participation opens doors to personal and planetary transformation—to heal together. In contrast, distancing or viewing ourselves as distinct from the crisis (and from the natural world) perpetuates disharmony and suffering.

## Bows to the Invisible

While outer solutions are critical to minimize climate "bleeding," these are bandages until we heal our web of relationships that precipitated the climate wound. We can approach this healing process as we would working through the challenges of any important relationship and be transformed in the same way any injury or illness can transform us. This way, we come back into sustainable relationships with one another and the biosphere (the global ecosystem) to which we belong and upon which we depend. If we cannot ultimately mitigate climate breakdown enough, healing our triangle of resilience relationships will best prepare us to weather the downturn.

The lack of critical thinking and emotional wisdom that has hastened the climate crisis is as unobvious to the naked eye as the cause-and-effect relationship between invisible greenhouse gas molecules in the atmosphere and the incidences of wildfires and floods. This book is dedicated to the unseen causes of climate crisis birthed deep inside us and largely forgotten by our linear, outward-obsessed, and emotionally immature Western culture. May this writing contribute to a sophisticated and holistic, inwardly rich and emotionally intelligent ethos to help us heal through climate illness and save ourselves and all of life *any* amount of undue suffering.

# Section I
# INNER AND OUTER CLIMATE CHANGE

# Chapter 1
# RADICAL RESILIENCE

*People choose no pain now, that's why we've done nothing about climate change.*[5]
~DR. JOANNE CHORY, THE SALK INSTITUTE

"Even though many are still either in denial or preoccupied by the daily struggle for survival, the most serious threat that humans have ever encountered in our 150,000-year evolution is global warming and severe climate change," says activist Ronnie Cummins.[6] UN Secretary-General António Guterres, who spoke at the opening of the 2018 climate talks in Katowice, Poland, called climate change "the most important issue we face."[7] Since 2017, millennials also consider climate change the most serious issue affecting the world today.[8] Belonging to Generation Z, the "Climate Kids"—including activist groups such as Fridays for Future, the Sunrise Movement, Youth vs. Apocalypse, and the Bay Area Earth Guardians—are sounding off their heart-wrenching, no bullshit message in the face of a dismal future and possible extinction.

These pronouncements and uprisings are reasonable responses to recent, alarming climate science and catastrophic global events (see appendix I). Deeply concerning ourselves with this crisis is a marginalized pursuit, and only handfuls of us take keen interest. We all need to be talking about climate crisis, and

---

5. Popescu, "This Scientist Thinks She Has the Key to Curb Climate Change: Super Plants."
6. Cummins, "Degeneration Nation 2018: The Darkest Hour."
7. Associated Press, "UN Chief Calls Climate Change 'Most Important Issue We Face'."
8. Loudenbeck and Jackson, "The Ten Most Critical Problems in the World, According to Millennials."

more importantly, feeling its effects. It's difficult to expect anyone living paycheck to paycheck or with other serious challenges to agonize over climate crisis. Paradoxically, however, empowering ourselves to climate activism can bolster our well-being, as climate prodigy and 2019 Nobel Peace Prize nominee Greta Thunberg did to overcome her climate-induced depression.[9] Perhaps we also fear the overwhelming emotions the difficult issues stir—for which we have no adequate forum to share our concern and feelings—and the accompanying sacrifices we'd feel compelled to make if we took the bad news to heart. In truth, we have not done enough, and the discussion to cure the climate crisis continues to focus almost exclusively on what must be done outwardly. Something deeper is missing from the equation.

Our collective inaction has propelled me to wonder what allows us to willfully, even nonchalantly, march toward collapse and our own demise. I have meditated on this question for years, searching for a radical etiology, or root cause for our folly. Even if we address the numerous cognitive biases with which evolution and cultural conditioning have wired us, we still haven't answered what it would take to empower enough of us to sufficiently care for the natural world and our own survival. We lack a strategy for how to care enough even to learn *why* we don't care enough (Resource 2: "Gardner"). We are still without a road map for how to become inwardly (and for many underprivileged, also outwardly) resourced enough, and therefore fulfilled enough, to do without many of the superfluities that exacerbate our Sasquatch-sized carbon footprints and perpetuate our complacency.

In the pages ahead we address precisely these issues by learning how to (1) psycho-spiritually cope with and passionately thrive through climate crisis, (2) become the kind of people *capable* of acting more wisely and effectively, (3) leverage the effects of climate crisis as an opportunity to profoundly transform ourselves and the world, and (4) increase our capacity for love and connection as climate chaos worsens. To engage these changes would be a humble gesture toward all we have hitherto treated so poorly. In this we find integrity and amends, to let everything breathe more easily as the short-lived sun of industrial civilization sets.

---

9. Watts, "Greta Thunberg, Schoolgirl Climate Change Warrior: 'Some People Can Let Things Go. I Can't.'"

## Triangle of Resilience Relationships

Drawing primarily from climate science, holistic medicine, depth psychology, neuroscience, the poetic tradition, and deep ecology, we will explore how we've arrived at our current precipice. We'll learn how to grapple with and grow from this dangerous predicament in the most honest, skillful, and whole-hearted way we can.

The climate crisis is generated both by our individual contributions and by corrupt governments and corporations. And while we've all contributed to the problem, the corporate elite are especially guilty; their negligence has manifested as murderous corruption, dishonesty, endless pollution, war-making, and mercenary fundamentalism. Most of the rest of us have succumbed to apathy, denial, and a lack of courage to rebel and deny our society's manipulative enticements and "do without" (live more modestly). On the bright side, recent climate strikes and resistance movements are beginning to move the chains. With this in mind, I propose three primary, invisible drivers for why we destroy the planet and continue to:

1. The first and foremost driver is our fear and failure to be sufficiently transformed by our emotional pain, past and present, including traumas large and small. This dynamic results in *hurt people hurt others*, including Earth, and is explored in section III. Climate crisis has been initiated and perpetuated by our collective, unresolved difficult emotions, especially our need to grieve. Psychological depth work, what I also refer to as death-and-rebirth work, helps liberate our vitality from past loss and wounding to break this cycle of needless destruction and demise.

2. The second driver is our disconnect from the natural world with which we have coevolved for millennia, a relationship elaborated in section IV.

3. The last driver is our loss of heartfelt, tightly knit community, which we shared for our entire history until it became eroded by a modern individualism. This dynamic is explored further in section V.

These three drivers—with self, nature, and one another—represent three primary relationships, our "triangle of resilience" relationships. Our neglect of these relationships is a radical cause for the symptom of climate crisis. Forsaking any of these relationships causes damage. And in the same way a robust union of these relationships confers exponential strength, abdicating two or more invites catastrophe. Consider that the atrophy of these relationships underlies apathy, war, rapacious capitalism, overpopulation, poor diet and lifestyle choices, laziness, irresponsibility, antisocial psychopathy,[10] religious fundamentalism, scientific illiteracy, and excess pollution—the many dynamics often attributed to our failed stewardship of the planet.

While these many symptoms arise from underlying relationship fractures, they also perpetuate and exacerbate our unsustainable ways and cause further damage to our triangle of resilience relationships, resulting in exponential decline. An example: greed and consumerism are often rooted in an impoverished inner life, yet indulging greed and consumerism further impoverishes one's inner life. Research supports this hypothesis and shows that yoking self-worth to financial success impedes the fulfillment of psychological needs—such as meaning and purpose, confidence, and having close relationships—that creates sustainable happiness.[11]

In contrast, revitalizing these essential relationships builds a triangle of resilience. Our triangle of resilience relationships dictates the unfolding of three major climate change dynamics. These relationships, when marginalized, are the underlying drivers for climate change's inception and perpetuation. When nourished, however, they are the best means we have to cope and thrive through climate chaos, and when they are robust and stable, these relationships are the best way to radically mitigate climate damage.

We must therefore practice desisting from the many expressions of relationship illness and, most importantly, restore our foundational triangle of resilience relationships. I don't propose this strategy as a panacea for all our inner and outer climate challenges, but to equip us with sufficient restraint and resources to renew ourselves and the world—to begin spiraling upward instead of downward. *Any* progress we make in these ways is significant.

---

10. Clark, "The Science of Raising a Friendly Psychopath."
11. Suttie, "How Does Valuing Money Affect Your Happiness?"

## Climate Initiation

Radical imbalance requires radical remedy. When no viable solution exists, we can embrace radical honesty and hold a tension of opposites in order to persevere and preserve a passion for life. The best way I know to do this is to welcome what I call the "spirituality of a broken-open heart"—an honest, Earth-based disposition that embraces both dark and light. It is to embody what Leonard Cohen described as "the crack that lets the light in." In a modern Western culture that worships steadfastness and constant productivity, such a sacred wound—on behalf of everything—isn't easy to bear.

The "climate crack" is not only a wound but an invitation into depths we otherwise would not venture into, where the most comprehensive healing can happen. In this sense, climate disruption challenges us to undertake a profound initiation. Because our culture has all but forgotten the value of initiation, we may fail to see the value—much less possess the savvy and behold the wisdom—to accept Mother Nature's kindness in disguise. The time is ripe to embrace holy struggle for the sake of deliverance to a livable future.

Through this climate portal into our hearts we are given the chance to tend our deepest wounds and restore our dignity with the natural world and one another. This is the opportunity climate crisis offers as it breaks our hearts. Through this transformation, we can reciprocate with a gift of care from our newfound integrity. We don't have to wait for climate change to wake us up, nor have we ever. We can enter this crucible, instead of turning away, when our hearts are broken open through any kind of death or loss. If we deny this grief-pain, as many of us have throughout our lives, we become disjointed and fragment the world as a result. Climate chaos, however, presents an ultimatum we can't ignore. We either deal with the shadow pain and deficiencies from which it arose, or we perish.

## Building Integrity

Triangles are the most sturdy and stable of geometric structures. Each side relies on the others for support, creating a strength greater than the sum of its parts. In reality, because each of our triangle of resilience relationships is multidimensional, each is a triangle in its own right. Joined together, they form a pyramid, whose base is the common ground shared by all life.

Reviving a triangle of resilience fosters integration. Integration builds integrity. Integrity guides humility, care, and regeneration in the form of courageous awareness and wise action. Take, for example, one facet of our triangle of resilience: healing through our core love wounds. Embracing this form of heartbreak takes (and builds) courage, helping us unlock our vitality and care, resulting in more wholeness and a richer inner life. Our resulting integrity helps us notice (awareness) what's unsustainable and tread more lightly (wise action). This process makes degrowth (needing and using less) easier, and is characteristic of regenerative living (less waste and emissions, more fertility and thriving). Our newfound awareness, vitality, and care also allow us to take bolder climate action. Noticing and addressing what's injured catalyzes renewal on all levels, as nature herself models for us via the cycle of death and rebirth. This fertile procession is eloquently represented by the Yin-Yang symbol, one of our constant metaphorical companions on this climate cure journey.

Figure 1: Yin-Yang

The elixir for developing integrity—what I call "becoming medicine for our times"—exists along a spectrum. It doesn't seem to be enough only to be close to nature,[12] nor only to do the necessary inner work or robustly connect with others in community. A combination of these capacities in varying proportions offers more promise for a well-fortified triangle.

If engaging in emotional work doesn't immediately appeal to you, getting out to nature more often and engaging more authentically with others can help soften your defenses, renew your perspective, and/or provide support you

---

12. I've met many a naturalist who is kind to the natural world but is unable to be kind to, and communicate effectively with, other humans.

didn't know you needed. Similarly, acting for the greater good changes how we think and feel. The catch-22 is that it often takes a level of inner work to build enough integrity to sufficiently free oneself from pain to be of selfless service in a self-centered culture. Moreover, acting without wisdom can be dangerous, even if it looks good on the surface or in the short-term (further discussed under the topic of *sacred permission* in chapter 8). Nonetheless, acting on behalf of regenerative values from a place of care is often a good enough effort toward climate cure.

I invite you to sit with these considerations, and if any ring true, to take the next steps into radical resilience. Whatever your unique recipe, together we can begin to shift the paradigm of our disastrous addiction to distraction and unconscious destruction. Please step out of status quo insanity and face this conundrum with me and the many others who can't ignore our screaming hearts and right minds any longer.

## Why Bother

None of what I suggest is utopian; it's too late for this. I propose what is *enough*, which requires change from many of us—enough to curb our diseased relationship with the natural world and with one another, for the sake of integrity, regardless of the outcome. Enough that we could move into a functional range of inhabiting the planet without slashing and burning everything to smithereens, or just not so quickly. *Enough* also means engaging 3.5 percent of the population in rebellion to turn the tides. This figure is based on research showing that "nonviolent protests are twice as likely to succeed as armed conflicts—and those engaging a threshold of 3.5 percent of the population have never failed to bring about change." [13]

Such protests can affect local or global policy. For example, a 3.5 percent threshold was reached during September 2019 when protestors in New Zealand took to the streets for the Youth Climate Strikes. [14] This was soon followed by the New Zealand government committing to an ambitious goal of net-zero carbon emissions by 2050. [15] If many groups worldwide rebel against their

---

13. Robson, "The '3.5% Rule': How a Small Minority Can Change the World."

14. Al Jazeera, "Thousands in New Zealand Kick-Start New Wave of Climate Protests."

15. Wamsley, "New Zealand Commits to Being Carbon Neutral by 2050—With a Big Loophole."

respective local governmental policies, a global shift could occur. This in fact is the basis for Extinction Rebellion's strategy: engaging collective civil disobedience to target local governments by demanding net-zero emissions by 2025. While parts of the biosphere might be too damaged to substantially recover from our lashings, this should not stop us from doing right. Rather, it should invigorate us.

You might have heard someone ask, "If our planet and humanity are lost causes and there's not much I can do, why should I care and waste my time learning, worrying, and getting upset about climate change?" Maybe you have even wondered this yourself. Sadly, acting from this perspective results in both inner and outer inaction and is precisely what has contributed to our current state—not only to the demise of the natural world but to our lost sense of belonging, which has eroded our ability to care enough to work through this mess together.

The non-discerning, binary nature of the above question also fails to appreciate the value of acting with integrity despite the condition of the world— that to live with dignity in heart and action always matters. For instance, we might change our behavior to ease the suffering of other life forms we are extinguishing with us. This could include something as commonplace as not driving and flying unless we must, or something as conscientiously rare as not making undue noise in a quiet place. All this requires commonsense care and a capacity for personal "sacrifice" we seem to lack. This broken integrity is the common "patient" inside us all that we must learn to collectively heal.

Reasons to learn about climate change and expose ourselves to the difficult truths are therefore many. While knowledge might sting in the short term, it can help us avoid—and avoid causing—more suffering in the long run. Knowing and naming the nature of the disease helps us best prepare for and prevent further damage. Also, if it were more likely that your lifestyle and well-being would be significantly disrupted earlier than you anticipated by a force other than the usual culprits that spoil plans, wouldn't you want an informed say in how you spend the rest of your days?

For all these reasons, I offer the following incentives for you to consider learning and *feeling* more about our climate predicament:

1. It's usually a good idea to be grounded in reality and to learn what's true, or what is most likely true. "The truth shall set us free," even if it's tough to accept. Radical acceptance of *what is* prompts our creative ability to arrive at nonlinear solutions to what undeniably seem like dead ends. One learns this when passing through any kind of heartache or descent into the underworld, especially when stripped of hope.

2. The lives of our children and grandchildren are lives many of us deem more valuable than our own. A major challenge is deciding how much climate information to share with children: what's appropriate for them to hear and what knowledge robs them of life versus contributes to their preparation through appropriate learning? Having conversations with fellow parents, psychologists, and asking for feedback from children themselves can help you arrive at the best decisions on this important issue (Resource 1: "Climate Reality Project" and Resource 3: "Hippo Works").

3. Sleepwalking into the future comes with high costs, as the last many decades demonstrate.

4. The allegory of a frog in a boiling pot of water demonstrates what happens when we don't pay enough attention and become too comfortable.[16] Like the allegorical frog, we can't see or grasp gradual climate changes (though they are progressing rapidly in meteorological time). Instead of apprehending and responding to these changes, we unconsciously habituate to them and remain idle. Staying informed about climate change news helps motivate us to jump from the pot before it's too late.

5. Learning how despoiled our world is motivates urgent radical acts of justice such as rebellion. Please consider joining Extinction Rebellion,[17]

---

16. Acaroglu, "Climate Change Is the Slowly Boiling Frog in the Pot of the Earth."

17. Extinction Rebellion, "#Whereisyourplan."

Fridays for Future,[18] or any other climate strike movements. Even climate scientists are joining and asking other scientists to join in protest.[19]

6. Exposing ourselves now to difficult truths helps us cope ahead and integrate climate changes already in the pipeline. Steady awareness allows us to more gradually metabolize the information and more likely future scenarios. It also helps us begin making sacrifices in our comfort level so we acclimate to living with less. These measures seem more prudent than suddenly being taken unawares by overwhelming news and traumatic climate events. *It's better to kneel now than fall from ten feet later.*

7. Learning about the likely future informs every aspect of our lives. Climate change scenarios span a range of possibilities and time frames; they are not black or white. Exposing ourselves to the latest science and global news as it unfolds can help guide us today and tomorrow: in the ways we interact with one another, how we spend our time, what we dedicate ourselves to, how we hold our hearts and our relationships, and what we cling to. For my part, climate change knowledge sways many of my decisions, especially big ones.

   For example, you might choose not to have children—as many are now choosing[20]—or decide to adopt. You might choose to work at an animal shelter or live in the country. You can choose to change the design of your dreams and let go of those that are unsustainable—all wisely informed by global climate status. Or you might choose to let go more completely, follow your uncanny callings, and see what magic awaits in the radical unknown.

8. I've heard many dismiss the far-reaching calamity of climate change with one pseudo-humble retort: "The planet will be better off when

---

18. #FridaysforFuture, "What We Do."

19. Gardner and Wordley, "Scientists Must Act on Our Own Warnings to Humanity." As conservation scientists and members of Extinction Rebellion, we encourage our fellow scientists to join us in embracing activism. In April 2019, over 12,000 scientists signed a letter endorsing the global school strikes, which are acts of civil disobedience, and praising the movement as 'justified and supported by the best available science' (Hagedorn, "Concerns of Young Protestors are Justified."). We ask that scientists take this one step further, and themselves join civil disobedience movements.

20. Timsit, "These Millennials Are Going on 'Birth Strike' Because of Climate Change."

humans are gone." Ironically, this view is hubristic and entitled. Who's to say we won't kill the planet, as we have almost everything else? Few realize, for example, that nuclear reactors take decades to decommission. Without an adequate power grid, or due to flooding from rising sea levels, they could melt down and unleash widespread, crippling radiation on life that remains for eons to come.[21]

9. Painful climate change news affects us emotionally. While this might hurt, a broken heart is also an opportunity. The grief of heartbreak, when held tenderly and wisely worked through, can transform and bring out the best in us. A poster in the Extinction Rebellion office in London reads: "Give yourself time to feel—grief opens pathways of love and melts the parts of you that are frozen."

10. Resisting a destructive and unsustainable status quo, as well as acting compassionately toward one another and the natural world, helps ease the suffering of all beings. Preventing needless suffering gets my vote every time.

---

• EXERCISE •

CHAPTER 1 JOURNALING

Take out your journal or notepad, place it in front of you, and write out your responses to the following prompts.

1. What message from this chapter stood out for you or spoke to you most powerfully?
   • Why did it speak to you so strongly?
   • What action—inwardly or outwardly—are you inspired to take as a result?

2. What holds you back from learning and engaging more about climate crisis?
   • For example, is it any combination of a lack of time, fear, hopelessness, or a lack of knowledge?

---

21. Flavelle and Lin, "U.S. Nuclear Plants Weren't Built for Climate Change."

• What changes or support do you need to engage more fully? How might you make these changes or enlist the support you need?

3. What steps are you willing to take to bolster your triangle of resilience relationships? List up to five superfluous activities you can let go of in order to dedicate yourself to your triangle of resilience relationships—to self-healing, nature connection, and building community.

4. What would it take for you to join a strike or rebellion movement such as Extinction Rebellion and/or introduce your children to any of the children's strike movements mentioned at the beginning of this chapter?

• What prevents you from doing so? How can you address your concerns and make time for this?

• Are you willing to investigate your concerns and any fears and try to work through them?

# Chapter 2
# THE INNER PATH
# TO SUSTAINABILITY

*There is no way to preserve anything approximating the status quo without turning into monsters or cadavers, and no way to survive that is not radical. In this future we will need to keep our eyes open and learn to calm ourselves only with truths.*[22]
~BEN EHRENREICH

We know a lot about how to reduce our carbon footprints, but relatively little about how to do so with less and work for free to save our lives. Ironically, we're so busy "surviving" that we're killing ourselves. Inner work undoes this catch-22. Such inner climate action is as important as outer, especially since no immediate climate solution currently exists and because "nothing like what is happening—and what needs to happen—has ever occurred in history," says meteorologist Eric Holthaus.[23]

In addition to a lack of guidance for how to cope, we have but a superficial understanding of how we got to this precipice. Surely there must be more to the story than burning fossil fuels, corporate greed, and political stonewalling? Understanding the unseen forces for how we arrived here—hidden in our very bodies and inherited from our storied evolution—can empower us to move beyond ignorance and compulsion to untangle our knotted hearts. Then we

---

22. Ehrenreich, "To Those Who Think We Can Reform Our Way Out of the Climate Crisis."
23. Holthaus, "U.N. Climate Report Shows Civilization Is at Stake If We Don't Act Now."

might begin to back away from the edge of the cliff and improve our experience here, as well as that of countless other species with which we share the planet.

On this journey together, we explore how climate crisis and its impending consequences can catalyze our greatest transformation. I introduce these perspectives and some navigational strategies just ahead. I also introduce salient themes to be developed in subsequent chapters where they are integrated into a cohesive whole. So, let's begin with an overview for how to holistically engage with our climate predicament.

## Radical Sanity

Healing climate crisis and our heart-minds shares the same strategy: facing reality with intellectual and emotional honesty while cultivating passion, meaning, and depth. This requires every inner and outer resource we have. Climate cure means we not only heal ourselves, but also help the rest of the planet flourish as much as possible. In this sense, climate chaos is a catalyst, an opportunity for regeneration, similar to other forms of heartbreak.

Conveniently, the honest, critical thinking and emotional intelligence we need to resolve our personal heartaches are the same capacities we need to reckon with environmental collapse. They are a form of "radical sanity" as we follow Ehrenreich's wise, challenging prescription to "calm ourselves only with truths."[24]

The word *radical* means "root," which connotes the roots of plants and trees that hold the Earth's soil, as well as our humanity, together. *Radical* also conveys severe or extreme, fringe or counterculture. Because the radical problem of climate chaos is rattling our many support systems, we must dig down and branch out in new directions that are foreign to our current sensibilities. Indeed, we must live beyond current societal norms—the taken-for-granted beliefs and business-as-usual practices we have grown up with that are, unfortunately, tearing down the world.

As a Chinese medicine clinician, I am trained to discern the root causes of disease, the same focus I apply to climate illness. This holistic medical system has its roots in our interdependence with the natural world. For this reason,

---

24. Ehrenreich, "To Those Who Think We Can Reform Our Way Out of the Climate Crisis."

and for its wise metaphorical foundation, Chinese medicine provides an excellent framework through which to assess human-nature dynamics. While outer fixes such as solar panels, carbon dioxide sequestering devices, and electric vehicles can stem some climate chaos, I propose that no external solution will ultimately be enough to stay away from the edge of the climate cliff. This is not only because we don't currently have a viable solution, but because until we deeply heal ourselves, we will repeat unsustainable patterns, just as we do in intimate relationships that, to be sustainable, require us to address the roots of our psyche. Until then, we will continue to follow the destructive pattern: hurt people hurt others.

## Becoming the Change

We've all heard the catchphrase, attributed to Mahatma Gandhi and often spoken in the context of stepping up to the plate to save the planet and ourselves: "Become the change you want to see in the world." While it's a fine bit of wisdom, Gandhi didn't say it. What he did say is: "We but mirror the world. All the tendencies present in the outer world are to be found in the world of our body. If we could change ourselves, the tendencies in the world would also change. As a man changes his own nature, so does the attitude of the world change toward him." [25]

The great hero for social and environmental justice tells us that personal and collective transformation go hand in hand. Gandhi suggests the locus for transformation is body-centered; this orientation is also Earth-centered because our bodies correlate with the body of the Earth. We are indeed *walking talking chunks of Earth.* But how exactly do we change, and do so deeply and comprehensively enough? The nuanced, uncommon explorations of this question in the pages ahead will likely surprise you.

A starting point is to embrace inner work that allows us to become a quality of people able to care enough to passionately and cooperatively address the collapse of human integrity and the environment. Caring enough is often made possible by privilege, by being fortunate enough to have a good life—one that feels worth living. Securing rights for marginalized groups is more than a

---

25. Gandhi, *The Collected Works of Mahatma Gandhi, Vol. 13.*

path to meet basic needs. It is also a means to provide broader opportunities often thwarted by a struggle to merely survive.

It's not possible for many to care enough for the natural world when their only means of survival lies in its destruction. Burning the Amazon jungle to clear space for raising cattle and soya, butchering elephants for their ivory tusks, or poaching exotic and endangered birds in the Indonesian rainforests and razing it for palm oil, are environmental violations driven by social injustice. Eighty-five percent of Indonesia's $CO_2$ emissions derive from destruction of the rainforest and its underlying nutrient-rich soil. This soil (called "peat") sequesters eleven times more carbon than the biomass above it.[26] Included in the social-environmental equation is the fact that indigenous peoples, who are often exploited, steward 80 percent of Earth's biodiversity.[27] Racial and social justice are vital for environmental justice and our collective survival. Said another way: "The urgency of climate change is also an urgency for racial justice."[28]

Caring enough invokes grief and other difficult and challenging emotions such as fear, remorse, anger, longing, and despair. As we will explore at length, these "dark" emotions have the sacred power to awaken us. To become more caring and sustainable, then, we must tolerate emotional pain, especially grief. When we compassionately face and allow ourselves to be transformed by our dark emotions, we become more psychologically regenerative, inwardly rich enough, to curb our need for outer riches. This is why I call emotional depth work "the inner path to sustainability." It's also why addressing climate collapse through care, and with a modicum of fright, is essential (discussed further in chapter 4).

We embark, then, on an inner journey into why we destroy the planet and the means by which we instead can fundamentally renew our relationship with Earth, ourselves, and one another. In this vein, we explore the shadow work (introduced below and covered at length in chapter 7) needed to become people radically different from the cultural status quo that got us into this mess.

---

26. Zuckerman, "As the Global Demand for Palm Oil Surges, Indonesia's Rainforests are Being Destroyed."

27. Food and Agriculture Organization of the United States, "6 Ways Indigenous Peoples Are Helping the World Achieve #ZeroHunger."

28. Holthaus, "The Climate Crisis Is Racist. The Answer Is Anti-Racism."

You may also be familiar with a quote commonly attributed to Albert Einstein: "We cannot solve our problems with the same level of thinking that created them." Except Einstein didn't say this. He did say something similar that was quoted in a 1946 *New York Times* article: "A new type of thinking is essential if mankind is to survive and move toward higher levels."[29] If we marry Einstein's genius to Gandhi's and adapt it to climate crisis, we get something like this: we must become a comprehensively new version of human being able to both think and feel differently to help transform our global climate predicament.

## Shadow Pain

In our quest to reckon with the hidden forces that have propelled us to such destruction and suffering, not just any kind of inner work will do. We need the sort that makes us more second-naturedly compassionate, so we don't have to struggle to muster enough kindness.[30] We need body-centered, somatic work that transforms our hearts to allow compassion to naturally flow from us, not just to try to become what we think is compassionate. This is the territory of radical transformation, of clearing *enough* of the hidden shadow pain that shrouds our hearts.

In my own life, for example, I felt generally angry and frustrated prior to enrolling in somatic (body-centered) therapy in my mid-twenties. I distinctly remember saying to friends, "I just don't think it's my lot to be a happy person." After a deep stint of grief work, however, I found myself significantly happier and more fulfilled.

From the outset, and for the purposes of our discussion, I want to distinguish *grief work* from the emotion of *grief*. I use the term grief work to refer specifically to healing our core, historical love wounds. This is to work through the painful losses of love and other sad or traumatic experiences we didn't get a chance to fully process—especially during childhood, but also as adults—usually because we weren't supported in our feelings. Examples of this wounding

---

29. *The New York Times Archives*, "Atomic Education Urged by Einstein; Scientist in Plea for $200,000 to Promote New Type of Essential Thinking,"

30. This mustering, however, is not useless. It is important when we find ourselves reacting in an inappropriately violent manner.

include being verbally or physically abused, not being appreciated and sup-ported, or being otherwise neglected or abandoned by a parent. Grief work entails mourning these losses, which we do by experiencing the emotion of grief. Grief also refers to the sadness we feel during current, or in anticipation of future, loss.

Grief work is the heart of transformational emotional healing. It is foun-dational inner work that sets the stage for and renews all aspects of our lives. Grief work is to go deep into the body and experience the places we have been disavowed, ignored, abused, or disenfranchised. During grief work we might feel not only sadness but a host of other attendant emotions, such as anger, rage, fear, remorse, helplessness, and even hopelessness.

During my process of grief work, I would sit quietly, feel into my body, and let it both express its pain and tell the story of what caused that pain. This journey took me from my present life all the way back to my mother's womb. I engaged this inner work for three years, after which I could not find any more heartache to render. Releasing this sadness and anger also allowed me to become more sensitive and empathic to others' pain. I consider this inner work with ourselves (triangle of resilience relationship #1) to be the heart, or main facet, of our triangle of resilience relationships.

While I offer several grief-work exercises in chapter 6, here's a taste of body-centered work to prepare for this deep inner work:

### • Exercise •
### Body Survey

Sit quietly or lie down and notice how your body feels, in an overall sense. Next, with your inner sensory awareness, slowly "feel into" your body from your feet to your head. Begin at your feet and notice how they feel. Allow yourself to rest in this experience of your feet being as they are for thirty seconds or so. Proceed this same way all the way up to your head, tuning into your calves, thighs, groin, hips, belly, chest, arms, neck, head, and any other places that you want to feel into. Allow your breath and your body to be relaxed during the exercise. All you are doing, for now, is noticing and making contact with how your body feels from your inner awareness of it.

Central to realizing a new level of compassion, then, is grief work. Until we release the backlogged pain of unconscious love wounds, it effectively possesses us and drives every aspect of our lives. Unattended, our love wounds block our capacity to give and receive love and cause us to violate and injure others, including the Earth. Until we deal with this shadow pain, we remain too self-obsessed (ironically enough) and unable to love enough, especially during times of decline.

Through grief work, we liberate our grounded care—our embodied human capacity to give and receive love—in the form of what I call our *finer jewels of being human*. These *finer jewels* are psycho-spiritual resources that have, in significant part, remained mired in our negative, shadow pain. Our finer jewels therefore correspond with our *positive shadow*—our inner storehouse of unacknowledged and often underdeveloped, life affirming capacities and aspirations. They include a stellar repertoire of virtues: our compassion, empathy, creativity, passion, honesty, patience, freedom, humility, perseverance, critical thinking, courage, care, wisdom, and a robust sense of meaning and purpose.

A profound and sustainable way to liberate our positive shadow is by reckoning with our *negative shadow*—our unacknowledged arsenal of pain and life-depleting attributes. Note, these positive and negative descriptors are merely that—descriptive. They don't assess intrinsic value. Like dark and light, each dialectic is valuable for its unique contribution to our wholeness. When both are left unconscious, they cause unnecessary suffering. When made conscious and worked with paradoxically, we get integration. Integration bestows the integrity of care.

## Embodied Spirituality

In the midst of climate crisis, we have the opportunity not only to radically renew our hearts and come together as never before, but to do so vis-à-vis our relationship with the natural world. For this, we explore how our negative shadow grows as a result of our disavowed pain and our disconnect from nature's rhythms and one another. We engage "inner activism" to deeply heal these essential relationships. I invite you to consider these severances as modern, virtually invisible illnesses—radical causes of climate disease. A catch-22, however, is that our fear of climate crisis can shut us down even further, preventing us from addressing these relationships and climate trauma itself. The first step to healing our relationship with climate trauma, then, is to notice and identify these hidden dynamics.

We also will have to communicate intimately and compassionately, as well as work humbly and cooperatively, with one another in any new world we create. This requires accountability to self and others, as well as being able to move through and let go of "small stuff" differences for a larger goal. Earnest inner and interpersonal work, especially via emotional intelligence and critical thinking, vitally prepares us for this level of regenerative community. This forges a new level of resilient relationships, unlike those that gave rise to our current atrocities. Case in point: during a local Extinction Rebellion meeting, one member commented how uniquely restorative and invigorating it is to work collaboratively for shared principles in a context other than a corporate setting.

To renew our connection with the Earth, I propose an embodied spirituality for becoming more fully human. In this Earth-centered orientation, we learn how to cultivate the inner and outer resources to comprehensively renew ourselves, as well as how to endure and mitigate our wholesale destruction of the biosphere. We discover how we can truly change, from the inside out, and radically heal our triangle of resilience relationships, all of which have served as dumping grounds for our disavowed shadow pain. This path is a soul-saving undertaking even in the absence of climate crisis.

If we miraculously escape the worst of climate collapse, having learned to grow our hearts as wide as the world will leave each of us a better person. To live with such integrity is a gift to everything amid our modern-day madness, no matter how lonely the journey. And to whatever degree we save ourselves and the planet, a resuscitation of our triangle of resilience—intimacy with ourselves, the natural world, and one another—potently prepares us to weather tougher times.

———

In the absence of integrity, the default urge to project and displace our inner pain tightens us like a coiled spring, a cobra ready to strike. And we lash out, unwittingly poisoning others, including the Earth. Yet we need not be condemned to this scenario; we can mindfully prevent the coil from tightening so much. This way, we reduce the cycle of needless suffering and harvest from pain our finer jewels. Reclaiming them predisposes us to a fulfilling, deeply joyous, yet also wholly heartbroken, experience of life. Such tension of opposites as dynamic paradox is a sure sign we are on the warrior path: dark and light, inner and outer, Yin and Yang, ever wedded in passionate reciprocity. This orientation allows us to act more regeneratively in the world because we have cultivated our finer jewels by participating in our own regeneration (psychological death and rebirth).

Reckoning with our psychological shadow paradoxically generates more grounded love and passion. This path of difficult descent and eventual renewal is mirrored in the Yin-Yang symbol (figure 1, page 14) pertaining to the Chinese medicine I practice. The Yin-Yang symbol is a perennial symbol of balance and wholeness. This elegant and wisdom-rich image shows us that Yang depends on Yin and Yin depends on Yang. Night and day, inner and outer, below and above, Yin and Yang—each depends on the other.

Yang is represented by the white paisley and Yin by the black. Cardinal Yang qualities include what is masculine, light, active, outward, and prolific. Cardinal Yin qualities include what is feminine, dark, quiescent, inward, and declining. Note that "masculine" and "feminine" connote archetypal qualities, not gender. Yin and Yang are dialectics, opposing yet perfectly complementary forces that support each other. Neither can exist without the other; when wisely integrated they create a thriving atmosphere.

In clockwise fashion, Yang constantly transforms into Yin and Yin transforms into Yang. Round and round through the seasons of life they cycle, as night turns to day and day into night. In this sense, and as we will explore in depth later on, this ancient symbol is more a verb than a noun. In sum, Yin and Yang encompass all our human capacities as well as all aspects of our world. Through the metaphorical lens of Chinese medicine, we learn that rejuvenating our sense of wholeness depends on all our relations and all our faculties—a necessarily Yin *and* Yang endeavor.

Chinese medicine's spiritual roots are a way to live in harmony with the ebb (Yin decline) and flow (Yang growth) of nature's seasons, which include our inner seasons of joy and sorrow, courage and fear, creativity and dissolution. Undertaking this inner path of emotional transformation while reconnecting with the natural world that models it for us—all within the context of heartfelt, tightly knit community—comprises our triangle of resilience for radical sanity in these harrowing times.

Our triangle of resilience relationships include both Yin and Yang capacities. One facet of the triangle, inner work, is a Yin endeavor. Nature connection and community are a blend of Yin and Yang qualities. The cultivation of both Yin and Yang resources via the power of the triangle empowers us to act. When we *act wisely*, we marry the Yin quality of wisdom with the Yang quality of action. Such integration is regeneration and the foundation for an Earth-centered humanity. While the atrophy of our triangle of resilience relationships is a virtually unseen driver of climate crisis, the bolstering of these hidden nourishments is the best means we have to cope, thrive, and heal through climate disruption.

## Magical Thinking and Ecocide

In a body-centered, Earth-based spirituality, we exist in constant interplay and attunement with the natural world. Outer reality directly informs our inner lives—and, ultimately, our actions. Unilaterally light-seeking and bliss-focused forms of spirituality tend to omit this vital intimacy between our bodies and the Earth, thereby leaving this vital link undernourished. Without our bodies, without our humanness and the Earth included in our daily meditations and blessings in action, we lose touch with what supports any form of spirituality.

In contrast with an Earth-based spirituality is "spiritual bypassing," which means seeking refuge in lofty spiritual ideals and ethereal states as a way to avoid—to bypass—difficult aspects of everyday life, especially difficult emotions (Resource 2: "Masters"). It is a largely disembodied orientation, often with roots in childhood abuse and neglect. Bypassing abandons grounded reckoning with ourselves, one another, and with the body of the Earth as a way to deny what pains us. As we have briefly discussed, when we avoid inescapable pain, we avoid sustainability and regeneration. And because this pain is unavoidable, we transfer it to others when we don't steward our core hurts. Spiritual bypassing is therefore another invisible contributor to climate crisis.

Consider too that our Earth-denying, privatizing Western culture also stems from collective love-wounding and is exacerbated by capitalism's insistence on excessive division and individuality. Parceling land, corporate mining and drilling of mountains and forests, damming rivers, private ownership of shared natural resources such as water and trees, and ideologies such as "every man for himself" all breed loneliness, alienation, disease, and egoism. These unsustainable patterns of behavior are passed down generation after generation until we are able to break the cycle by mending our triangle of resilience relationships.

Reestablishing our primary relationships with self, nature, and one another ensures our actions are coordinated with cues we receive outwardly, so that human-to-nature and human-to-human wellness are constantly updated and restored. To do this, we must become more sensitive to the natural world and intimate with our dark emotions that signal us to imbalance, which I will guide you through in upcoming chapters. If we're attentive and receptive, for example, we may notice birdsong and insect chatter declining after pesticide is sprayed. We may also notice how we feel, and are called to act, in response to the damage. We may feel sadness, anger, and despair when a mountaintop is leveled for coal, or a river and its inhabitants are poisoned from mine tailings. We might become aware that we pause less frequently to speak with each other; and when offering support, we often try to "fix" instead of listen.

Being an inwardly sustainable person includes having the sensitivity and presence to embrace all our emotions and to notice subtle changes in the world. In their book *Active Hope*, Joanna Macy and Chris Johnstone counsel, "Repressing emotions and information dampens our energy. It is enlivening to go with, rather than against, the flow of our deep-felt responses to the world."[31] Doing so, we can synthesize a wise, holistic, curative response. The more we understand and tend to the biodiversity of our inner lives, the more care and wisdom we generate. Allying this inner, regenerative soul-work with its outer correlates of regenerative farming and honoring all forms of life, for example, begins to metamorphically knit a resilient world back together.

---

31. Macy and Johnstone, *Active Hope: How to Face the Mess We're In without Going Crazy*, 70.

## Blind Inheritance

Many of us feel overwhelmed enough without having to contemplate the real possibility of getting wiped off the planet. Indeed, we may not be equipped even to contemplate such a large-scale future catastrophe because we've been psychologically wired since hunter-gatherer times to focus on immediate survival needs. Far-off projections, such as slowly rising temperatures over the course of decades, does not push our survival-instinct fear buttons. In an article titled "Humankind Is On the Road to Nowhere," author and columnist Norman Pagett enlightens us to these invisible dynamics: "But nature still cares only that we survive the present, and our hunter-gatherer instinct concurs; in evolutionary terms, action on a threat that is not imminent is still a waste of precious energy, the fact that we have a surplus is taken as confirmation that we need do nothing, because there will always be more. That is why we perceive the dangers of climate change, overpopulation and energy depletion and our other potential problems as being beyond our event horizon, so the majority of us obey primitive instincts and ignore them."[32]

The blind inheritance to which Pagett refers has helped me realize part of why I regularly pore over climate change news. It's as if I'm trying to beat it into my head and heart through repetition in order to overcome my default predisposition to ignore it. I'm trying to bring the event horizon closer, so I can feel appropriate urgency for it.

Pagett's quote also invokes a big problem with climate science reporting: many climate projections are made for the year 2100. Even a decade into the future, let alone 2100, is far too futuristic to rouse our concern about catastrophic climate change—because our brains aren't wired to apprehend or care about such distant possibilities. Nobel Prize-winning behavioral scientist Daniel Kahneman concurs: "A distant, abstract and disputed threat just doesn't have the necessary characteristics for seriously mobilizing public opinion."[33] Some have even criticized the proverbial 2100 date as a way to transfer the burden onto younger generations and to excuse ourselves from grappling with it.

---

32. Pagett, "Humankind Is on the Road to Nowhere."
33. Mui, "3 Reasons There Might Be No Path to Success on Climate Change."

We need more immediate projections and more media coverage about disasters unfolding now in less fortunate parts of the globe, because catastrophic climate crisis strikes somewhere every day—too often just a little too far away. Fires destroying close to five million acres of forest in the Amazon and some thirty million acres in Siberia in the first part of 2019 grabbed the world's attention. We need regular reminders of current disasters like these, because we easily forget. Unless we are scared enough (and skillfully mobilize our fear into wise action), our passionate care remains underground, and we continue business as usual.

## Fulfillment as Sustainable Happiness

Famed Russian novelist Leo Tolstoy believed maintaining the vital link between humans and nature a primary condition for happiness. Tolstoy speaks to the equivalent of preserving our second triangle of resilience relationship. Spiraling into egoic pursuits that excessively despoil the natural world disavows this symbiosis.

Pleasure and experiencing beauty are as important now as ever, to recharge and keep our spirits up. In addition to difficult reality, we can also live in celebration with friends, family, and the providence of the natural world that remains. But too much celebration while the house (Earth) is burning down renders us distracted, ineffective, and addicted to surrogates for "happiness." It's still deceptively easy to think we can ignore inconvenient climate change news, especially if we believe that flicking a switch, popping a pill, or going shopping can make it all go away, however momentarily.

Ironically, our "happiness" culture might be in good part responsible for our crisis, since perpetual, superficial happiness goes hand in hand with too much consumerism, pollution, and denial. Rather than deal with sacred heartache, we too often try to pleasure it away. While pleasure makes life worth living and soothes its harsh turns, when we use it to avoid too much difficulty, we brew disaster.

In contrast, we are rewarded when we embrace our pain. In his poignant book *Original Blessing*, Reverend Matthew Fox writes, "Pain destroys the illusions of false, that is elitist, pleasures. It burns from the inside out. It therefore sensitizes us to what is truly beautiful in life."[34] Our denial of pain not only atrophies our stewardship of the natural world, but also denies our experiences of one another as sacred. It creates a shadow that goes on growing while we simultaneously generate more avoidance to keep it at bay. And we lose yet again when we deny our pain because we don't get to unearth our finer jewels, which emerge from embracing the depths of our hearts. So, we pursue more and more happiness, more "elitist pleasures," until our souls are buried beneath so much compulsive pleasuring that happiness becomes not a slice of life, but a covertly fear-driven addiction.

I wonder if Reverend Fox's use of the word "elitist" is coincidental or uncannily prescient for yoking corporate, elitist-manufactured, unnecessary products with not being sensitive to "what is truly beautiful in life." In the lexicon of Chinese medicine, this kind of avoidant pleasure-seeking is understood as too much Yang-light (pleasure) casting too big a Yin-shadow (pain). Such addiction robs us of essential psycho-spiritual gifts—from both these domains—conferred by our positive (Yang) and negative (Yin) shadows.

When dark and light fall too far out of balance, chaos ensues as a healing crisis, to transform pain into a more sustainable form of happiness—fulfillment. Fulfillment requires we lovingly embrace personal and collective heartache as a more humane reckoning with everything alive. It takes wisdom and courage to choose such a path over a steady diet of sugary pleasure in the form of protracted avoidance and smiley faces that disguise our suffering. This inner path to sustainability yields a richer life, a full-course meal of meaning, depth, and soulful community rather than that which avoids, appeases, isolates, and burns us — and the planet — out.

## Leveraging Chaos

The great depth psychologist Carl Jung realized "When an inner dynamic is not made conscious, it occurs outside us as fate."[35] The wake-up call to heal our collective pain-shadow of trauma thunders now as the specter of climate

---

34. Fox, *Original Blessing: A Primer in Creation Spirituality Presented in Four Paths, Twenty-Six Themes, and Two Questions*, 76.

35. "Jung: 'When a situation is not made conscious, it happens outside, as fate.'" *Collected Works 9ii: Christ, A Symbol of the Self,* Par. 126.

trauma descending upon us from outside. In other words, climate breakdown is a reflection of our broken inner lives.

The question is: *will* we—and more poignantly *can* we—clear what's inside and among us to help courageously endure and comprehensively cure this disaster with passion and wisdom? In the spirit of unique opportunities made possible by crisis, I propose that facing the massive initiation that is climate catastrophe can guide us to this necessary inner and outer (r)evolution. Reciprocally, embracing our historical wounds can help us confront, grapple with, and better cope and thrive through this mess.

Within the problem is the solution, and in the case of climate emergency we have to go deep within to find it. Such inner work in turn makes us more *emotionally bioavailable* to care about the condition of our world. Indeed, climate crisis and our personal woes intersect in our hearts. Climate change causes loss, which is why consciously dealing with our personal, historical losses prepares us so well for dealing with climate-related losses. The more we heal our personal histories, the more resilient we become to face climate crisis and its ongoing pain-making. The more resilient we are to face climate trauma, the more we can effect a cure. Reciprocally, engaging with and feeling climate trauma can help us become aware of our personal love wounds, bring both to light, and heal through them. These dynamics connect our inner landscape— our inner earth—with the earth we live on, creating common ground and the realization that renewing both occurs via the other.

At a minimum, this inner-outer recognition can be a silver lining, a consolation for our current tragedy. At most, it is a way to become the people we've always wanted to become and create a more beautiful world. Likely, we will continue landing somewhere between the tragic and the beautiful. So, while this formula may not create the optimal world we'd like to live in, it offers us a better chance to salvage our best selves and minimize suffering for other forms of creation in the process.

———

While we don't need outer crisis to address our hurts, this is often how deep healing happens. We can leverage existential climate pressure as an ally to address what we have avoided, often for generations. Again, this is similar to how a challenging romantic relationship encourages us to work through our limitations to create more goodness and love. Building emotional intelligence can fortify us to explore the historical reasons for why we avoid all manner of initiatory difficulty. Such inner work helps us to confront our fears and process our backlogged pain. This way, and in true Yin-Yang balance, our inner and outer worlds constantly inform and support each other for mutual benefit.

Our predicament was dire prior to the inauguration of the forty-fifth United States president. With the result of the 2016 election, the gas pedal of denial, ignorance, and malevolence is now pressed ever further to the metal, accelerating the unraveling of our biosphere.[36] We can't face or endure this alone. We need each other, which is why gathering in community—face-to-face and heart-to-heart—is essential (more on this in chapters 10 and 11). We have no choice but to collectively address the injunction climate crisis presents. It's now or never to engage with our inner and outer darkness as we never have, for the heavens are truly burning and the tides literally overflowing.

If nothing else, we now have a great excuse to abandon less meaningful pursuits. It's time to get down to sacred business so we can live and love more passionately than ever before, especially if it seems too late. For this, we turn to building deep emotional intelligence and working more effectively with fear and anxiety so we can engage more robustly with deeper inner work, climate activism, and community building.

---

• EXERCISE •

## CHAPTER 2 JOURNALING

Take out your journal or notepad, place it in front of you, and write out your responses to the following prompts.

1. If you want to become more a part of the solution, close your eyes and allow your awareness to be simultaneously present in all parts

---

36. Oppenheimer, "Avoiding Two Degrees of Warming 'Is Now Totally Unrealistic'."

of your body (refer back to and practice the Body Survey exercise). Ask yourself this question: "How do I envision becoming the change I want to see in the world; what calls my passion forth?" Sit quietly with these contemplations and, when ready, begin to write about what surfaced for you. Feel free to pause at any time, close your eyes to feel into the question again, and then resume writing.

2. Which emotions do you experience when interfacing with climate change? Do any of these emotions prevent you from becoming more engaged with climate action? After you've identified any of these emotions, sit with your eyes closed, feel the place where you feel each emotion in your body, and note any memories that arise in relation to sitting with or contemplating these emotions. Perhaps a childhood memory arises, or an incident at work, or details from a relationship. What comes to mind? For now, just note what comes up and write it down in your journal under "Chapter 2."

# Section II
# FOUNDATIONAL WORK

# Chapter 3
# THE YIN AND YANG
# OF EMOTIONAL INTELLIGENCE

*There is something infinitely healing in these repeated refrains of nature,*
*the assurance that after night, dawn comes, and spring after winter.*[37]
~RACHEL CARSON

In this chapter we explore how to work with the difficult emotions necessary for all aspects of climate resiliency. I present this material via the perennial, wisdom-rich metaphors of holistic medicine because this is the best eco-psychological model for comprehensive human-nature healing I know.

Difficult emotions arise as we engage with both climate crisis and our historical love wounds. As we've discovered, these inner and outer domains interface with each other. Embracing these states simultaneously helps us heal our hearts as well as the world. The emotions we need to reckon with climate breakdown and mobilize for climate action are the same emotions we encounter dealing with life's many challenges and disappointments, including reckoning with our past love wounds. Wisdom for how to work with these emotions is also invaluable for cultivating and sharing our unique gifts with the planet and our loved ones. Embodying and skillfully working with sadness, anger, fear, remorse, despair, and other difficult emotions are therefore adaptive for coping and thriving on multiple fronts.

---

37. Lear, *Rachel Carson: Witness for Nature*, 213.

# Ten Benefits of Difficult Emotions

Difficult emotions help us:

1. Heal through past and current trauma, including losses caused by climate change.

2. Rebirth our finer jewels of being human, such as compassion, empathy, creativity, and wisdom.

3. Overcome fear and denial (what I refer to as our *fear-mark* in the next chapter) to face difficult reality, including distressing climate change news and reports.

4. Better empathize, communicate, work cooperatively with one another, and resist business as usual.

5. Live more fully in the present moment.

6. Be more receptive to signals from our environment so we can extend a healing response.

7. Engage tough love and tend to what is ailing without turning away, thereby increasing our sense of oneness and our capacity to love when what we love is ailing. (If love is only a positive, feel-good experience, then we miss out on the experience of love when things fall apart.)

8. Cope and thrive with having less, producing less, and consuming less (minimalism and degrowth).

9. Lower our carbon footprints by allowing us to make peace with naturally cycling fallow times and not compulsively "progressing" and "succeeding" 24-7.

10. Live poetically and passionately so we can nourish ourselves with sustainable beauty and pleasures through thick and thin, thus precluding our need to purchase, plunder, and lump too many things onto our lives.

Our emotional intelligence toolbox also includes learning how to work with strong emotions without letting them totally derail us. This strategy is consistent with that of prevailing psychological wisdom for how to face and metabolize emotional pain by keeping one foot in difficulty (pain, trauma, and overwhelm) and one in resiliency (regulation, mindfulness, and nature/community connection). This approach respects both chaos (difficulty) and order (regulation), Yin and Yang respectively, in order to integrate what feels broken and unmanageable into a more beautifully complex and full-spectrum whole-ness. With emotional intelligence we harness difficult emotions as fuel for care, activism, and building community.

Still, we often don't have control over our emotions. We may encounter stints of overwhelm or lapse into extreme emotional states. I have personally found these intense forays valuable for moving fully through the depths of pain and being rebirthed into new levels of integration, even though they compromise my usual productivity.

Heartache from both personal or climate loss can transform us into people more richly connected to the rest of life. Each of us will have our own sensibil-ity and tolerance for how deeply and how long we go into such healing crises, for which emotional intelligence tools are invaluable.

## A Holistic Lens

Yin and Yang comprise the primary metaphorical design of Chinese medicine. The Five Elements—also called the Five Phases—are an extrapolation of Yin-Yang dynamics, represented in figure 2 below. The Five Phases are Wood, Fire, Earth, Metal, and Water. These phases refer both to the composition and forces of the natural world, as well as to human beings as expressions of nature. They therefore represent our total interconnection, our holistic entanglement, with the natural world.

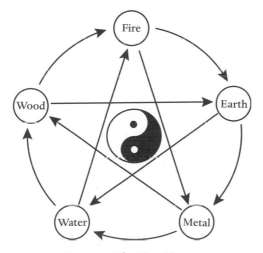

Figure 2: The Five Phases

I like to refer to the elements as "phases" because this speaks to their dynamic, transformational nature, as represented by the clockwise arrows in the schema above. This way, we can think of the Yin-Yang symbol and its Five Phases as verbs. The model of seasonal transformation (both in the outward seasons of the yearly cycle and via our human, psycho-spiritual "seasonal moods") from one phase to the next is the essence of human-ecological regeneration and resilience in mind, body, and spirit in concert with the natural world.

According to Chinese medicine, each of the Five Phases corresponds with a season and an emotion. The Fire phase corresponds with summer and joy, Earth with late summer and worry, Metal with autumn and grief, Water with winter and fear, and Wood with spring and anger. The phases and their corresponding seasons and emotions are divided among Yin and Yang, in the spirit of balance. The Metal and Water phases pertain to Yin and decline, represented by the black paisley; the Wood and Fire phases pertain to Yang and growth, represented by the white paisley. The paisleys are depicted in miniature at the center of the image with their white (Yang) and black (Yin) halves corresponding with the seasons and emotions they represent (figure 2). The Earth phase, representing our planet and Mother Nature, is considered a balance of Yin and Yang energies (figure 3).

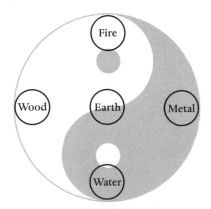

Figure 3: The Five Phases with Earth at center

Older pictograms of the Five Phases show Earth at the center, seen above in figure 3. While figure 2 differs from figure 3, each highlights a distinct Yin-Yang dynamic. When Yin and Yang are in balance, the Earth between them that they mutually create is supported and thrives! The same is true for humans, and we must find this thriving *in relation with the natural world*, not in a human-centric bubble. This is why Yin-Yang and the Five Phases provide the quintessential model to understand and engage with emotional work to heal all aspects of ourselves in relationship with the natural world, including climate crisis.

Grief and fear correspond with the Yin seasons of autumn and winter and are therefore Yin emotions. Grief is a downward, sinking feeling, and fear contracts us. Downward and inward are both cardinal Yin attributes. Anger and joy, on the other hand, correspond with the Yang seasons of spring and summer and are therefore Yang emotions. Anger and joy are both upward and outward emotions; upward and outward are cardinal Yang characteristics. Yin-Yang and the Five Phases eloquently capture eco-human dynamics of interdependence and regeneration in a healing context. They are therefore a dynamic lens through which to understand not only human-nature dynamics but all our triangle of resilience relationships, to help us heal through climate crisis.

We can see the results of our Yin and Yang emotions in the world and in the dynamics of climate change. Our emotions are, in fact, nature's passion coursing through us in all its varied expression. How we work with and employ emotion through our actions in turn affects the whole of nature. It's no accident that we feel more joy in the warm ease of summer, more melancholy and sadness as leaves fall in autumn, more contraction and fear in the depths of winter, and more anger and frustration as we grow from the darkness of winter into the buds of spring. Nature's signature is in us and in the more-than-human world; we are one.

## Adaptive Hurt

As the primary drivers for our lives and the litmus test for our wellness, our emotions inherently join us with the natural world to ensure a sustainability of mutual wellness. When human culture becomes too solipsistic and anthropocentric, our emotional intelligence informs us of this imbalance via our difficult emotions. Because we are connected with the natural world, when it hurts, we hurt. This confers a survival advantage, as we're prompted to heal what cries out for help. In contrast, denying painful emotions leads to an imbalance of the Five Phases inside us, eventually translating to disharmony outside us. Our sadness, anger, anxiety, and even feelings of hopelessness and depression—when skillfully worked with—can be sane, adaptive responses to climate distress. Our emotions alert us to the problem; how we respond is our choice, and this is where the rubber meets the road.

Minimizing unnecessary busyness and distraction to reduce unnecessary stress allows us to be more emotionally aware and integrated, both of which liberate time and energy for climate activism. These two undertakings—creating time and energy and mobilizing emotional work (inner activism)—are precisely the measures that have personally prepared me to engage in building community, climate rebellion, and eco-restoration efforts.

When we are stressed and distracted by everyday living, we can't easily connect with our more vulnerable feelings of sadness, fear, and even anger in response to climate crisis. Assuring that we can harvest the holistic wisdom in difficult emotions—which resets our inner compass and rebuilds a bridge of connection with the living planet—is foundational for restoring our relationship with all aspects of the world we inhabit. This way, we are more able to notice and act when our relationship with the biosphere goes awry. Yin-Yang and the Five Phases therefore provide a radically sane medium for regenerating our triangle of resilience relationships.

Jung believed we are all whole within, but to actualize this potential we must make our unconscious conscious. Because Yin (the unconscious) and Yang (conscious awareness), along with their respective phases, represent our wholeness, incorporating and welcoming all the phases' corresponding emotions of joy, sadness, pensiveness, fear, and anger into daily life is to live more fully and, ultimately, sustainably.

## Emotional Flow

In the same way the yearly seasons flow into and support one another, so too do their associated emotions flow through us when we acknowledge and embrace them with skill and wisdom—with emotional intelligence. Experiencing all the phases' associated emotions is essential to our being fully and compassionately human, and to our ability to extend compassion to the Earth. This could be another reason the Earth phase was originally placed at the center of the Five Phases, indicating its centrality to our well-being (see figure 3).

Welcoming and skillfully engaging with our dark emotions ensures the smooth flow of vital energy, or *Qi* (Chi), as it is called in Chinese medicine. This flow is the transfer of energy and matter from one of the Five Phases to another along the wheel of Yin and Yang (see figure 2). You can also think of *Qi* as the vital energy in all our emotions, as well as the wisdom released through our finer jewels when we work through the knots and sludge of our emotional pain. When our *Qi* flows—up through the Yang phases and down through the Yin phases of our lives—we find vitality in both joy and sorrow, and maintain a sane connection with our world.

At times, embodying our emotions might *appear* imbalanced. But as long as an emotion is allowed its season and is skillfully worked with, it can transform into more wisdom and wholeheartedness. When we consciously embody and allow our natural ups and downs, we join the cycle of the phases, as each emotional phase arises and gives way to the next. This constant transformational cycle—the verb of Yin-Yang and the Five Phases—can paradoxically impart a sense of stillness and effortlessness, especially when we genuinely accept tough times. We experience this cycle daily when we rise to be active (Yang) and then lie down to rest at night (Yin). We also experience it during and after creative flow states such as dancing, creating a poem, or trekking through the woods. All include tough and easy patches, as does any meaningful activity in life. Both effort (Yang) and surrender (Yin) are required.

## • EXERCISE •
## YIN-YANG BALANCE

To shed light on your personal Yin Yang balance, reflect on the following Yin and Yang qualities. Elaborate on what you realize, and note where you could create more balance for yourself—not per societal norms or what you are "supposed to do," but by what feels intuitively, somatically "right" or true for you.

• Do you feel that you are too mentally and physically active (Yang activities) and that you need more rest and relaxation (Yin activities)?

• Are you more comfortable feeling and expressing the Yang qualities of judgment, anger, and criticism than you are the Yin qualities of grief and compassion?

• Do you feel you spend too much time extroverted (Yang) as opposed to introverted (Yin), or vice versa?

• Are you able to patiently sit with difficult emotions (Yin), or do you feel a need to impulsively and immediately express and distract yourself from them (Yang)?

———

While the cycle of the Five Phases is a fixed progression of the yearly cycle, this is not always the case in our emotional lives. Any emotion can arise in us at any time. Anger can turn to fear, then to grief, and then to joy. The progression of our emotions does not necessarily follow the Five Phase cycle of the seasons shown in figure 2. The Five Phases simply represent a fullness of emotional experience and offer wisdom for how to embrace and balance all our emotions, in whatever season they may arise. We should not contrive our emotional lives to fit the literal cycle of the Five Phases. The lesson is to attune to the intimations of transformation, overall balance, inter-support, and wholeness amongst all the phases, and to note their influences and gifts throughout the seasons of our lives.

Because difficult emotions impart wisdom, tending to our shadow through emotional honesty—which is to consciously feel our true feelings—contributes  to regenerative acts more than maniacal progress. Regenerative action, for example, is painfully absent among many of our current world leaders. It is common in those fighting for justice, who communicate well through thick and thin to build community, and work sustainably with the land.

Emotional balance means living in a functional, Yin-Yang dynamic of repose and action, reflection and expression, death and rebirth. My unique recipe for emotional intelligence, informed by holistic medical wisdom, includes the following ten ingredients:

## Ten Steps for Emotional Intelligence

1. Feel your true emotions and feelings (for this discussion, *emotions* are acute reactions to events, and *feelings* are how we feel in the longer term, after reflecting and integrating emotional experiences).

2. Know which emotions you are feeling. Name them.

3. Determine whether it's appropriate to surrender to the emotion or to mitigate it (more on how to discern this in the forthcoming chapters on fear and anxiety).

4. Identify any helpful information an emotion has to share with you.

5. Discharge or express strong emotion in as nonviolent a way as possible.

6. When appropriate, feel and "be with" an emotion or feeling without immediately acting on or expressing it.

7. To the degree appropriate, allow yourself to be affected and changed by emotions and feelings, such as receiving the experience of grief without analyzing it.

8. Gradually process and integrate emotion by pacing yourself according to what you can handle (a process called "titration" discussed later in this chapter under "Titration and Healthy Denial"), and reach out for support when metabolizing overwhelming emotion and feelings.

9. Allow emotions and feelings to have their time and their season, and to pass on their own terms, coaxing and curbing them when appropriate (described shortly).

10. Reflect on the results: what worked well and what didn't. Sometimes this takes a while to reveal itself and requires patience.

---

• EXERCISE •

### EMOTIONAL INTELLIGENCE REFLECTION

Reflect or journal on the following questions for each of the Ten Steps for Emotional Intelligence:

1. What is your opinion of each of the steps, and which do you find valuable?

2. How much do you already practice each step, and in what specific ways can you increase practicing any that you feel to be helpful?

3. Recall a recent challenging emotional experience. Review each of the Ten Steps above and list those you applied to the situation. Also, identify which ones you didn't apply and consider how each of these might have saved you unnecessary suffering.

―――――――

Treating the world with care relies on emotional intelligence. We pause long enough in self-reflection to generate sufficient wisdom to act with integrity for ourselves and for the whole. Creating a sustainable outer world from solid emotional work and clear thinking (Resource 2: Weber, "Re-thinking") provides enduring security for equitable prosperity—more compassion and equality for all. This allows for more inner growth, which in turn leads to a more enjoyable and fruitful outer life. A fertile, positive feedback loop is created.

Since positive feedback loops will be discussed throughout this writing, I want to briefly define the term. A positive feedback loop occurs when a given condition A amplifies condition B, which in turn amplifies condition A, thus amplifying condition B anew, on and on in an exponentially intensifying cycle. Some positive feedback loops create beneficial (fertile) results; others lead to disaster.

An example of a beneficial positive feedback loop is the example just mentioned: inner work (condition A) influences our actions to benefit others (condition B), which in turn supports our inner life (condition A), which creates even more benefit to others (condition B). In contrast, the wildfires that began in Australia in late 2019 are an example of a disastrous positive feedback loop. These wildfires were fueled by climate change (condition B), yet the fires themselves (condition A) exacerbate climate change (condition B), which in turn amplify the incidence of wildfires (condition A).[38] Healing climate crisis requires we create regenerative positive feedback loops between ourselves and the natural world, and that we desist from Earth-destroying ones.

―――――――――――――――――――――――――

38. Stone, "Climate Change Fueled the Australia Fires. Now Those Fires Are Fueling Climate Change."

When either Yin or Yang is deficient (underrepresented), a distorted manifestation of the other results. Too little Yin creates a relative excess of Yang, and vice versa. On a physiological level, if we are deficient in Yin hormones, vital fluids, and sleep, we tend to develop what Chinese medicine calls *Yin-deficient heat signs*. This often manifests as headache, night sweats, temporary flushing, and restless irritability. If we are deficient in Yang hormones, metabolic energy, and physical activity, we tend to develop *Yang-deficient cold signs* such as chills, low appetite, weight gain, lethargy, and depressed mood. On an emotional level, denying (Yang) joy leads to (Yin) despair and apathy. Too much (Yang) anger and not enough (Yin) grief leads to excess (Yang) violence and destruction. Further, symptoms of Yin and Yang excess and deficiency create infertile (inappropriately destructive) positive feedback loops leading to more imbalance, which is why it's important to address them sooner than later.

In sum, we see how the interdependence of Yin and Yang can work for or against fertility and renewal. Inner, positive feedback loops of physiological dysregulation and emotional denial can render us less capable of caring for the world, leading to destructive positive feedback loops in the body and in the environment. These proverbial chickens of biospheric imbalance come home to roost, dysregulating us even further and creating a larger, novel feedback loop of destruction and violence between humans and the environment. In contrast, by following Yin-Yang wisdom and welcoming all its seasons to the guesthouse of our hearts and minds, we create a regenerative, positive feedback loop with the natural world. An embrace of all Yin and Yang emotions also helps us maintain harmonious, regenerative relationships with each other as we work through difficulties, celebrate goodness, and remain humble for the greater good.

## Grief, Anger, and Integrative Activism

Because emotional intelligence contributes to our own and the natural world's health, wisdom for how to work with emotions is part of holistic medicine. Yin-Yang emotional intelligence includes an equal appreciation of each of the cardinal emotions in the wheelhouse of the Five Phases as required to live regeneratively within a balance of death and rebirth for ultimate flourishing.

What's more, each emotion serves to keep other emotions informed and in check, similarly to how the light of awareness keeps in check and informs us of our unconscious psychological shadow in order to curb our malevolent urges and perverse progress. This checks-and-balances system is known as the Control Cycle in Chinese medicine. It helps integrate the phases by guiding medical treatment and harmonizing our psyches, the very qualities we need to cope through and heal climate crisis at its root.

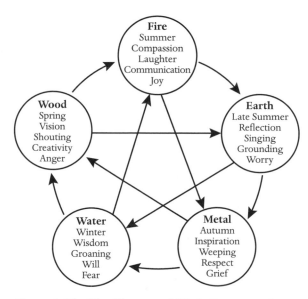

**Figure 4: The Five Phases and Their Correspondences**

The Control Cycle is depicted by the inner arrows, in the form of a star, among the phases, as seen above in figure 4. Yin's grief and Yang's anger, for example—pertaining to the Metal and Wood phases, respectively—must exist in dynamic balance. As you can see, these emotions lie on either end of the arrow extending from the Metal to the Wood phase. A significant excess of either of these emotions, when consciously or unconsciously used to avoid the other, creates enduring imbalance and throws off the smooth flow of the other, disrupting harmony inside, and eventually outside, of us.

In contrast with the Control Cycle, the Generation Cycle is depicted by the outer arrows in figure 4, indicating a healthy flow of transformation from one phase to the next in a clockwise direction, similar to the flow of the seasons of the year. The Control Cycle imparts a Yin, restraining effect on our lives, while the Generation Cycle imparts a Yang, procreative effect. This Yin-Yang balance is key to sustainable living, as we both curb and progress in all ways.

In section I, we learned some of grief's benefits. Grief's cardinal function is to keep fertile darkness—namely our emotional pain—moving and transforming. For this, all we need to do is feel our grief—to mourn. But grief, and grief work, are not just about expressing sadness and "dying through our pain" like this. They include feeling and expressing anger; after all, anger is one of the five stages of grief. We can feel sadness and anger for what we've lost and in response to what has hurt us, including ecological or interpersonal losses and injuries.

Another often overlooked, valid form of expressing anger is sitting with anger, neither repressing nor directing it outwardly. This way, anger expresses itself inside us, as it simmers and "boils off," allowing for a more gradual, measured release. If we find our anger is festering more than simmering and diffusing, we might not choose to express it appropriately and safely. Noticing this dynamic and sensing how to express anger is an example of emotional intelligence. So is noticing the results of doing so.

———

Let's explore in more detail how grief interacts dynamically in relation to its Yang brother on the other side of the Yin-Yang spectrum: anger. When we can't feel and process (Yin) grief, the resulting buildup of backlogged pain often propels us to lash out inappropriately in (Yang) anger. This dynamic is represented by the diagonal arrow from Metal to Wood becoming weak (figure 4), resulting in a lack of healthy restraint on the Wood phase and its associated emotion of anger. This lack of "control" (read: healthy check) on the Wood phase allows its corresponding emotion of anger to grow unrestrained.

The holistic model of the phases and their correspondences shows how energy manifests through any of the correspondences. Grief and autumn correspond with degrowth, while spring and its creativity correspond with growth. Thus, an inability to grieve leads to unregulated growth of all kinds. Dysregulated (extreme or misplaced) anger combined with a failure to grieve correlates with greed and pernicious outward growth, as we observe in out-of-control industrial production and consumption. This is an example of how our collective emotional imbalance creates social and environmental imbalance.

Similar damage occurs in reverse. If we can't feel and express healthy anger, it becomes repressed. A common result of this is a retreat into hopelessness, silent grief (or depression), complacency, and impotence. When the Wood phase is repressed this way, it is said to "overact" or "insult" the phase responsible for controlling it, in this case the Metal phase. This overacting (by way of repressing healthy anger) opposes the Control Cycle. Wood's kickback on the Metal phase can result in repressed grief, which might cause us to feel apathetic and lethargic, purposeless or depressed (symptoms of both repressed anger and blocked grief). Stifled grief in turn generates more anger, and without a healthy means to express this anger, leads to violent destruction of what we love, all of which fuels climate imbalance.

In this we see the intricate interdependence and the cause and effect relationship among our emotions, and how their repression and overindulgence lead to careless polluting and ecocide. In this case, an intolerance of—and inability to healthily express—the Yang emotion of anger leads to an excess of Yin grief. If we can't grieve, more anger builds, and the vicious positive feedback loop persists until emotional intelligence comes to the rescue. Our inability to express healthy anger causes injustice and malevolence to persist unchecked and unchallenged. This is what happens when anger does not rise up to serve its sacred activist role of protection and boundary-setting. Examples are the ongoing desecration of natural refuges and discrimination against indigenous peoples when enough of us don't collectively speak up for their rights.

Skillfully expressing anger in a manner that is not manipulative or abusive is an art worth mastering and an essential tool for bringing about social and environmental justice. When expressing anger to others, we can express our upset and even raise our voices. We should use "I" statements as much as possible, abide by the facts, and refrain from name-calling and personal attacks that shame and belittle another. An example, said in a low or loud voice, might sound like: "I am really upset you didn't pay me back and I don't like how you repeatedly ignore my requests for repayment. I really don't like being taken advantage of like this."

If we can also contact our care and love when we are upset, and allow these more Yin tender feelings to infuse our Yang anger, we create an amalgam that empowers both polarities for passionate, meaningful communication. This is usually easier, and more authentic, once we've vented our initial anger-fire, which is why sitting with and venting strong anger before confronting another (when possible) is often helpful.

---

### • EXERCISE •
### EXPRESSING HEALTHY ANGER

The next time you need to express your anger to another, first do a practice delivery in private. Begin by writing or speaking out your raw anger as a stream of consciousness, without censorship. Pause and rest as you need to. Take a break when you have finished.

Before expressing your next practice round of anger delivery, see if you can identify what you care about that your anger is protecting; anger often defends something we value. Reflect or write about your care and allow yourself to feel that care and love. If you care about the person you are upset with, see if you can feel your care for them along with your anger. In your next practice round of expressing your anger in private, try to allow your vulnerability and sense of hurt come through and influence the delivery of your anger.

If this integration of Yin (care) and Yang (anger) emotion feels good to you, when and if you feel ready to express yourself to the person who hurt you, try delivering your upset in this integrated way. If you journaled your practice sessions, consider first speaking it out in private.

---

Anger is also vital for motivating rebellion unto revolution. We want to be careful, however, not to always express our anger impulsively, through aggression and resistance. We can also express it wisely by harnessing anger's passion and applying it skillfully to each situation. Combined with the Yin emotions of grief and fear, the Yang energy of anger is a key ingredient for climate activism. It's the cayenne pepper that gives the needed kick to the hearty soup of change-making. Anger, and a dash of fear, kicks us in the ass to get up and do something. Grief curbs anger's intensity and destructive capacity—when appropriate—and infuses it with compassion, patience, and wisdom. The result is integrated, measured action informed by wisdom and possessing the necessary passion to let others know we mean business.

Utilizing the healthy volition in anger propels us to rebel against climate crisis and challenge our governments (especially local) to make desperately needed top-down policy change. I discuss this further in the context of Extinction Rebellion in chapter 11. The same mobilizing energy of anger also propels bottom-up, personal lifestyle changes for consuming less (degrowth). Rising up in outrage to protect what we love shares energetic poetry with the Wood phase energy of sap rising in spring. It is an example of sustainable action. Also embracing grief (downward and inward energy) prevents our outrage (upward and outward energy) from becoming excessively volatile, sabotaging anger's protective role.

Via these Five Phase dynamics, we see how an embrace of both grief and anger regenerates us and the world we inhabit. Please don't worry if you don't fully grasp the Five Phase details I'm describing here. The takeaway is that all emotions—not just anger and grief—need to be skillfully worked with because each has a sacred role to play in both personal and planetary wellness. Understanding the Yin and Yang dynamics of emotion places them in a holistic context that connects our inner lives with the outer world in shared oneness. When we successfully enact emotional intelligence, we create positive feedback loops for increased eco-human thriving.

———

It's worth mentioning that feeling all our emotions does not mean we wallow in or immediately act on these emotions. More important is that we embody, work with, and then act on them—this is the heart of emotional intelligence. Case in point: in a discussion of emotional responses to climate crisis, a colleague asserted that grief is not the emotion we need to be feeling right now. I responded that this assumes we have the choice *not* to feel grief. Indeed, we often don't have this choice, and embodying our grief can actually help us generate a clearer, more genuine, and passionate climate response.

In a letter responding to the suggestion that climate scientists tend to repress grief on the job, professor Andy Radford acknowledges that unacknowledged grief "can cloud judgement, inhibit creativity and engender a sense that there is no way forward."[39] In the same letter, its coauthor, Dr. Steve Simpson, adds: "Instead of ignoring or suppressing our grief, environmental scientists should be acknowledging, accepting and working through it."[40]

The suggestion to avoid grief also overlooks the importance of grief's role in curbing anger, as previously discussed, as well as grief's compassion-generating and wisdom-birthing power. When grief is repressed, it can transform into anger and rage via the reciprocity of Yin-Yang, whereby one extreme transforms into the other. This fuels war-mongering, imperialism, domestic violence, bullying, and injustice of all kinds. Especially for men, anger is easier to express and is less stigmatized than grief. Arizona-based psychologist Todd Linaman speaks to these many dynamics: "For many people, chronic anger is an expression of unresolved grief. They may unconsciously exchange the emotions most often associated with grief because it makes them feel weak and vulnerable. Anger, on the other hand, serves as a sort of force field that shuts us down so we don't have to go any farther in the grieving process. It allows us to turn our uncomfortable feelings outward onto others. While this can affect anyone, men, in particular, struggle with expressing deep, personal grief."[41]

We might feel grief or anger for a few seconds, or it might flood our psyche for weeks and months. Still, we can take measures to reduce our emotional suffering and employ emotional passion to our benefit. With practice, we become more skillful at finding balance between sitting with our emotions and expressing ourselves in the moment. We can pay more attention to subtle messages—such as "whispers" from our deeper self—for when to let insults go and when to take them to heart. We become more attuned to knowing when to be patient and when to be spontaneous—*everything has its season*. Each situation, and each of us, merits unique balance in this regard—a personalized, seasonal prescription for psychic and ecological sanity best guided by an amalgamation of established wisdom, trial and error, and our own intuition.

---

39. Weston, "'They Should Be Allowed to Cry': Ecological Disaster Taking Toll on Scientists' Mental Health."

40. Ibid.

41. Linaman, "Is It Anger or Unresolved Grief?"

# Full-Spectrum Love

Let's recap. Healthy grief opens and softens our hearts so we can intimately know for what, and how deeply, we care. Healthy expression of anger creates boundaries to appropriately protect what we love. Clearing our pain via grief is as important as venting pain via anger. Held in dialectical balance, these interdependent emotional energies help curb and thereby bend the otherwise straight lines of Yin and Yang into the integrated circle they comprise together. This way, anger and grief support one another and contribute to a thriving inner and outer world, represented by Yin and Yang in dynamic balance. Holistic emotional intelligence requires learning how to face, embrace, modulate, integrate, and express emotion for love in action. Use the Ten Steps for Emotional Intelligence listed at the beginning of this chapter to guide you.

The Yin-Yang symbol also beautifully represents love in the form of grounded care. Such full-bodied love is all the seasons and their corresponding phases wholly embraced so they can robustly sustain one another along the Control and Generation cycles depicted in figure 4. An embrace of each phase and its corresponding emotion allows the cycle to turn. Whole-bodied love, then, includes anger, grief, fear, joy, and all our other emotions wisely worked with. This is the soulful "better living through chemistry" we have been missing in the industrial age.

To be sustainable, love must be more than a feeling or a willful effort. It must amount to more than trying to be nice and peaceful. Shadow work and integration of our dark emotions is the long-term strategy for sustainable joy and truly loving, regenerative acts. While superficial love is often unaware of its shadow, deep, wise love includes what is sacredly dark, difficult, and fertile. *Love is enough*, but it must be this kind of full-spectrum love. Without this, what I call *climate bypassing* results—the denying of difficult emotions that arise in relation to climate change that leads to our ignoring climate crisis and prevents us from wholeheartedly engaging with it.

We recall a core message of holistic medicine's metaphorical framework: we are intertwined with the natural world in a reciprocity of oneness. The Five Phases, including their emotional correspondences, represent this interrelationship. Hopefully, you can now more deeply grasp how a lack of emotional intelligence has driven our current climate predicament. You might also better understand how emotional intelligence is foundational for radical regeneration of humanity and the natural world. These latter assertions will be more robustly evidenced in the chapters ahead.

## Cognitive-Emotional Process Tools

This discussion of welcoming emotion warrants an important caveat: it's not always helpful to unconditionally embrace emotion, especially if we are excessively out of balance. In these instances, denying an emotional excess in order to preserve equanimity and remain more functional is often more appropriate. Examples include clinical anxiety and depression, emotional dysregulation from substance abuse and triggering events, and extreme stress. In these cases, rather than using a psychodynamic, depth-oriented, transformational approach appropriate to grief work and healing old love wounds, we most often want to "fix" these imbalances via mitigation, as we do physical imbalances. Here, the psychotherapeutic modalities of cognitive behavioral therapy (CBT) and dialectical behavior therapy (DBT)[42] are more appropriate psychological healing approaches. CBT and DBT address changing how we think and behave as a way to better regulate how we feel. A combination of depth and cognitive approaches may also be helpful. Engaging in depth work when cognitive behavioral work is called for, or vice versa, can lead to harm. Guidance from a psychotherapist in these instances is recommended.

A *psychodynamic* approach to psychotherapy can be understood as exploration of the relationship between conscious and unconscious cognitive and emotional dynamics that shape our motivations and personality. CBT and DBT generally do not prioritize or look for meaning in thoughts, emotions, and even personal narratives, while psychodynamic work does. Although CBT and DBT help us regulate our emotions when we feel too far out of balance (dysregulated), they can be incorporated into psychodynamic work to help "titrate" (gradually process and integrate) strong emotional experiences and gain overarching perspective, as I'll discuss further along. Just as we welcome all of our emotions, all these therapeutic modalities are important for cultivating emotional intelligence and

---

42. Grohol, "What's the Difference Between CBT and DBT?"

resiliency, for letting the seasonal vicissitudes of Yin and Yang become sustainable enough to transform and not derail us.

## Titration and Healthy Denial

"Titration" is a term borrowed from chemistry. As applied to psychological work, it means to gradually digest difficult, strong emotions, a little at a time, so they don't overwhelm and derail us. Titration often happens automatically, such as when we instinctively buffer ourselves from feeling the full impact of grief, anger, or anxiety all at once.

Let's explore how to titrate anger without dangerously repressing it. Raw, volatile anger often has few remunerating physiological benefits, except for when it saves our lives! Letting ourselves get too angry too often damages our health and our relationships. We can practice reducing anger's intensity (and that of other emotions too) through deep breathing, exercising, and reducing general stress levels. As shared earlier, we can also sit with and feel anger, without expressing it outwardly. Consciously taking a "time-out" from a heated argument to simmer down also helps us titrate, and thereby regulate, our anger. This way we feel and discharge anger over a longer time span while not letting it precipitate hurtful actions. This is not repression but skillfulness. It is both self-care and care of others so we are not at the behest of anger's destructive, greedy, self-perpetuating demands.

To prevent emotional overwhelm and aid in its titration, we can engage in *healthy denial*. This means we can take breaks from focusing on overwhelming emotional states by, for example, *deliberately* distracting ourselves. Neurochemically, anger inhibits activity in our prefrontal cortex, a region of our brains involved with self-reflection and the critical thinking needed to ascertain facts and regulate ourselves. If we feel overcome by rage in a disagreement with a lover or at the corruption and inaction of our government on climate change, for example, we can take a time-out or choose an activity that distracts us from our anger. This helps our reasoning, prefrontal cortex to come back online so we can reflect on the facts, which is difficult to do in the heat of upset.

We can also titrate grief. Grief is heavy and can leave us depleted and unmotivated. Going out to dinner with friends, watching a movie, or taking a walk to get breaks from protracted grief are all forms of healthy denial that help us release and recharge. They leave us better equipped to resume the griev-ing process as necessary. I find that paying attention to my body's sensations helps me determine when I need breaks from grief. This indicator is similar to other bodily cues, such as those for hunger or the need to get up from writing to move around. Just because I distract myself and take a break from full-on grieving doesn't mean the grief leaves me. It's there in the background, always, and I allow it to be, consciously straddling a tension of opposites between it and other emotions, including joy.

Healthy denial is never meant to become perpetual denial or suppression. As a general guideline, denial of or distraction from emotion is healthy and helpful when conscious and intermittent, and unhelpful when unconscious and persistent. It's important to come back again and again to a fuller embrace of grief, for as long as it persists. Doing so helps grief pass more readily, sanely, and organically from an acute stage into the background of our lives. Equally, we should be mindful not to embrace grief too tightly just for the hope it passes sooner. Too much eagerness to get through grief blocks us from fully embodying it, and, paradoxically, perpetuates it. Rushing the process also deprives us of grief's sacred gifts to us, which include dissolving our pain and releasing our finer jewels of being human as a greater capacity to love. Because climate grief is ongoing and perpetual, we should also get used to this sadness and not be in a rush to get somewhere, save to net-zero carbon emissions!

## Clearing Our Hearts

In the spirit of resolving past and present pain to nourish our triangle of resil-ience relationships, let's take a look at some more real-life dynamics. Many of us grew up unable to express ourselves sufficiently or to regulate overwhelming experiences, and to this day we may feel repressed, numb, and unrequited. The initial work to heal this is to express ourselves and to seek out the company of those who can hear us—including ourselves. By showing up for ourselves and by finding others who will hear and acknowledge us, we can rewire our brains, heal our hearts, and begin to change our experience from emptiness and apa-thy to fulfillment and purpose. Identifying our unhelpful habits, releasing back-logged emotion, and changing our patterns and choices all create space for new and nourishing experiences to enter our lives. In the process, little or "nothing" is left behind, as this poem "Rest of Longing," which I wrote from the midst of emotional death and rebirth work, conveys:

### Rest of Longing

*Trust those places*
*With no way out,*
*The dark corridors*
*Of your longing.*

*In fact, entrust them more*
*Than you give to daylight*
*Which disappears*
*With fall of night.*

*Only hidden light*
*That waits for you in shadows*
*Can reveal the invisible*
*Passage from darkness*
*That leaves nothing*

*Behind.*

Both the release of backlogged emotion and the fulfillment of our need to be heard and acknowledged can happen beautifully and simultaneously in therapy. We can supplement therapy by acknowledging ourselves each day through supportive self-talk, tending to emotions that surface, journaling, and other forms of self-care that give us nourishing respite from inner work and allow our difficult emotions to transform us.

---

• EXERCISE •
## EMOTIONAL SELF-CARE

Which of the following activities do you feel would help you be kinder to yourself in the midst of healing your heart?

• **Soothing self-talk:** Repeat some kind, affirming words to soothe and encourage yourself. Examples include, "It's okay, you're going to be better for this." Or, "I love you, hang in there." You can express such affirmations silently or by saying them out loud to yourself. Hearing yourself say the words often has more impact.

- **Be with feelings:** When difficult emotions surface, allow yourself to pause what you're doing and be with them. If feelings are overwhelming, how can you receive support, and what are some healthy ways to reduce their intensity?

- **Write it out:** Pick up your journal or some paper and write your feelings and other expressions or insights as a way to be present with yourself. You may want to seek the unconditionally listening ear of a friend as you share and process your feelings and thoughts.

- **Your Own Wisdom:** In what other ways can you be kind to yourself during this time of self-healing? Which do you feel ready to enact?

We can also engage in other forms of creative self-expression such as singing, expressive movement, and having fun. All these allow us to express, release, recharge, and bear witness to ourselves, so we can love ourselves into more wholeness, and by extension heal the world into greater balance through our presence and love in action.

Viewed through the lens of Yin and Yang, we have to empty ourselves (a Yin-clearing experience) of backlogged pain that clutters and stymies our heart in order to replenish (a Yang-filling experience) with something new and good. Ideally, we want to enter the depths of our pain so we can fill from that same depth. This joins conscious Yang experience with subconscious Yin depths, as we fulfill our quest for individuation, integration, and Yin-Yang's perennial promise for regeneration. This way, Yang-release and Yin-fulfillment happen simultaneously—our neuronally-encoded memories and attendant repressed emotions of the past are activated, released, and reconfigured by empathic, new learning in the present.

## A Higher Road

Once we have integrated enough of our previous emotional wounds, we may feel sufficiently empowered in our sense of self, in our sovereignty. As a result, we may not feel compelled to express all our emotions. It's easier to let go of smaller insults as an adjustment we make for the greater good. We will still feel all our feelings, but choose not to express them outwardly, or to do so in edited form. We are more able to "take the high road" without feeling repressed or unduly compromised in the process. This way, we can bring our relationships with ourselves and others to a new level.

Taking this higher path will not feel like an unreasonable sacrifice because the work we do to clear our emotional backlog helps us be more mindful of, and less charged about, our emotional triggers. We're not so ruled by them that they powerfully and negatively potentiate our present experience. None of this means we tolerate abuse, meanness, and other violations in the present.

While expressing and releasing backlogged emotion leads to more liberation and joy, a compulsive need to constantly express and act out "our truth" can be a self-indulgent trap and ironically, a burden and an obstacle to growth. After enough truth-telling, another kind of freedom might present: to *not* fully embody and take to heart each feeling, but instead to let go of the "small stuff." When we grow in emotional intelligence, we have the self-awareness to choose restraint as a response. It can be a welcome relief not to have to indulge our truth of disparaging thoughts and difficult feelings, and thereby not toss logs onto the fire of conflict and misunderstanding. This might look like not having to be right, loosening our boundaries to allow more connection, and holding back anger in disagreements.

## Holding Space

Having the genuine capacity to moderate or forego acting out emotional reactivity and "truth" allows us to be of more service. We enact these restraints to the extent we are able to without doing ourselves harm. When we can gracefully set aside our own upset and offer an empathic, non-reactive response, we help others find sanctuary in their own projections and displaced emotions which arise from wounded and dysregulated states. This is not codependency but mirroring integrity and self-sovereignty. The ability to show up and help others regulate is a potent heart-gift as climate crisis worsens, and will be increasingly so in the more challenging years to come. This is why healing our historical pain now must be a top priority.

As emotional dysregulation increases due to climate chaos, those of us able to hold neutral space and reflect care to others in distress provide vital medicine for our times. For myself, witnessing another settle into their vulnerability, open their heart, and find new strength gives me profound satisfaction. Deeply hearing the truth of others during the climate change discussion and support groups I facilitate is an especially nourishing experience. I also have been fortunate to be on the receiving end of this kind of compassion, which has helped me "pay it forward" by embodying it with others.

As collective fear, dysregulation, and trauma increase with global climate change fever, we will need more of us to bring coolness, wisdom, and comfort to chaos. These latter Yin dispositions help balance dysregulated Yang chaos and violence. Many have enacted this succor for displaced victims during recent wildfires. On my home turf in Hawaii, I and a dozen other lava flow evacuees were welcomed in by a loving couple who gave us a place to stay on their farm. They asked for nothing in return, and we all found unique ways to contribute as best we could. Their big hearts and gestures of loving-kindness not only helped me immensely during a devastating time of loss, but impressed and changed me in ways I'm still discovering.

Loss, when endured with an open heart, fortifies us to be a harbor for ourselves and others in challenging times. We can be the safe, nurturing, Yin-holders for grief and remorse as well as the strong, Yang-pillars to resist injustice and violence. Until we have substantially unburdened our hearts by working through our core love wounds, it can be challenging to show up for others as much as we'd like. We might even be repulsed by their wounds. As Father Gregory Boyle, founder of the largest gang member rehabilitation center in the world, aptly states: "…if you don't welcome your wounds, you may be tempted to despise the wounded."[43]

## Full Circle

When we view our own emotions as forces common to all of nature and its seasons—in the frenzied and creative buzz of springtime, in summer's bright and easy joy, in autumn's falling leaves and gradual descent inward, or in winter's

---

43. French, "Father Gregory Boyle, Author of New Book, to Pasadena Audience: Consider Radical Kinship and Compassion."

foreboding, desolate landscape—we foster wholeness vis à vis our relationship with the Earth.

Emotions also underlie our beliefs and decisions, heavily influencing our actions. This understanding has been borne out by pioneering neuroscientist Antonio Damasio, who has shown that emotion, often imperceptible to us, governs our decision-making. [44] Because our actions impact the natural world we depend upon for our wellness, we had better sort out our emotional lives if we want to work harmoniously together and act wisely to heal climate change. In a paper published in "Critical Psychology," ecopsychologist Dr. David Kidner highlights the link between our capacity to feel and averting ecological disaster. He writes: "… our current reliance on cognition and our corresponding marginalization of sensing and feeling, in addition to undermining human well-being, may be ecologically catastrophic." [45] To be clear, we need both clear thinking and robust emotional lives working in harmony for a better world.

Because Yin and Yang are inextricably interdependent, they mutually support and balance each other. We have seen this to be the case with grief and anger, a dynamic duo for environmental activism and coping with all manner of upset and injury. We can especially remember balance between grief and anger (and other emotions) in response to climate change injuries, political shenanigans, the challenges of working together to resist and reform, and our personal relationship struggles. Letting go of the small stuff and taking the high road helps us stay focused on our most heartfelt goals. In the next chapters we will explore the dynamics of fear and anxiety and how to "mine and manage them" to better weather and thrive through climate crisis.

When we embrace all Five Phase emotions and express them skillfully and appropriately, we create more harmonious relations with all our triangle of resilience relationships—with ourselves, with those we love, and with the natural world we must learn to bless … again and again.

---

44. Camp, "Decisions Are Largely Emotional, Not Logical: The Neuroscience Behind Decision-Making."; Purves, "The Interplay of Emotion and Reason."

45. Kidner, "Depression and the natural world: toward a critical ecology of psychological distress."

## • EXERCISE •
### CHAPTER 3 JOURNALING

Please also refer to the additional in-text exercises for this chapter.

Take out your journal or notepad, place it in front of you, and write out your responses to the following prompts.

1. How could you simplify your outer life and decrease unnecessary stress? How can you reduce your overhead and financial spending to make more time for inner and outer activism?

2. Turn back to the start of this chapter and review the Five Phases and all their characteristics. Which phase/s most strongly represent your personality, and which phase/s don't? Write down the characteristics from each phase with which you most strongly identify, as well as those with which you don't identify. Then, for each characteristic you identify with, briefly journal about how you would like to encourage or discourage it in your life. Do the same for the characteristics with which you don't identify.

## Chapter 4
# WORKING WITH FEAR

*Having so recently been one of the underdogs of the savannah,*
*we are full of the fears and anxieties over our position,*
*which makes us doubly cruel and dangerous.*
*Many historical calamities, from deadly wars to ecological catastrophes,*
*have resulted from this over-hasty jump.*[46]
~YUVAL HARARI, *SAPIENS*

In the previous chapter we explored the Yin and Yang dynamics of anger and grief, which pertain to the Metal and Wood phases of Chinese medicine, respectively. We also saw how working wisely with these emotions influences our ability to show up for our triangle of resilience relationships and climate action. Now we turn to building emotional intelligence around fear, the emotion pertaining to the Water phase. We will examine how fear often dictates what we notice and our capacity to engage with what matters.

Consistent with the dark depths of the Water phase, there is arguably no difficult emotion more foundational, powerful, and challenging than fear. Fear also underlies our resistance to experience other difficult emotions such as grief, anger, remorse, despair, and even joy. Together with grief and anger, fear completes the triad of difficult primary emotions pertaining to the Five Phases, all of which must be worked with to attain full-fledged emotional intelligence and truly holistic climate cure.

---

46. Harari, *Sapiens: A Brief History of Humankind*, 12.

Self-healing through grief work is most effective when we know how to manage our unhelpful fears, including anxieties. Fear and anxiety prevent us from productive inner work with other challenging emotions, making us "cruel and dangerous"[47] to ourselves, the natural world, and one another. The corollary is also true: bolstering our triangle of resilience relationships while our fears and anxieties are active is invaluable for managing these heightened states. We should therefore simultaneously seek to improve these relationships while we work to mitigate fear and anxiety.

What follows is an orientation to the dynamics of fear and how to work with them in the context of relating with ourselves, others, and the ongoing environmental crisis.

## Helpful vs. Unhelpful Fear

An allegory from Eastern spirituality lends insight to distinguishing between helpful and unhelpful fear, as well as to how our awareness can help us successfully navigate this emotion.[48] The parable tells of a monk returning home after work. He comes upon what he thinks is a snake in the road and becomes fearful of being bitten, unsure if he can pass. He proceeds carefully and discovers what he thought was a snake is actually a rope, perhaps dropped by a previous traveler.

All fear reactions are *initially* helpful because they alert us to possible danger. But perceiving a rope to be a snake is *ultimately* an unhelpful fear—which we can also call an *irrational* or *unrealistic* fear—because it is a misperception of reality. This causes us to recoil and react unnecessarily, expending valuable energy and ultimately limiting us. Conversely, fear reactions in response to real danger—which we can also call *rational* or *realistic* fear—are ultimately helpful. Encountering a snake or feeling scared of a quickly moving avalanche are real threats that produce helpful realistic fear. Helpful fears propel us to immediate action that keeps us safe.

Fear is hardwired in us, meaning we don't have conscious control over it when it first arises. In the moment, we can't think our way out of it, nor would we want to. We are wired to react with fear to all possible danger because it's not adaptive to stop and analyze whether a threat is truly dangerous or not.

---

47. Harari, *Sapiens: A Brief History of Humankind*, 12.
48. Chu, "The Snake Rope: Essential Buddhist Teaching in a Simple Story."

By the time we figure it out, we could be dead. Failing to jump away from a rustle in the brush or crouch when we hear a loud noise doesn't maximize our survival chances. So, when immediately threatened, we react to save ourselves from possible injury. In fact, such fear reactions (similar to reactive anger) shut down our capacity for conscious reflection, rendering us unable to think clearly or do anything but instinctively react to save our lives. As soon as this initial fear response subsides, however, our reasoning faculty returns and we can assess the danger. The immediate knee-jerk mechanism is valuable because expending some time and energy reacting to a potential fear is a small cost compared to the alternative of being seriously harmed.

Because we are not evolutionarily equipped to immediately distinguish between ultimately helpful and unhelpful fears, we must fill in this missing aptitude with conscious discrimination. We do this by intentionally reflecting as soon as possible—but only once we are safe from danger—to determine if the threat is real or not. This way we conserve energy and learn the truth about the threat, which informs our next actions. So, while we can't prevent our immediate, prerational (hardwired) fear reactions, we can choose not to exacerbate them. This allows us to *respond* more than merely *react*.

If we don't learn to surmount our unhelpful fear of ultimately harmless threats, the fear can also leave us with false beliefs about reality. This leads to more stress and more inefficient behavior that exact a toll on us and on the environment. Had the monk fled in the opposite direction the moment he saw the "snake," rather than investigating from a safe distance and learning there was no real danger, he might have experienced excess, unnecessary stress every time he walked that path in the future. By stopping to observe and apprehend reality, the monk saves himself from perpetuating false beliefs about the rope and feeding irrational fear. We can do the same for any fear we experience by not assuming or coming to a conclusion until we have had the opportunity to check the facts.

When we carry unrealistic fears about climate change, submit to knee-jerk reactions, and persist in acting on false beliefs, we render ourselves similarly ineffective in responding to reality and behaving in helpful ways. Let's look at both a personal and a climate example of irrational, unhelpful fears and how to manage them.

• Exercise •
## Fear Imagination

Imagine yourself in the following personal and climate situations.

**Personal Fear:** Your spouse doesn't come home one night and the next day you ask where they were. You spouse responds, "I slept with someone else last night." Your initial reaction is fear, then maybe anger. As you imagine your partner with someone else, where they might have absconded, and who this lover could be, you find yourself becoming even more fearful and incensed until you totally freak out.

Your initial fear is your hardwired reaction, which you can't help. But the sooner you can notice yourself reacting, the more pain you can save yourself. Once the initial rush subsides and you take a few deep breaths, you have a golden opportunity. This is when your awareness comes back online and you can check for a rope or a snake, in this case to make sure you heard your spouse correctly. If you never bother to learn they actually said, "I helped someone else last night," you dig your own hole and fill it in quickly! This is why we check the facts before getting carried away by initial reactions based on false understandings.

**Climate Fear:** You open your front door, walk outside, immediately smell smoke, and see a lurid orange color in the sky. Because you're living in the age of climate chaos, you assume a wildfire is nearby and coming fast and furious toward you. You panic, pack your bags, and drive as fast as you can out of town.

You can't control your initial fear reaction once you assume fire is on its way. But if you don't pause to fact-check what incited your escalating terror, you could end up in Timbuktu with no gas left in your car—or your adrenal—tank. Bothering to discover that what you smell and see is actually smoke from the neighbor's barbecue and an unusually colorful, but benign, sunset saves a lot of fossil and physiological fuel. Can you think of similar situations where you assumed incorrectly, reacted with fear, and it cost you dearly?

The aforementioned fears are not "snakes" but "ropes." Accurately apprehending reality and checking assumptions saves lots of stress and suffering over nothing. Similarly, being forever afraid to ask a special someone out on a date, or to shrink from giving an important climate change presentation, are not helpful fears. Confronting them feels scary but isn't truly dangerous. While you might endure some initial stress, persevering through these types of fears—by feeling the fear and doing it anyway—often results in worthwhile encounters with valuable benefits. The more we face our irrational, unhelpful fears—however gradually—the better we become at dissolving apparent limitations so we can live more freely, fully, and effectively.

---

One reason climate disruption is so difficult to apprehend is because it is part rope *and* part snake. It requires we pay attention, mitigate unhelpful fear, embrace helpful fear and other uncomfortable emotions, skillfully discern and face climate facts, dismiss climate lies, and not run and hide unless we are in immediate danger.

Ironically, irrational fear and unmanageable anxiety can also result from denial and insufficient knowledge about climate crisis, stymieing our ability to act. Complacency founded on not recognizing a real threat (wrongly perceiving a "rope" instead of a "snake") leads to inaction, just as that frog stays put in a pot of water slowly coming to a boil until it's too late to jump out. This dynamic parallels one form of "convenient" climate change denial whereby deniers misconstrue helpful, realistic fears (snakes are indeed snakes) as unrealistic fears (snakes are just ropes). Deniers try to lull us, and themselves, into complacency by falsely discrediting climate science, which has unequivocally demonstrated that climate change is severe, and we are causing it.

Climate deniers' arguments might stem from:

1. A need to allay their own fear.

2. A wish not to be inconvenienced by mobilizing for climate crisis.

3. An unconscious desire to perpetuate their own privilege and lifestyle.

The antidote to this denial is the courage to:

1. Face the facts, feel, and work with the fear.

2. Take effective action and embrace the inconvenience.

3. Accept that sacrifices and big changes are needed.

## Fear-Mark

When our irrational, unhelpful fears remain unconscious or unexamined, they gain control over us, govern our behavior, and limit our ability to be honest, courageous, and caring. I call the threshold at which fear disables us our *fear-mark*. It is analogous to the visible mark water makes against a hard surface when it persists at a given level, such as on the inside of a barrel or on the wall of a dam.

Our fear-mark is the degree of fear we can tolerate while remaining rational and skillful in our response to information. Said another way, it is the degree of fear beyond which we will *not* pay attention to helpful information. The more emotionally intelligent and gritty we are, the higher we can raise our fear-mark. The higher our fear-mark, the more effective we are at interfacing with climate chaos. Such courage grows with practice and support. If, however, we surpass our fear-mark without sufficient resilience, we shut down and go into denial and/or fight-or-flight reaction.

Our fears are often unconscious. We are not specifically aware of what we fear, nor of our underlying perceptions and beliefs that generate the fear. Until we develop awareness, our fears rule us. When we fear feeling the pain necessary for self-transformation, our fight-or-flight reflex is triggered. We may try to escape the pain (flight) or fend it off (fight). Flight can take the form of denial, and fending off can manifest as rage and violence onto others. This is one way that fear leads to genocide and ecocide. We also can't engage in deep emotional healing such as grief work, or take meaningful action—which both necessitate *being with* the challenging emotion or experience—if we are afraid of the pain we *believe* we will encounter by doing so.

Disarming unconscious, irrational fear first requires we notice when we are hindered by it—discerning that a rope is not a snake. Then we can choose to tolerate feeling the fear, ascertain its source, discern its veracity, and decide on an appropriate response. The way forward through irrational and unhelpful fear is, when we are ready, to "feel the fear and do it anyway." In contrast, when facing realistic, helpful fear, we want to heed its warning with appropriate action, as calmly, quickly, and efficiently as we can.

## The Neurobiology of Fear

Fear arises from our midbrain, from a region called the amygdala. The amygdala is part of the limbic system, also referred to as our "emotional" or "mammalian" brain. Confronting and moving through unhelpful fears is difficult because doing so is counterintuitive; we have to act against powerful instincts telling us something horrible is about to happen. Our bodies may tighten, knees quiver, throats constrict, hearts quicken, and our palms and brows become sweaty. All this screams to us, "Get ready to fight for your life!" Or "Stop, don't go there, run away!"

Instinctual fight-or-flight reactions can include fighting, fleeing, freezing, or fawning ("playing possum"). Fight-or-flight inhibits our neocortical conscious awareness (a higher, frontal brain function), placing us at the whim of instinctual reactions (lower, midbrain, and brainstem functions) which are only helpful when facing immediate peril. When our lives or welfare are truly at risk, our fear is adaptive and helps us survive. When our lives are not at risk and we have misperceived a threat, we fare better when we muster the courage to face and overcome our fear of "ropes." Our capacity to thrive—whether we get that date or deliver that climate crisis presentation—depends upon our ability to proactively confront our irrational, surmountable fears.

Fear and anxiety have archaic origins in our brain's tri-tiered architecture. We evolved neural fear wiring to increase our chances of survival in the face of mortal danger, as when our ancestors mounted an empowered adrenal response to fight off predators. This hardwired fear response enabled immediate, knee-jerk, lifesaving reactions that are still helpful today when we encounter real dangers. Unfortunately, identical fear reactions are triggered whether we're avoiding a snake, giving a public talk, or courting a new romantic interest.

We have not adapted a more discerning response system to different classes of threats. Industrial machine noises, for example, are like ancient, alarming rustles in the brush. Our amygdalae don't distinguish buzz saws, leaf blowers, and trucks' reverse bells as ultimately nonthreatening because these grating intrusions didn't exist when fear became an adaptive facet of our neuroanatomy. Today, our nervous systems perceive these stressors as dangerous, spiking our adrenaline levels (even if we don't realize it) and reacting to them as, for example, prehistoric undulations in the grass, falling rocks, charging animals, or lightning strikes. In excess, all such reactions exact a toll by way of energy waste, oxidative stress, and hormonal dysregulation. This constant wear and tear on our bodies wears us out, which is part of why quiet environments are restorative and healing. Silence itself has a downregulating effect on our nervous systems and has been shown to grow new neurons in the hippocampus, a brain region associated with the amygdala that is involved with emotional memory.[49]

Neocortical critical thinking helps us regulate our midbrain knee-jerk fear responses. Using our intellectual faculties for insight into our emotional responses allows us to work skillfully with them, as well as not suffer unduly at their behest. When we consciously determine that a false-alarm fear reaction (fearing a rope) is *just a feeling*, not an actual threat to our lives, and that overcoming it might improve our lives, we can begin to move beyond our current fear-mark. Acting counterintuitively, we can move beyond our gut, fear reactions. This is also just one example of how relying on our intuition and gut feeling is not always in our best interest; if we did, our unhelpful fears would win out every time. We'd be perpetually defeated, and our world would shrink to a small corner. Recognizing that an irrational fear is surmountable gives us the extra confidence to feel the fear and act anyway.

Irrational fear is real until it isn't. Anyone who has suffered trauma and healed through subsequent post-traumatic stress disorder (PTSD) knows this. A caveat: anxiety disorders—with their perpetual manifestation of sudden, unhelpful fear—require specific treatment and support. Cognitive behavioral therapy (CBT) and dialectical behavior therapy (DBT), mentioned previously in the context of clinical anxiety and depression in chapter 3, are particularly helpful to overcome unhelpful fears. Employing a technique called "exposure therapy," our nervous systems can habituate to and normalize anxiety. This way we learn that we are bigger than our irrational fears. So, as we courageously and skillfully face our fears, let's remember to be patient with ourselves and others along the way.

---

49. I. Kirste, et al., "Is Silence Golden? Effects of Auditory Stimuli and Their Absence on Adult Hippocampal Neurogenesis," 1221–1228.

## Overcoming Climate Fear

Fear is the primary emotion underlying climate denial and inaction. We are afraid of the anxiety we would feel if we paid attention to climate news, and are also afraid of feeling sad, angry, and despairing. We fear responsibility, and the comfort we would feel obliged to sacrifice if we stepped up to action. We might also fear feeling guilty and remorseful for having not done enough previously to mitigate climate breakdown, and for the pollution making we cannot yet renounce.

Working with fear is therefore the linchpin for coping through and engaging with climate crisis. And while we cannot control feeling afraid, we must face our unrealistic fears. Franklin D. Roosevelt had it right. In his famous speech of 1933, he said: "...the only thing we have to fear is...fear itself—nameless, unreasoning, unjustified terror which paralyzes needed efforts to convert retreat into advance."[50] He delivered these words on March 4 ("march forth"), the only day in the calendar that's a marching order! Roosevelt's insight is as apropos for climate emergency as it was during the Great Depression.

When we have wisdom, tools, and support to work with fear and other difficult emotions, we don't have to fear the fear of feeling them. When we no longer feel compelled to avoid challenging emotions at any cost, we can become more climate-engaged. Further, when we realize these emotions contain the seeds of our better selves, we have every reason to say *yes* to growing from them. Fear is then not an obstacle but a portal into regeneration.

Despite popular belief, fear and love are not mutually exclusive. When fear motivates us to right action, this is love in action. A healthy dose of fear that does not permanently scare the bejeezus out of us can be just the emotional spice we need to stimulate fulfilling change, especially since so many of us still don't know just how dire our climate situation is.

Working through fear, and both seeking support from and offering support to others to face reality, raises our emotional intelligence. In the face of environmental and political chaos and mounting natural disasters, many are paralyzed by fear that, unless consciously worked with, can defeat and sabotage what

---

50. Roosevelt, "Inaugural Address, March 4, 1933," in *The Public Papers of Franklin D. Roosevelt, Volume Two: The Year of Crisis, 1933,* 11–16.

could help us protect what we love. And when we lack sufficient care, as is collectively the case today, wisely channeled fear can work in a pinch to rouse us.

---

• EXERCISE •

FEAR-MARK CHALLENGE

On a fresh sheet of paper, list three or more climate-related fears you have. These can be anything from being afraid to live close to the ocean or read climate science news, to being afraid to talk with your climate denying relatives or march in a climate strike. Rate each fear on a severity scale from one to ten. Now think rationally, trying to ascertain how realistic each of these fears is; how much danger does each truly entail? Next, for any that are unrealistic fears, imagine doing what you fear. If it's too scary, begin with the least severe fears. Write out a first-person account of actually doing it, or you can try painting, acting it out, or telling the story of your fear to a friend as if you were doing it now. Do this several times and then rate each fear again. Compare these values with those from when you began the exercise; notice if your fear-mark increased or decreased.

---

## Climate Warrior

I wonder if fear dominates the cultural climate change narrative because it's so easy to disseminate, whereas building robust care requires challenging engagement with fear. In his essay, "Grief and Carbon Reductionism," Charles Eisenstein dissuades us from climate fear when he writes, "People are not going to be frightened into caring."[51] This polarization, however, presupposes fear and care to be mutually exclusive. They are not.

When skillfully worked with, fear can provide the spark in our hearts for the fuel of love (Resource 2: Weber, "Coronation"). Fear—as the fundamental, implicit will to survive—is integral to care. In a New York Times Opinion column about climate change titled "Time to Panic," author David Wallace-Wells proposes that fear may be the only thing left that can save us from climate catastrophe.[52] Fear, as a component of care, is needed for climate cure: enough

---

51. Eisenstein, "Grief and Carbon Reductionism."
52. Wallace-Wells, "Time to Panic."

fear to wake us up and even more passion to live meaningfully, join forces, and incite positive action.

Helpful fear keeps us focused on reality and guides us to right action. An activist colleague of mine attributes her waking up and getting involved with climate action to being scared. Fear has also helped me to care and engage with climate justice. Again, we don't have control over getting scared, any more than we do being sad, mad, or glad—unless we shut down our hearts. Not shutting down means welcoming heartbreak and becoming wounded climate healers.

In his video, "Amazon Rainforest Fires," Eisenstein mischaracterizes anger and doesn't acknowledge it as an honest response to harm. He, therefore, also fails to illuminate anger's crucial role and importance for activism generally. Instead, he encourages we favor grief.[53] But this separation of grief and anger illustrates another false dichotomy. We must not only feel anger, but mobilize its energy full circle in service of compassion and justice for all. As we learned in the previous chapter, anger—one of the well-known "five stages" of grieving—is a valuable component of grieving and part of our natural response to loss. Anger also helps us to keep excess grief in check, exacts justice, and protects us from more loss.

Understanding and experiencing firsthand the surprising, invaluable benefits of anger, grief, fear, and all of our difficult emotions, require deep insight and courage. While we don't get to pick and choose which emotions we feel in the face of climate breakdown, we can decide which emotions we feed. We can infuse the wisdom inherent in every emotion through our actions. We are better off working with broad emotional intelligence for whatever shows up than we are ignoring essential aspects of our hearts. In the face of climate crisis, we can't expect to activate our full selves unless we work with and are transformed by what pains us.

We can—indeed, we must—skillfully employ fear, anger, despair, and remorse for climate resiliency. Think of it this way: fear (and some care) will get you to the emergency room to save your life, but care (along with a modicum of existential fear) is needed to live well. Fear is more helpful for treating the branch stage of climate crisis (the acute stage when concern spikes). Care is more important

---

53. Eisenstein, "Amazon Forest Fires - Avoid This Trap."

for the longer-term, root solution (the chronic stage, or how we can cultivate enduring love in action). Each emotion has its place and each is needed for both the acute and chronic phases of climate illness. Each is essential to our whole hearts, which we wildly and beautifully craft through the work of courageously welcoming initiation into climate warriorhood.

We should not shrink from fear, but embrace it for its holy function of alerting us to danger and to help us heal ourselves and the world. Ironically, one fearful and inaccurately polarizing perception of fear is that we must either surmount it or be paralyzed by it. But this view is distorted; there is another option. We can choose to carry our fear, as we do some love wounds, so we neither deny nor become overtaken by it. We can also cultivate resilience to be *with* rational, helpful fear rather than hide or run from what scares us.

The amalgam of fear plus care produces passionate compassion—the Yin and Yang, the urgency and love—needed to heal through climate crisis. Fear alone doesn't have the heart to regenerate. Care alone is usually too mild and not acute or urgent enough. Fear wakes us up and mobilizes us, while care provides the genuine desire to heal what's been injured. To become sanely afraid (to save our lives), I invite you to read the climate science in the appendix, listen to experts speak on the issue, and discuss concerns with others who are climate-aware. This will keep your survival fear stoked—which, with practice, you can skillfully manage—for we are cognitively biased to forget climate crisis exists at all! You can also find support for this journey in your triangle of resilience relationships. All this can help you courageously embody your fierce love, fueled by healthy fear, to join others and protect what matters to you. This makes an integrated climate warrior.

Counterintuitively and methodically inoculating ourselves against what scares us, by biting off small bits at a time, makes fear easier to manage and integrate into our climate-ready tool kit. This strategy is part of exposure therapy, mentioned previously. It is also a form of emotional titration, discussed in chapter 3, that helps us gradually metabolize stress. Faced in small, measured doses, the fear no longer feels so overwhelming. For example, we can face the scary prospect of learning about alarming climate change news by exposing ourselves to it a little at a time. Preparing like this for stressful future events is also a way to "cope ahead." It's wise to begin this process now, instead of waiting for the probability of being overwhelmed by future circumstances. Gradually learning about how bad the climate situation is allows us to maintain psychic balance over the long run and mount a more effective, informed response.

We can take inspiration from heroic examples of working with fear, seen in those who act for the greater good even when the threats are real and their lives are truly at risk. As activist and film producer of *Art of Courage* Jon Quigley says, "It's every moment where a human being faces a fear and they stand up for something that they believe is more important than their own safety."[54] Mohandas (Mahatma) Gandhi, Nelson Mandela, Martin Luther King Jr., and the many valiant souls who worked secretly to save Jews during the Holocaust are examples. Modern day whistleblowers and indigenous activists protecting native habitats, as well as climate scientists Jon Box and Michael Mann—who have risked their lives to publish outspoken climate change findings despite death threats and financial ruin—are shining, contemporary exemplars of this bravery.[55]

## Room for the Dark

Environmental changes and personal revelation go hand in hand because we are a part of—not overlords of—the natural world. When nature hurts, we do too. Emotional intelligence is the keystone that determines our capacity to face difficult inner and outer realities. Overcoming our fear of feeling bad—sad, angry, scared, remorseful, despairing, or anxious—is the portal into broad-spectrum emotional intelligence. It is to say *yes* to benevolent, fertile darkness; *yes* to heartbreak and more wise Yin-Yang transformation.

Saying *no* to facing our fears means saying *yes* to the consequences of denial. Denial and intellectual dishonesty forged from fear set in motion all manner of calamity, especially evident in the myriad interconnected positive feedback loops contributing to climate chaos. Below are six compelling follies to deny climate crisis exists or to believe "everything will be okay." Curiously, these same denialist "benefits" or "unjust privileges" (if one's goal is to "feel fine") are also conferred when we embrace denial's opposite polarity: climate

---

54. *Art of Courage*, film directed by Kellee Marlow and Véronica Duport Deliz.

55. Richardson, "When the End of Human Civilization Is Your Day Job."

doom. Either extreme of doom or denial (as we explore in detail in chapter 5) provides ample justification to not care enough and allows climate disease to progress without our helping touch.

## Six Climate Denial Follies

By denying climate crisis, we:

1. Escape healthy and adaptive climate anxiety, grief, outrage, fear, worry, and despair.
2. Justify polluting as much as we want.
3. More easily justify abandoning compassion and empathy for others' suffering.
4. Allow the burden of repair to fall on others making heartfelt sacrifices.
5. Continue business as usual and not be inconvenienced.
6. Preserve the privilege of greed and financial gain by way of continued pollution and exploitation.

The totality of all these follies has delivered us to the precipice of extinction. This is the consequence of ignoring the truth so we can avoid feeling pain and continue to unsustainably enjoy ourselves. Instead, we could muster the courage to face the truth and not soft-heart ourselves into illusions.

---

• EXERCISE •
### CLIMATE DENIAL REFLECTION

For this exercise, we remember that we are all in denial of climate crisis to some degree and that *some* of this denial can be helpful. So, there is no judgment here, and if you judge yourself, let that go.

Referring to the Six Climate Denial Follies, which in particular motivate you to stay in the dark, to any degree, about climate crisis? For each that you choose, write a few lines about your fear and what motivates you to justify your denial (again, no judgment here). Note: you don't need to change any of these motivations; this exercise is simply to be honest with yourself. No one has to know but you.

Confronting and acting on climate change means that we face our deepest collective shadow, our deepest fears. We are challenged to relinquish what is most difficult to give up: our comforts, luxuries, and wishful idealism for a bright future. The etymology of "sacrifice" derives from the root *sacer*, meaning "sacred or holy." Understanding sacrifice this way transforms our sense of privilege into humble respect. Climate awareness, activism, and sacrifice of our standard of living affect every aspect of our psyches. Best-selling climate change author and activist Naomi Klein believes our fear of sacrificing privilege pertains primarily to "the radical redistribution of power and wealth necessary to heal the planet."[56] The prospect of degrowth (creating a "lower" standard of living for the privileged) confronts us with what is most threatening, what would ensure contact with our existential angst and despair, and what we would have to face absent our familiar defended power and imaginary dominion over nature. The disavowal of this universal responsibility becomes the displaced angst the rest of us have to grapple with on a daily basis, in good part because we can't, and won't, live in as much denial.

Climate crisis is the current form of our centuries-old and ignored fear-driven shadow, and it's knocking on all our doors, imploring us to emerge from the dark. It asks we relinquish our unsustainable fear of ourselves and malevolent control over others. Because climate crisis challenges us in our most vulnerable places, it is as commensurately difficult to heal as its underlying causes in the form of our inner, psycho-spiritual deficiencies (which our finer jewels fulfill when we liberate them through shadow and death-and-rebirth work).

You and I add to denial when we defend against, instead of surrender to, what is painfully true. Yet, even for those of us who are climate-aware and have faced a good share of our darkness, the task is still monumental. We therefore all need *some* denial. The devil in the details, however, is the degree to which we are, and remain, in ignorance.

---

56. Reese, "Naomi Klein: We Are Sleepwalking Toward Apocalypse."

# Depression

I include depression in this chapter because fear and depression share the poetics of darkness. When we fear and do not face our darkness, it consumes us—internally, externally, or more commonly both. Depression (a Yin imbalance) and its sibling, anxiety (a Yang imbalance), are currently the most common mental illnesses in the United States. As environmental collapse and fear escalate, so do eco-depression and eco-anxiety. While depressed feelings are a natural, even sometimes adaptive, response to climate crisis, it's important not to attribute depression caused by other factors to the state of the world. This can disempower and distract from seeking proper treatment, because depression has many etiologies (causes).

Depression and loss are a taste of death. Some don't survive the dark depths of major depression, and end their lives as a result of not receiving needed support and timely, appropriate treatment. My personal experience with clinical (severe) anxiety and depression several years ago was the most harrowing challenge of my life. I didn't think I would live through it.

Even though I had worked with patients suffering from anxiety and depression, it wasn't until my own experience that I truly understood how horrific these conditions can be. Personal collapse through anxiety and depression forever changed me (Resource 2: Weber, "Anxiety"). There is no longer an intact, previous version of myself. Instead, I inhabit and reckon with a new version of myself: part old, part new, part unknown. Sometimes I feel homesick in my own body, longing for times past, a kind of body-mind solastalgia (feeling homesick when home). This post-collapse state bears resemblance to that reported by some inhabitants of Greenland, where climate change has proceeded more rapidly than in other places on the planet, leading to devastating changes. They no longer trust the land (part of their extended "body") and acknowledge that much of their heritage will never be the same. It rains in winter, when it should be snowing, and snows during the summer. Greenlanders can no longer rely on the ice, their solid ground. In addition to eco-anxiety and eco-depression, they also experience eco-grief, eco-PTSD, and solastalgia, all due to climate change.[57]

---

57. McDougall, "'Ecological Grief': Greenland Residents Traumatized By Climate Emergency."

A common feature of depression (and sometimes anxiety) is *anhedonia*, defined as the absence of pleasure or an inability to enjoy what once gave joy. One may lose the capacity to feel and give love, experience beauty, vitality and happiness. All these qualities are essential for a meaningful life. Anhedonia is just one aspect of why clinical depression and anxiety are so devastating. I invite you to pause for a moment… and imagine being unable to experience beauty, love, and joy. Perhaps you have even experienced it in real-time?

My collapse into depression marked the only time in my adult life I wasn't inspired to write, and it was writing that had helped guide me through many previous devastating descents into grief. Depression sucked the life out of me in a way I'd never experienced. Anxiety freaked me out to the point I thought anything I wrote could be misleading or harmful. Support from others was essential to my getting through this dysregulated phase. The importance of community has been embedded into my heart as a result.

If you have passed through inner collapse due to significant anxiety or depression—and especially if you have learned successful self care for how to get through these states—this may serve you well through outer collapse further along the climate crisis pipeline. Your wisdom can also help support others who suffer. In this vein, I have assembled a list of psychotherapist-reviewed and vetted depression coping tips (Resource 2: Weber, "Healing").

The degree to which we experience future collapse—and this is not currently, precisely knowable—could resemble that of apocalyptic movies such as *Mad Max* or *Children of Men*. To whatever degree greater cataclysm comes to pass, learning how to persist through dark times when nothing looks bright will help you. Glitz-addicted, happy-crazed, and drug-abusing modern culture prepares us not at all for this darkness descending upon us now. Ironically—and as I've tried to communicate throughout this writing—these death-wishing-in-disguise cultural norms have created and perpetuated our current climate calamity.

One of the best-known accounts of grappling and surviving through atrocious darkness—and therefore its relevance for climate resiliency—is Holocaust survivor and psychiatrist Viktor Frankl's book *Man's Search for Meaning*. I also highly recommend depression survivor and psychologist Andrew Solomon's TED Talk, "Depression, the Secret We Share." Dr. Solomon describes depression as the "flaw in love" and a "slow way of being dead."[58] He also alludes to life in a concentration camp, as well as global warming. As discussed previously, Greta Thunberg fell into depression upon learning about climate crisis. Her rise to greatness from those depths is a testament to overcoming adversity for us all, not to mention doing so while still a child—deep bows, Greta.

Anhedonia—characteristic of both depression and to a degree, societal collapse—seems ironic given the Western obsession with worshipping and consuming pleasure and beauty. But when we plot this dynamic along the spectrum of Yin and Yang, it's not surprising. The beauty and pleasure our culture worships are largely superficial and non-regenerative, surrogates for more meaningful experiences in the form of fulfillment. When either Yin or Yang is excessive, the other polarity also soon accumulates, unless healing intervenes. As a result of our linear, aggressive pursuit of superficial pleasure and beauty (Yang), we are now experiencing a death (Yin) resulting from an absence of the enduring and soul-affirming versions of these virtues. Underlying this collapse is fear, especially of facing our pain, which is what's required for creating regenerative pleasure and beauty.

While grief is difficult and can be harrowing, depression is a different animal. Grief is a healthy response to loss, which often eventually renews us.[59] Severe depression is usually not so fertile or renewing. Depression is widely misunderstood and has many etiologies. Its unique message, if there is one, depends on its causes, and these are not always identifiable. For me, anxiety precipitated my depression and neither held a significant, curative message. Yet, when lifestyle issues or past trauma cause depression and one is able to heal and make changes, the disease can be transformational and even lifesaving. Equally, depression can be little more than an imbalanced disease state from which we need to rally and recover by any means possible—just as we would from diabetes, the flu, or a heart condition. Any part of the human body can malfunction or fall ill, and this also applies to our brains.

---

58. Solomon, "Depression, the Secret We Share."

59. Save, for example, in what is called "complicated grief," in which grief becomes protracted and comorbid (co-occurring) with other conditions, such as anxiety and depression.

# Absurd Medicine

To face the challenges of dark times and allay fear, the importance of having a sense of humor, especially for the absurd, is crucial. Celebrating absurdity can break us out of mental and emotional ruts and help us to live outside the prison of our usual patterns, if only momentarily. In this freedom, we can discover alternative perspectives that ease the weight of woe.

Humor can also be an indispensable coping tool and antidote for anxiety and depression. While what we have done to the planet is utterly tragic—and it is devastating—we can *also* inhabit a polar opposite, Yin-Yang perspective in the midst of it all. We can stand back and view our experience here as a comedy of the absurd. In *Man's Search for Meaning* Dr. Frankl says, "It is well known that humor, more than anything else in the human makeup, can afford an aloofness and an ability to rise above any situation, even if only for a few seconds."[60]

Humor, then, is another honest psycho-emotional tool to maintain perspective and emotional regulation. This is not humor used for the wholesale denial of difficult reality or to minimize the urgency of climate crisis, but rather to lighten our psychic load as we heal and mobilize. My own kinship with absurdity helped carry me through my losses in Hawaii. I grieved heavily and at the same time was able to bust out a chuckle now and again after the lava destroyed all that I'd built and there wasn't a thing anyone could do about it.

It's absurd, and a bit insane, how we live—what we create and lose, how we start over, and how we convulse over what really doesn't matter as much as we think it does. While this overarching perspective does not dismiss or diminish in any way the pain of loss, the point is we can hold enlivening, uplifting qualities in dynamic tension with our pain. We ought to carry a hearty dose of absurd and irreverent humor into the future along with our gravity. It's possible to view the unraveling of everything as a ridiculous movie, and temporarily escape the realm of "reason" and believability. To keep our physical and psychological heads above water through turbulent times, employing all and any helpful faculties toward facing helpful fears and cultivating radical resilience is good medicine.

---

60. Frankl, *Man's Search for Meaning*, 63.

• EXERCISE •
## CHAPTER 4 JOURNALING

Please also refer to the additional in-text exercises for this chapter. Take out your journal or notepad, place it in front of you, and write out your responses to the following prompts.

1. List three of your greatest helpful (rational, real) fears and three of your greatest unhelpful (irrational, surmountable) fears.

   • How does each affect your triangle of resilience relationships (with self, nature, and others), both positively and negatively?

   • How does each influence your engagement outwardly and inwardly with regard to climate crisis?

   • Recalling the wisdom in fear discussed previously, how has each of your rational, helpful fears served you and the world at large?

   • Write out a brief strategy for how you might skillfully face your irrational fears, such as by gradually exposing yourself to them and procuring any support to move through them.

2. On a scale from one to ten, how compassionate are you with yourself regarding your fears? Do you judge yourself for having them? How can you become more compassionate toward the part of you that fears?

# Chapter 5
# MINING AND MANAGING (ECO) ANXIETY

*Over the past decades our culture has gone apocalyptic*
*with zombie movies and Mad Max dystopias,*
*perhaps the collective result of displaced climate anxiety ...*[61]
~DAVID WALLACE-WELLS

To this point, I have generally encouraged embracing all our emotions, save for in certain cases of mental illness, unhelpful fear, and when we are too overwhelmed. Anxiety is an emotion we want to acknowledge and investigate but not always feed or wholly heed and believe. In this chapter, we will learn what anxiety is as well as how to maximize anxiety's boons and let go its banes.

Climate anxiety is synonymous with eco-anxiety. In tandem with eco-grief, climate anxiety is arguably the most distressing emotion we encounter in the face of climate breakdown. While the Diagnostic and Statistical Manual of Mental Disorders (DSM-V) has not yet identified climate anxiety as a specific condition, a 2017 American Psychological Association (APA) report discusses eco-anxiety and defines it as "a chronic fear of environmental doom."[62] While climate disruption elicits all our difficult emotions, anxiety can be the

61. Wells, "The Uninhabitable Earth: Famine, Economic Collapse, a Sun that Cooks Us: What Climate Change Could Wreak—Sooner than you Think."

62. Whitmore-Williams, et al., "Mental Health and our Changing Climate: Impacts, Implications, and Guidance," 68.

most debilitating. British ecopsychologist Jayne Rust reflects: "I think it is a massive thing to live with the suspicion that (as some of my younger clients have said), 'We're completely screwed.' I suspect it might be part of the reason for binge-drinking epidemics, and other addictions, for example (Resource 2: Moss, "The Extraordinary Science"). There is a general feeling that the future is so uncertain and it's extremely hard to live with."[63]

Eco-anxiety, if managed, is adaptive in the face of ever greater, looming climate catastrophe. An anxious response to this real threat is not pathological.[64] Anxiety, however, is not a black-and-white phenomenon. It can feed on itself unless we notice, intervene, and lessen it. We can respond to helpful anxiety and mitigate unhelpful anxiety so it is no worse than it needs to be. If we don't, needless suffering results.

A fear of eco-anxiety is one reason some choose to deny how severe climate change is. Disavowing climate crisis allows us to continue business as usual and shields us from distressing emotions, including eco-anxiety. Yet, this strategy is lethal. It's akin to ignoring cancer; do that for long enough and you die. Our planet, and humanity, is in stage IV climate cancer. We've ignored its progression to the edge of extinction. Even if we try to ignore climate crisis, a background anxiety surrounds us, as we know and sense to varying degrees the predicament we are in.[65] This is helpful, adaptive anxiety; embracing it helps mobilize us to ward off catastrophe.

## Fear or Anxiety?

Anxiety and fear are related but different. Fear in its pure state relates to an immediate, in-the-moment threat, such as jumping away from a snake on the road. Anxiety relates to what has not yet occurred and may only be vaguely identifiable. For the purposes of discussion, in this chapter I sometimes use the terms interchangeably. Professor Shaharam Heshmat, PhD, points out that anxiety is driven by "what if" thinking.[66] Much eco-anxiety is preoccupation with

---

63. Fawbert, 'Eco-Anxiety': How to Spot It and What to Do about It."
64. Lawton, "If We Label Eco-Anxiety as an Illness, Climate Denialists Have Won."
65. U.S. Senator Bernie Sanders, Facebook, March 31, 2019, *https://m.facebook.com/story. php?story_fbid=10157792158047908&id=9124187907&ref=m_notif.*
66. Heshmat, "Anxiety vs. Fear: What is the Difference?"

future, catastrophic events: *What if the glaciers melt and sea levels rise hundreds of feet? What if the Amazon rainforest dies? What if we reach 1.5 degrees Celsius rise above pre-industrial levels?* For these kinds of anxious wonderings, we can heed what astrophysicist-turned-climate scientist, Peter Kalmus, says, "I've trained my brain to not torture myself about things that are outside my control."[67]

Anxiety triggers the "alarm system" in our brains and can cause us to perceive situations as more dire than they are. Severe anxiety may cause us to feel something horrible is always around the corner, or that we are going to die. Anxiety is both cognitive (disturbing or stressful thoughts) and somatic (visceral bodily sensations). Some of anxiety's mental indicators are black-and-white thinking, catastrophic thinking, disoriented thoughts, uncontrollable and intrusive thoughts, and the inability to "think straight." Physical symptoms include palpitations, irritability, an inability to relax, a burning sensation, nausea, dizziness, or disorientation. Due to anxiety's mind-body nature, employing both cognitive and somatic techniques is usually most helpful to reduce anxiety's severity.

Anxiety is distinct from worry, which is less acute than anxiety. I tend to feel worry in my forehead and in the front of my head, while anxiety often surges up the back of my neck or pounds my heart hard and fast. Relative to fear, anxiety is heady, ethereal, thin, and dispersed. Fear feels thicker and deeper, in my gut. That's why we say "free-floating anxiety" but not "free-floating fear."

Joseph LeDoux, a pioneering neuroscientist who has performed groundbreaking research on fear, says, "The human being is an anxiety machine ... anxiety is the price we pay for that ability to imagine the future."[68] He adds, "That's what anxiety is, an imagination of a future that hasn't happened yet, but that you are concerned with, worried about, dreading, and so on."[69]

Much of Dr. LeDoux's work revolves around the amygdala, the same area of our brains, mentioned in chapter 4, that mediates fear as well as anxiety. Stressful events, especially looming uncertainty, danger, and the threat of loss or death, trigger the alarm response of our amygdala. Our amygdalar alarm response was eminently functional during our cave-dwelling past and days on the open savannah, but hasn't evolved for modern times. It still reacts as if we are going to be

---

67. Corn, "It's the End of the World as They Know It."
68. "Neuroscientist Joseph LeDoux on Anxiety and Fear," New York State Writers Institute."
69. Ibid.

maimed at every turn. Anxiety's overreaction is key to why we must learn to intervene and work skillfully with anxiety to reduce unnecessary stress.

Anxiety incommensurate with a threat is an overreaction of our nervous and endocrine systems that's similar to the exaggerated immune response of an allergic reaction. Lousy allergy symptoms are due to our body's overreaction, not the actual harm posed by the allergen itself. The disorientation and tension of anxiety is our nervous system's overshoot. Each of us experiences this maladaptive evolutionary inheritance to different degrees. After all, this anxiety is part of what makes us human. While there may be lurking danger, and there always is to a degree, an excessively anxious reaction distorts our perception of reality, making it seem worse than it is. In some cases, as with some anxiety disorders such as PTSD, no current external threat exists at all.

## Understanding Climate Anxiety

At its root, anxiety triggers our fear of dying. Coming to terms with our eventual death can help us mitigate some degree of climate anxiety. In my own anxiety over the future, I notice I unconsciously conflate some of my climate anxiety with my general fear of dying. This awareness allows me to untangle some of my fear of a premature death and the great suffering it might entail from the fear of death inherent in being human. For this reason, I think it's important to confront our fear of death to help ease some climate anxiety.

Of course, we are all going to die, and some fear of death is hardwired in all humans. Yet, climate crisis throws an extra dose of fear into the mix. We can differentiate two fears (technically anxiety) of death: the first is of death by ordinary causes, which for the sake of naming, we can call "natural death anxiety." The second is a fear of a premature and more gnarly demise due to climate crisis, which we can call "climate death anxiety." Climate death anxiety exponentially amps up our fear of natural death and greatly exacerbates our generalized anxiety surrounding death.

While we may not be able to make a big dent in our fear of death from either cause, it's important to separate our fear of climate death from our fear of natural death. Lumping these together can potentiate our anxiety around natural death and also lead to perceiving climate breakdown with excessive *emotional reasoning*, a psychological term meaning to arrive at (usually false) conclusions based on the intensity of emotion, rather than the veracity of facts. Saying to ourselves and one another, "We're all going to die anyway" reminds us that death is scary even without climate crisis. Working with our fear of natural death to alleviate unnecessary suffering in anticipation of, or during the acute process of dying, can help modulate our fear of climate death.

Death Café (Resource 5: "Death Café") is a community forum that can help us process fears about and come to terms with death and dying. Death Café is therefore helpful for coping with climate anxiety. I've attended several cafés in my town, and facilitated one. I find them personally invaluable and especially relevant for coping with climate fear. Coming to terms with death—or becoming less afraid of it to any degree—helps reduce climate anxiety and our fear of loss and dying from it … or from anything else.

Climate crisis is the perfect arena for anxiety to run rampant, yielding both bane and benefit. Climate anxiety is our reaction to what hasn't happened, what could happen, and to what degree it might all come down at any point in the future. Climate distress confounds us because it creates *reasonable fear and both helpful and unhelpful anxiety*. Again, it is part "snake" and part "rope." We are in danger from it right now, even if we're not actively fleeing a storm surge or heat wave. When we're not faced with such an urgent manifestation, the climate crisis still presents a chronic background fear—or more accurately, anxiety—that causes us to pay attention, wake up, and be ready for action. This is why our adrenal glands secrete adrenaline in response to anxiety, and the adrenaline then contributes to our lived experience of this emotion.

Climate anxiety is adaptive because it's highly probable that increasingly dire manifestations of climate crisis will befall us in the future. It's healthy to worry enough to heed the very credible reality of future harm. It's possible, but less likely, that worse (or the worst) may never come to pass. We don't want our angst to grow to the point we suffer panic attacks, freeze with inaction, or go into wholesale denial as a result of overwhelm. So, working with both climate fear and anxiety is a tricky balance which requires careful cognitive and somatic awareness, as well as skillfulness, self-care, and interpersonal support.

Understanding the dynamics of anxiety, and in particular the unremitting threat that drives climate anxiety, gives us the critical thinking edge to be skillful in our response to anxiety. Remember, we can't avoid feeling anxiety, but we *can* prevent it from overwhelming us. Therefore, when anxiety surfaces, don't try to repress it; employ strategies to regulate it, such as the Twenty-two Anxiety Tips at the end of this chapter.

Sometimes our reaction to climate change is bona fide fear, as when we are in the midst of immediate danger. When the fire came to Ojai and the lava began barreling down the mountain in Hawaii, I fled in fear. When our lives are in immediate danger, this fear is invaluable. We want to heed our fight-or-flight response, which includes options to fight, flee, freeze, or fawn (also sometimes called "flop"). Because I could not fight the fire or lava, and I didn't even consider freezing or playing possum, I fled! In contrast, if a mountain lion charges you, the advice is to stand your ground and fight, not flee. Different threats require unique, and sometimes counterintuitive, responses. Knowledge is critical not only for coping with anxiety, but for saving our lives.

When we experience anxiety about a *possible* future event, and there's no immediate danger of dying, we don't have to panic in the moment. Nor do we want to go into denial and never prepare or act. Mitigating and regulating our anxiety reaction so it becomes a *measured response* as opposed to a *knee-jerk reaction* is paramount. I therefore recommend this anti-denial prescription for climate anxiety mitigation: *Welcome enough anxiety to alert, learn, and mobilize; then follow up with needed, measured, swift action.* Notice, this prescription includes both critical thinking and emotional regulation.

## When Anxiety Strikes

To harvest good from anxiety's haranguing assault, we must hold a dynamic tension of opposites. This Yin-Yang dynamic of interfacing with anxiety informs how to best work with it. It comprises a three-pronged strategy, or "Three-Step Anxiety Strategy," which is adaptable to each unique situation.

### Three-Step Anxiety Strategy

1. **Selective Listening:** Tolerate anxiety's discomfort and seek to harvest valuable information from its warning. It's "selective" because we choose to heed what's true and helpful.

2. **Regulation:** Practice mitigating anxiety's physiological responses and let go of unhelpful, obsessive thoughts (via the "Seven Body-Centered Self-

Care Tips for Acute Anxiety" just a few pages ahead, and the Twenty-two Anxiety Tips at the end of this chapter).

3. **Measured Action:** Take appropriate action, which includes verifying if the stimulus is a true threat (a "rope" or "snake").

---

### • EXERCISE •
### THREE-STEP ANXIETY PRACTICE

Describe three issues that cause you anxiety. To whatever degree you are comfortable, feel them in your body as you describe them. Then, for each anxiety, proceed through the Three-Step Anxiety Strategy above to practice learning from and reducing your anxiety reactions.

---

Reviewing climate science is remarkably valuable for the third step, Measured Action, because it shows us why to concern ourselves, what to address, and how best to proceed. Please be aware that sometimes anxiety can be too intense in the moment to practice step one to glean any valuable information. In this case, we can practice step two, Regulation, and when ready, return to Selective Listening.

Let's look at how we might apply this strategy to a specific climate example. Say I learn that climate change is predicted to cause the sea-level community where I live to be inundated with water within two to three years. Since there is no immediate threat, I might begin by verifying the information. Then, I might choose to take some long, deep breaths. Next, I might engage in soothing self-talk, take a walk, or share my worry with a good friend. I might say to myself, "Jack, your community is in danger and it's probably a good idea to plan to relocate. Our climate is out of whack and this likely means there are also other dangers." Next, I can notice which unhelpful thoughts or images continue to plague me and practice letting them go. This is a technique called "thought diffusion," to be discussed shortly. Working to let these thoughts go, I might say to myself: "Just breathe, we don't know when this will happen, if it will happen, and it's not happening right now. Just chill for now." Since the prediction is a couple years out, I can then plan any actions, such as researching where to move and/or meeting with a realtor. I might also check the integrity of my home's foundation and talk to my neighbors.

## The Problem with Panic

Unless we check and moderate our alarm response, our anxiety can worsen into panic, an extreme form of anxiety. Panic is helpful when our lives are in immediate, grave danger, if it causes us to respond immediately and decisively. Otherwise, a panicked reaction is not helpful, and can even be harmful in the face of immediate danger. For example, when evacuating a building during an emergency, it's paramount to exit in organized fashion, and not push or trample others. We must be mindful to pause and evaluate knee-jerk responses and enact counterintuitive responses when necessary to ensure our own and others' safety.

Since global climate change is vast in scope compared to a building evacuation emergency—but arguably less urgent in this very moment—panic is not needed or helpful. Being aware, regulating our physiology, and acting wisely are. Again, step two, Regulation, can help avert panic, making it easier to glean any valuable information from the anxiety. "Chilling down" like this is appropriate when there is a solution at hand and/or the threat is not impinging upon us at this very moment in a life-or-death way. Channeling helpful anxiety into proactive climate activism makes the best use of eco-anxiety and integrates all three steps of the Three-Step Anxiety Strategy.

If we aren't able to reduce our anxiety and it elevates to panic, one possible outcome is a panic (anxiety) attack. Panic attacks are scary but pose no immediate health danger. (A caveat: because panic attacks and heart attacks can have similar symptoms, when in doubt, seek immediate medical attention.) Soothing a panic attack—as with unwinding anxiety generally—begins with recognizing we are having a panic attack. Next, soothing self-talk and deeper, slower breathing to calm down, sorting out fact from fiction, calming herbs, supplements, or prescription medication, and the support of others are among the methods available to ease attacks. Tincture of time is also helpful; panic attacks usually last about ten to thirty minutes and almost always less than an hour. Remembering the sensations are temporary can be enormously helpful for getting through an attack without aggravating its symptoms. Consulting a mental health professional is advisable, as is seeking medical care if symptoms do not improve, or if they feel notably different from typical panic attack symptoms.

# Catastrophic Thinking

Anxiously believing the worst when there's no confirming evidence is called *catastrophizing*. Catastrophizing, or catastrophic thinking, is a form of distorted, anxious thinking. In the *New York Times* column titled "Time to Panic,"[70] author David Wallace-Wells says catastrophic thinking about climate change is now reasonable and appropriate. In the article, he references a United Nations climate change report and the permission he perceives it gave scientists. He writes, "The thing that was new was the message: It is O.K., finally, to freak out. Even reasonable...This, to me, is progress. Panic might seem counterproductive, but we're at a point where alarmism and catastrophic thinking are valuable, for several reasons."

It might be helpful to freak out momentarily, but it's not helpful to do so enduringly and without modulation. This latter view is echoed by Debbie Chang, a climate change emotional support group leader: "...panic is not a good emotion to act from...If it's [the climate movement] driven by the panic, we won't be able to do much."[71]

While Wallace-Wells is right to sound the alarm bell, he might not have considered that catastrophic thinking is, by definition, irrational. It's a cognitive distortion. According to Dr. John Grohol, catastrophic thinking is "an irrational thought a lot of us have in believing that something is far worse than it actually is."[72] Even if Wallace-Wells is colloquially advocating panic as a call to action, it's still a bad idea. It's far more helpful, once panic or anxiety arises, to engage the Three-Step Anxiety Strategy. It's a good idea to be realistic and alarmed about, and take to heart the likelihood of, worsening future damage, and also to take action. But thinking catastrophically is not reasonable or a healthy strategy, nor is protracted panic. This leads to psychological paralysis, panic disorders, and nervous breakdowns.

Wallace-Wells is correct to say that panic may "seem counterproductive"; it usually is—unless we are facing an overwhelming threat and the risk of injury or death in *this very moment*. In his article, Wallace-Wells mentions four justifications

---

70. Wallace-Wells, "Time to Panic: The Planet Is Getting Warmer in Catastrophic Ways. And Fear may Be the Only Thing that Saves Us."
71. Arciga, "Climate Anxiety Groups Are the New Self-Care."
72. Grohol, "What is Catastrophizing?"

for catastrophic thinking (1) climate change is a crisis because it is a looming catastrophe that demands global response, (2) thinking this way makes it easier to clearly see the threat of climate change, (3) complacency remains a bigger problem than fatalism, and (4) fear can mobilize and even change the world (he cites Rachel Carson's groundbreaking book *Silent Spring*, which led to the DDT ban, as an example). Yet, all four of these alleged rationales can be addressed by skillfully working with anxiety and fear, without panic or catastrophic thinking. Catastrophic thinking does not make "it easier to clearly see the threat of climate change."[73] It is self-exacerbating, distorted thinking.

Catastrophic thinking compels us to seek data to justify our extreme emotional responses. It's important, however, to be rational about *likelihood* and then determine if our alarm response is commensurate with the probability of the occurrence of the anxiety-inducing event. Let's say I'm freaking out about wildfires this summer. I might justify the severity of my response with the facts that $CO_2$ levels just hit 415 ppm, we are in severe drought, and fires ravaged nearby areas last year. But this data does not make it advisable to freak out. Sometimes we exaggerate or even call speculations "facts" to justify our reactions. For example, during evacuation from the lava flow in Hawaii, a panicked neighbor told me that Highway 11 to town was cracking because the magma was just beneath the surface, pressing up from below, and these cracks meant the whole road was going to "blow." This wasn't factually accurate, and it never happened.

To quote from a *Grist* article where meteorologist Eric Holthaus interviews David Wallace-Wells: "The question is whether fear is the right emotion to play on to get people to sit up, listen, and take action. According to Holthaus, who's been writing about climate change for more than a decade, it's not. To him, it's best to accept the scientific consensus and inspire our fellow humans to roll up their sleeves and ensure we do whatever it takes to decarbonize the global economy rapidly."[74]

While fear is an important player, it doesn't have to be a primary motivator. Holthaus's perspective wisely engages the Three-Step Anxiety Strategy and makes the best use of anxiety by transforming it into action. Holthaus also

---

73. Wallace-Wells, "Time to Panic."
74. Grist staff, "To Fear or Not to Fear."

invokes *care* in his alternative to Wallace-Wells's fear. Abiding the wisdom that there is a kernel of value in all emotion most of the time, and leaning toward the "both/and" wisdom of Yin-Yang, I encourage us to welcome both fear/anxiety and care, with an emphasis on care. Managing and channeling our unhelpful fear delivers better quality care and results. To care, we have to love, and to love deeply enough, we must have sufficiently healed our hearts and made friends with our difficult emotions. As discussed previously, possessing *enough* of this deep, automatic care is the key emotional intelligence aptitude needed to empower significant climate mobilization.

## Somatic Anxiety Strategies

Our brains have evolved a pessimistic bias, which ensures survival over that conferred by an optimistic disposition or, unfortunately, even a carefree and realistic one. It takes a lot of cognitive work to overcome the distressing consequences of these ancient hardwired tendencies. For this we use the newest addition to our brains—the neocortex—to utilize self-awareness for subsequent behavior modification. We therefore get to practice being rational and realistic, as well as act counterintuitively, to short-circuit our exaggerating, sometimes catastrophizing neurobiology.

Learning how our brains generate bias can help us notice when our alarm system has tripped and moved us into fight-or-flight mode. While we can't halt the initial rushes of adrenaline, we *can* practice not exacerbating our distress. Below are some additional pointers for de-escalating anxiety before it gets the best of us. These "Seven Body-Centered, Self-Care Tips for Acute Anxiety" are adapted from psychotherapist Pete Walker's "Thirteen Steps for Managing Flashbacks,"[75] and can be integrated into step two of the Three-Step Anxiety Strategy discussed previously.

## Seven Body-Centered, Self-Care Tips for Acute Anxiety

1. If you are feeling fearful or anxious, name the emotion, saying, "I am feeling anxiety (or fear)."

---

75. Walker, "13 Steps for Managing Flashbacks."

2. Gently ask your body to relax: feel each of your major muscle groups, and your hands, and softly encourage them to relax. Tightened musculature sends unnecessary danger signals to the brain.

3. Try easing back into your body. Fear launches us into "heady" worrying, numbing, and spacing out.

4. Breathe deeply, slowly, and steadily to help come back "into" and anchor yourself in your body. Holding our breath signals danger to our brains.

5. Slow down: rushing and time pressure press our mind's panic button.

6. Bring your attention back to what you are doing to soothe yourself. Wrap yourself in a blanket (special "weighted blankets" are very helpful to some), listen to favorite music, snuggle with a stuffed animal, hold a friend's hand, or ask them for the support you need.

7. Feel any anxiety in your body but don't react to it, even though it signals danger. It's not the anxiety that hurts us as much as reacting erratically or self-destructively to it.

---

• EXERCISE •

BODY-CENTERED ANXIETY PRACTICE

Refer to the list of anxieties you created in the Three-Step Anxiety Practice, and/or describe three other anxieties you have been struggling with. To whatever degree you are comfortable, feel them in your body as you describe them. Then, for each concern, proceed through the Seven Body-Centered Tips for Acute Anxiety above as a self-care practice to reduce your anxiety.

---

## Exposure and Habituation

As mentioned in chapter 1 (item 6 in the list of incentives for learning about climate change on page 18), sometimes we want to purposely elicit our anxiety response. Learning about climate crisis and engaging in some mentation of likely or probable future scenarios can help us habituate to possible future reality. One way to do this is to bite off bits at a time. This is a form of exposure therapy, which helps our brains adjust to anxiety by incrementally exposing ourselves to distressing triggers. The aim is to eventually minimize our fear or anxiety response. We can titrate our emotional responses to learning about climate change by taking smaller bites and assimilating the information before we face more of it. This approach doesn't deaden us to current news and calls to action; it brings us more sustainably in alignment with them—both intellectually and emotionally.

To avoid overwhelm during habituation, it's important to proceed at your own pace. Exposing yourself to distressing reality will increase your anxiety. This is the objective. You want your anxiety to be at a level that challenges you but from which you can recover without undue difficulty. To help, you can employ the seven checklist tips just mentioned and the Twenty-Two Anxiety Tips at the end of this chapter. It's also helpful to have support from others, such as empathic, climate-aware friends, to help "hold" and process the information and its impact. You might also consider working with a psychotherapist.

## Anxiety Break

We can do a lot to minimize unhelpful anxiety. Using gentle awareness can help us notice:

1. When we go into fear-anxiety states, which may feel like we want to fight, flight, or freeze.

2. Notice thoughts and conclusions that arise from these feeling-states and whether they are true, reasonable, or helpful; choose not to believe extreme or irrational thoughts (with practice, we become more familiar with the "flavor" of these).

3. Choose to engage self-care activities and mind-body practices to decrease stress and increase long-term resilience.

If, on the other hand, a situation presents solid evidence for alarm, we can believe it and follow our fact-vetted fear response to immediate safety. In the absence of evidence, we can rely on our best sense assessment, which includes heeding reasonable intuitive conclusions. This said, we have to be careful about following intuitive reasoning into anxiety state rabbit holes, because anxiety is very compelling—it easily convinces us to believe worst-case scenarios and to ignore real evidence to the contrary.

This chapter concludes with a list of anxiety coping tips, but first I want to present a critical thinking and emotional intelligence strategy for how to interface with the broad spectrum of predictions about our climate future. Many assumptions about this future result from knowing something, but not enough, about climate change. Limited understanding compels us to fill in the gaps with inaccurate and exaggerated ideas and beliefs, often generated by emotional reasoning. Our unconscious assumptions and unchecked reactions to these beliefs and ideas cause many of us undue anxiety. Wisely assessing our climate trajectory puts into practice many of the anxiety dynamics discussed to this point.

## Navigating the Doom and Denial of Climate Crisis

When we look to the future, the unknown stares back, unnerving us. Our brains abhor gaps in knowledge as much as we dislike missing stepping stones between one side of a stream and the other. Just because we don't like gaps, however, doesn't mean we should arbitrarily fill them in. We should resist making imaginary assumptions with false, albeit comforting, stories and beliefs.[76] Doing so may help us allay our anxiety in the moment but ill serves us in the long run.

Nobody knows the precise design of all future climate scenarios. There are too many potential and unidentified x-factors that even over a short period of time—say one year—could shift the balance significantly toward worsening or improving climate conditions. For example, the super-carbon-sequestering bio-engineered "Ideal Plants" that world-renowned botanist Dr. Joanne Chory is working on at the Salk Institute could make a big dent in sequestering atmospheric carbon dioxide.[77] On the other hand, sudden methane releases from a quickly-disappearing Arctic permafrost, or collapse of the Amazon or Siberian rainforest, could spell disaster. Human extinction is not guaranteed, nor is our escaping this mess alive. The weight of evidence, as the climate science discussion in the appendix makes clear, tilts heavily in favor of cataclysm. The less we do to drastically alter our current trajectory, the more this likelihood increases.

---

76. This is a "God of the Gaps" logical fallacy.
77. Popescu, "This Scientist Thinks She Has the Key to Curb Climate Change: Super Plants."

To collectively alter our current course, each of us can contribute our unique and most passionate gifts to the climate conundrum.

Future climate scenarios encompass a spectrum of shades-of-grey possibilities, though one guarantee is the effects of climate change will get worse. "The world is headed for major upheaval, it's merely a question of the scale," reports *The Guardian* in a discussion with top scientists.[78] We are due for worse if only because we are locked into a decade of more warming even if we stopped our emissions today.[79] We currently have no means to pull out the excess $CO_2$ we emitted ten years ago, and global emissions have been increasing annually right through 2019.[80]

Even though carbon dioxide levels are projected to decrease by up to 8 percent by the end of 2020 due to the COVID-19 pandemic lockdown, according to a United Nations report, levels would need to continue to decrease each year thereafter through 2030 by 7.6 percent over the previous year's level in order to remain below a relatively catastrophic 1.5 degree celcius temperature rise over preindustrial levels.[81] This is a mighty task, and an unlikelihood, when the world is collectively gung ho to reopen and get back to business as usual (Resource 2: Weber, "Lockdown, With Benefits").

The grey shades, therefore, include the as yet unknown precise nature and extent of future malady: how much nonhuman life will be lost, what the climate refugee situation will bring, what kind of social disorder will ensue, which and how much of food crops will grow, and who and how many among us might perish.

As I mentioned in the first chapter, those of us committed to more deeply investigating climate news and climate change science are few and far between. And those of us sufficiently educated in climate science seem to swing between insistent optimism and staunch pessimism about the future. Those less knowledgeable about climate change details, which is most of the population, are

---

78. Ibid.

79. Ricke and Caldeira, "Maximum Warming Occurs about One Decade after a Carbon Dioxide Emission."

80. Kelly Levin, "New Global CO2 Emissions Numbers Are In. They're Not Good."; Plumer, "Carbon Dioxide Emissions Hit a Record in 2019, Even as Coal Fades."

81. United Nations Environment Programme, "Cut Global Emissions By 7.6 Percent Every Year For Next Decade to Meet 1.5°C Paris Target - UN Report."

more likely to hang in the greys of the spectrum. I hypothesize this is because once we learn what's really going on, fear kicks in and pushes us to extremism. We see this happening during the COVID-19 pandemic as well. The most honest stance toward the future is likely one of holding the evidence in dynamic tension without swinging to an as yet unevidenced extreme conclusion. Enough is unknown, in fact, that qualifying and quantifying each future scenario would be not merely laborious and unproductive, but likely impossible. We lack all the data required to be precise enough. Indeed, the devil is in the details.

An example might help. I'll use numbers after the following statements of degree to indicate their intensity: zero indicates the least extreme and least likely amount of climate damage to occur, and ten is the most likely and extreme amount of damage. The scale represents objective and hypothetical consensus assessments, not personal and subjective ones. We know our predicament is bad (8–10), pretty darn bad (8.8–9.5?), but we don't truly know just how bad (9.5–10?) or not as bad (7–9?) it is. Words cannot qualify these numerical designations precisely; the numbers are more accurate measurements of degree than more vague references of "bad" and "very bad," for example. A similar vocabulary problem for the Intergovernmental Panel on Climate Change (IPCC) results in its failure to relay climate science accurately to the public.[82] So, our very language limits our ability to communicate precisely the likeliest shade of grey. More lack of precision stems from the uncertainty that what we ascribe numbers to will indeed come to pass.[83] The ultimate purpose of this numbering exercise is to train the brain to be specific and not to generalize and thereby polarize. Abiding shades of grey, we minimize emotional reasoning and catastrophic thinking, helping us to moderate doom and denial.

After researching the latest climate science over the last several years, I had an epiphany. While learning some intriguing new neuroscience and watching

---

82. Herrando-Pérez et al., "Statistical Language Backs Conservatism in Climate-Change Assessments."

83. Note, this grey spectrum of dark to light and its corresponding numerical degrees is accounted for by the shades of grey (degrees of black and white) of Yin-Yang circle described previously.

my own behavior and that of many of my peers, a possibility (6–9 certainty?) occurred to me: *the hidden driver swaying our assertion of a particular extreme climate future is less a matter of certainty and veracity of that position than it is a discomfort with persisting in the anxious unknown.* An unconscious need for control in "knowing" can also contribute to the polarization. Our general incapacity to hold a tension of opposites prevents us from residing in the most accurate reality: a degree of both certainty and unknowing, and tolerating probabilities. A related tension of opposites is the ability to continue to do good in the world while soberly accepting a dismal future forecast. Cleaving to both is to abide cognitive dissonance; practice makes progress, I have found.

Averting truth due to anxiety or fear is consistent with what I described in chapter 4 as our fear-mark. Those who know enough about climate change (and each person has a unique threshold for "enough") tend to gravitate toward extreme optimism or extreme pessimism to avoid the anxiety of not knowing. The optimism might sound like: *Oh, there's nothing to worry about.* The pessimism could be: *Nothing will stop our extinction and nothing we do matters.* Notice, each position contains the extreme and irrevocable "nothing."

The excessively optimistic position is simply naïve. The pessimistic speciously predicts the precise design of the future without allowing that we might enact a cure and can do a lot, in the name of compassion, to make life easier for ourselves, one another, and other species—our triangle of resilience relationships. Many seem unable to hang out in the 8–9.5 intensity range, and I am regularly practicing this myself. If our anxiety is great, and we have scant tolerance for it, we might even deny climate change altogether.

———

In a recent article, "A World Without Clouds," three leading scientists are asked their opinion about our climate future. Their responses vary from "I'm worried…Are you kidding" to "pretty—fairly—optimistic."[84] This suggests that others' opinions—even experts' opinions—don't matter as much as we'd like to believe even our own do. This must include my own, so please take my perspective for whatever sense it makes. I propose this recipe for accuracy and

———

84. Wolchover, "A World without Clouds."

honesty: assess the preponderance of scientific evidence (appropriately adjusted for critical thinking, e.g., weighing the conservatism of the IPCC and scientists generally, as discussed in the appendix), scrupulously check personal emotional biases and cognitive assumptions, and welcome a dose of the unknown. Again, we could make a game-changing discovery to wholly mitigate climate change at any time. Or, tipping points and exponential changes could tilt the scales into runaway chaos. We just don't know at this point, though the darker scenario has *a more likely probability* based on trending evidence.

If we can learn to tolerate more anxiety as well as fear, grief, anger, despair, and even remorse, we can openly face climate reality honestly and courageously. This requires more emotional and cognitive integrity, which we can cultivate with practice and support. Most of us have little experience supporting one another by embracing our shared present and future with such honesty. In sum, this is what we need to do now: soberly face the facts (intellectual honesty); embody and welcome, or at least bear our difficult feelings (emotional honesty); and support one another and work together through the pain and best forward strategies.

To avoid placing their certainty in jeopardy, or risking anxiety and a drop in dopamine-driven pleasure, rosy optimists don't let in facts that contradict their position. Doomsayers (aka "doomers") dislike positive news (placing a need to be certain or right above their own survival advantage), also because it compromises their certainty and introduces all the uncomfortable emotions that accompany not knowing. Either polarity serves to avoid dwelling restlessly in the anxiety of not knowing.

I got real-life practice hanging out in the unknown during the lava flow in Hawaii. During one stretch, the lava was erupting almost daily from newly formed fissures, bursting suddenly from the ground in molten geysers. This was unnerving, to say the least, as lava has no mind for neighborhoods, homes, and roads. No one knew where it would erupt next. The fissure sites, as well as the direction of the flow, regularly foiled predictions. Months of this helped me learn how to tolerate my own anxiety (and everyone else's), as well as to surrender a little more to the possibility of destruction and death—which is what anxiety, in its preeminent expression, helps us avert.

———

Because climate science indicates a worsening of our situation, doomsayers seem to live closer to reality, despite their general refusal to let in positive news. It's the rare person who can deeply acknowledge climate reality and not polarize their view. It's a rarer person who can acknowledge a well-informed 8–9.5 position and not knee-jerk into an unrealistic, fear-driven 9.5–10.

Hope makes optimists feel less anxious and doomsayers more anxious. In response to the doomsayers's pattern of rejecting hopeful evidence, I coined the term *reverse hopium*. I define the term *hopium* as "unrealistic positive hope to make us feel better in the face of bad news; a cognitive opiate to reduce existential angst." *Reverse hopium* I define as "unrealistic negative hope that denies realistic hope to make us feel better in the face of distressing good news; a cognitive opiate to reduce existential angst." This is hopium's Yin-Yang polarity. Both forms of hopium serve to bolster certainty and allay anxiety from not knowing. Both include aspects of black-and-white thinking and miss the grey zone of what's more likely to be realistic. Both take Yin *or* Yang positions instead of an appropriate shade of Yin *and* Yang commensurate with the evidence. And because new evidence is constantly discovered, we have to stay informed and be flexible to adjust our points of view and beliefs accordingly.

Hopium believes *everything is going to be okay; there's no need for worry.* Reverse hopium believes *nothing is going to be okay and there's no hope.* Notice the "everything" and "nothing" in the first and second statements, respectively. These extreme positions are fueled by emotional reasoning. Let's look at a specific, real-life example: The scary news (and it is worse than this, as the climate science section in the appendix elucidates) from the IPCC is we have only until 2030 to reduce our carbon footprint by 45 percent before we experience the strong likelihood of significantly more catastrophic climate effects.[85] Hopium glosses over the danger and assumes we'll figure it out somehow. Reverse hopium concludes we're screwed no matter what and helpful acts don't matter. Notice, *both extremes absolve their adherents of any meaningful action,* allowing them to continue business as usual, since there's no need for concern

---

85. IPCC, "Summary for Policymakers of IPCC Special Report on Global Warming of 1.5°C approved by governments."

(optimist), or there's no hope whatsoever (doomer). Both the optimist and the doomer tend to defend their point of view "to the death." This "fight" seems to be part of the fight-or-flight response that allays the anxiety invisibly driving the extreme beliefs. Because both polarities are emotionally reasoned, this results in a degree of inaccuracy that is likely defended by an unconscious "fear of death."

Reverse hopium's stance can resemble the kind of thinking we experience when, frustrated in an argument, we resort to histrionic pronouncement as a way to unconsciously tie up our jumble of hurt feelings. For example, say you remind me that I forgot to take out the trash and, emotionally triggered, I snap back, "Oh yeah, I'm a total screw-up and can't do anything right." This extreme, shut-down reaction distances me from deeply feeling emotion: anxiety, shame, guilt, anger, or grief. Practicing awareness when we are triggered—pausing, deep breathing, and reflecting for accuracy before making such retorts—not only helps our personal relationships but trains our brains to respond more accurately and responsibly to threatening climate crisis news.

In similar emotionally-reasoned and knee-jerk fashion, reverse hopium would react to the distressing timeframe from the IPCC by inaccurately concluding, "Oh yeah, we're all screwed and there's no hope for us." In contrast, emotional resiliency allows us to be with our difficult feelings to allay our distress and decrease the internal pain-pressure driving us to emotionally reason ourselves into unnecessarily perilous conclusions. This is why emotional intelligence is essential for being grounded in reality, in compassion for ourselves and one another, as well as helping us take meaningful action.

Current climate reality offers mostly bad news, some good news, and much that is unknown. With practice, we can modulate and become comfortably uncomfortable with not knowing; learning this skill is an aim of this chapter. It is a courageous spiritual practice to live in accord with what is most likely true. Most of us don't want to wait for any degree of mastery by growing *through* what feels bad (psychological rebirth). Nor do we want to make the effort to accord with what's most likely true, or to put in the work to become emotionally intelligent and resilient. But just as we tolerate the suspense of watching a thrilling movie or sporting event, await the outcome of a medical exam, or try to keep cool during a natural disaster, we can practice these tolerances. And we can do so in preparation for the biggest screen of all: our planet and its tempest climate story. This way, we might avoid depression, panic, denial, *and* hopium for good or bad news, any of which renders us more unrealistic, unprepared, and unwell.

———

Clearly we are in climate trouble (8 9). Big trouble (9.3-ish?). Irreversible, severe, climate change-driven damage has already occurred and will continue, and worsen. There is realistic hope we won't experience the worst-case climate possibility, but only if this hope is what author and deep ecologist Joanna Macy calls *active hope*—positivity coupled with commensurate, wise action. Fortunately, the world seems to be waking up and helpful action is rising. What the result will be we don't get to know.

Whatever the future brings, I propose we practice with our whole hearts to fiercely hold a tension of opposites rather than take polarized stances. Extinction of most life on Earth or our saving most of it may come to pass, but not because of any information we are sure about today. Holding a tension of opposites is what the late Jungian psychoanalyst and elder Marion Woodman said being human is all about. It's to live with gaps in knowledge and an only partially visible path leading from today to tomorrow.

Throughout our evolution we've had to contend with anxiety. Prehistorically, we feared being eaten alive at every turn, and our angst was greater than during current, relatively cushy industrialized times (though the chickens of the Industrial Age are now coming home to roost). The latter have spoiled us for what is more the historical norm. Allow this perspective to help you dig down and better tolerate these harrowing climate times. We have good reason not to panic, and also to be critically concerned about premature demise or extinction.

When my beloved grandmother was ill at ninety-two years old, I remember *feeling* sure she was about to pass on. Indeed, she seemed to be. Instead, she made several comebacks, felt better for stints, and lived to be just short of 100, against many odds. Scientist and passionate environmentalist David Suzuki similarly discusses the resilience of the natural world in a story about the salmon native to his wilderness—their numbers plummeted one year and he figured them goners. But they returned the next year in record numbers.[86] So, if you find yourself dismissing possibilities of renewal in the midst of climate crisis, please reconsider.

For this climate story, we get to actively participate in the outcome of its most epic episode. While we're inside this unfolding, we can still step outside it for perspective. An overarching view is as important as constant engagement in the details of climate drama. A wider perspective helps us modulate unnecessary anxiety. Because we are left with a good dose of unknowing, and because some degree of unknowing (maybe a 5–7?) seems most honest, learning to manage our anxiety is paramount, for which I hope this chapter helps.

At the end of the day, we are left with the perennial wisdom we glean even in the absence of climate crisis and our unknown fates: *carpe diem*. This injunction comes with an extra infusion of poignancy in the face of climate breakdown. So, let's embrace the day and live as effectively and fully as we can for the benefit of everything—with a sober, wary eye to the future and a hearty embrace of the present.

---

• Exercise •
## Doom and Denial Inventory

Write down your doomsday (informed by reverse hopium) or denialist (informed by hopium) views, if you can indeed identify the latter, about our climate future. Using the critical thinking perspectives just shared, how might you modify your views about our climate future? List any previous catastrophic thoughts you now feel differently about and what caused you to shift your mind.

---

## Twenty-Two Anxiety Tips

Several years ago, I passed through a period of intense anxiety which lasted for months. My obsessive-compulsive disorder (OCD), an anxiety disorder, had become triggered after decades of dormancy. I was unaware it was occurring because I had never before experienced this particular manifestation of its symptoms, and I didn't know how to manage it. During this time I often

---

86. Rae, "Why It's Time to Think About Human Extinction / Dr. David Suzuki."

felt like I was dying, which I later learned is how our brains interpret severe anxiety. There were long stretches of time when the only anchor I had was my breath, and while this wasn't much consolation, I stayed close to it for what seemed like dear life. For days and weeks, I persisted breath-to-breath, fearing every next moment. In hindsight, and in reality, *it felt and seemed like* all I had was one breath to the next, moment-to-next-moment.

Digging myself out of that hole—in which I was also plagued with major depression—was the most trying experience of my life. During my recovery, I gained some potent insights and tools to work with anxiety and depression. My in-the-trenches practice with anxiety ended up helping me and others when our community was threatened by lava during the volcanic eruption. That event, while devastating and nerve-racking, was a cakewalk compared to my personal collapse. Thankfully, I was able to use wisdom that I gleaned in working with anxiety during the eruption, and to share it with others in a time of urgent need.

The anxiety tips that follow are a synthesis of my personal practice to manage anxiety. They're an amalgamation of insights from psychologists, what I offer to patients and friends, and some of what I shared with neighbors during the lava eruption. Notice, I say "practice." Managing anxiety is an ongoing mind-body practice, and framing these tips as exciting challenges for emotional intelligence encourages us to keep at it. I invite you to refer to this list as frequently as needed. Coping through anxiety depends on our awareness to manage it, for which the support of others can be invaluable, especially those who have had successful personal experience. Remember, practice doesn't make perfect; it makes progress!

I decided to include the least obvious and the most important tools I've learned. These are in addition to strategies already mentioned and more popular self-care practices such as exercise, yoga, tai chi, humor, eating well, not sweating the small stuff, getting out to nature, and taking any doctor-prescribed medications. I believe the tips below are helpful for any kind of anxiety and truly aid us to "be here now." They are unlikely to eradicate all anxiety and some may not work in all situations. All will become more valuable as climate chaos worsens and brings more uncertainty and angst.

## Anxiety Tip 1: Awareness

Notice what anxiety feels like. Become familiar with its physical sensations and mental dynamics (or gymnastics!), mentioned toward the beginning of this chapter.

When you notice you are feeling anxious, name it and say to yourself, "This is anxiety" or "I am feeling anxiety." Dr. Matthew Lieberman at UCLA calls this "affect labeling." His research shows that labeling or naming emotion decreases activity in our brain's emotional center, including the amygdala. "This dampening of the emotional brain allows its frontal lobe (reasoning and thinking center) to have greater sway over solving the problem"[87] and returning to a regulated state.

Recognizing and naming anxiety connects mind and body. Relating objectively to unhelpful, dysregulated anxiety as an experience that is happening to us, and not as an essential part of "who we are," creates an I-thou relationship with anxiety. Identifying the issue this way allows us to work with it strategically and effectively. A more balanced and rational, witnessing part of us can manage the distress. In the same way, objectifying diseases like cancer, diabetes, or depression can also be helpful (as explained in chapter 4).

## Anxiety Tip 2: Breathe Deeply and Slowly

This tip is at the top the list because if you glean nothing more from this section, conscious breathing alone will save you lots of suffering. Deep, slow, steady, diaphragmatic breathing is the simplest, most accessible, and quickest way to allay anxiety and stress. It creates a foundation for dealing with all forms of anxiety.

If your breath feels stuck and you can't breathe down into your abdomen, a few strong attempts (but not so forceful as to hurt yourself) with the emphasis on the inhale can often undo the blockage. I also find vigorous exhaling out my mouth, rather than my nose, works as a kind of exhaust pipe to blow out stress.

In addition to breathing deeply and slowly, another strategy is to consciously breathe ALL the air out before the next inhale. Not being able to

---

87. Abblett, "Tame Reactive Emotions by Naming Them."

"catch your breath" often happens because you haven't exhaled completely. Pause at the bottom of the exhale and gently allow the next inhale to begin spontaneously. It may be helpful to count to four or six and be mindful to make the inhalations and exhalations even and equal in duration.

## Anxiety Tip 3: Gratitude

Naming and *feeling* what we are grateful for can ease and calm. No matter how bad things are, we can always find something, no matter how small, to be grateful for. Maybe it's simply being able to breathe, having one person who supports us, or having food for the day.

## Anxiety Tip 4: Take Action

Taking action in response to helpful anxiety empowers us to mitigate real, impending danger. Boarding up your windows before a hurricane to prevent damage and looting, or clearing brush around your home to reduce fire risk, are good examples. Climate activism and joining a climate movement has helped many cope with eco-anxiety, including some members of our local Extinction Rebellion group.

## Anxiety Tip 5: Get with People

The importance of community resilience cannot be overemphasized. Support from other caring humans is a vital defense against climate anxiety. So, find and get with your people!

The care of others helps us regulate and process our feelings and thoughts, both overtly and by holding attuned attention. If you can't be in-person with others, getting on the phone or chatting on video are good, too. The company of animals and the natural world is also essential, but feel-good human interaction is paramount.

It can be difficult to find others who prize tightly-knit belonging, so community is not always possible. It's imperative, therefore, that we do all the inner work we can on our own and with the natural world. Note, Climate Change Café (Resource 5: "Climate Change Café") meets the need for like-minded community for support around climate crisis issues.

It's also incumbent upon us to do our best to show up for others. Practicing kindness and compassion toward others is especially important in these distressing and anxious times.

## Anxiety Tip 6: Mind Control

When you notice yourself repeating the same worries inside your head, practice tough love with yourself and stop the compulsive pattern by interrupting it. This gives your mind a break from itself. For me, saying, "Stop thinking about that now" allows me to get out of "looping" thoughts, which can rapidly spiral and worsen anxiety. Use deep breathing (tip 2), distraction (tip 15), thought diffusion (tip 9), as well as any other helpful, healthy means you know, and seek support from others to help interrupt onslaughts of anxious thoughts.

## Anxiety Tip 7: Bad Chickens

Don't count your good or bad chicken-ideas before they hatch. Sometimes we have to go hour-to-hour, or minute-to-minute, or even breath-to-breath, not knowing the outcome. Watch out for catastrophizing or coming to conclusions prematurely. Breathe, be in the moment, and take concrete steps to address anything solvable.

## Anxiety Tip 8: Black-and-white Thinking

Black-and-white thinking is a modern epidemic. It occurs particularly when we are triggered or catastrophizing. Notice it and find the shade of grey that is more grounded in reality. For example, I recently heard a popular climate collapse advocate say (and I paraphrase) that any attempt to offer a bright vision of the future at this point is an exercise in delusion. Note the binary nature of this statement, which fails to take into account either the x-factors that could positively tilt the scales or the good we can do to make things better, even in the midst of calamity.

## Anxiety Tip 9: Thought Diffusion

Thought diffusion is de-emphasizing the importance of thoughts and allowing thoughts to come in and out of awareness (a.k.a. proverbial "clouds" floating by) without attaching to them or letting them spin us out. While some thoughts require attention (*I left the bath water running!*), most aren't helpful when we're feeling anxious, triggered, and/or exhausted. We can remind ourselves, "These are just thoughts." We can reassess and address any remaining issues when we feel more rested, calm, and supported.

## Anxiety Tip 10: Anxiety Lies

Just like depression, anxiety lies. When we can't control our anxious thoughts, we can mitigate them. When anxiety abates, we're able to see how unrealistic and silly many of our anxious thoughts are. We can practice discernment, and come to recognize the "flavor" of our unrealistic, exaggerated, anxious thinking more easily over time. Using thought diffusion, we can then disregard them as best we can.

Not all anxious thoughts are lies. Identifying the flavor of *untrue* (or unreal) versus *trustworthy* (true) anxiety helps discernment.

## Anxiety Tip 11: Anxiety about Having Anxiety

When we grasp that anxiety takes a toll on us—in the form of forgetfulness, sleep deprivation, exhaustion, undue stress, or just plain feeling bad—we might get anxious (secondary anxiety) when we notice we are becoming anxious (primary anxiety). Primary anxiety is already bad enough. Before we practice not reacting to primary anxiety, we can address any secondary anxiety around the existing anxiety. Noticing when we are anxious about being anxious, we can gently talk ourselves out of the added layer of anxiety, and gradually come to rest in the primary anxiety. And we can employ any of the tips on this list to get us there. Support from a therapist is also helpful for reducing anxiety around anxiety.

I find it most helpful and effective to simply *notice* when I become anxious about being anxious, and gently let this secondary anxiety go. Getting too action-oriented to escape anxiety can get us more enmeshed in what we're trying to escape, like wrestling with glue that only gets us more stuck in it the longer we futz with it. Returning to deep breathing and exhaling from the mouth (tip 2) to release tension are helpful companions for noticing and untangling primary and secondary anxiety.

None of this is easy and it's always a practice—a work in progress. But I can personally attest it's possible to reduce secondary anxiety to primary anxiety and then reduce primary anxiety to common, helpful anxiety.

## Anxiety Tip 12: Vent

Release stressful feelings, frustration, and physical anxiety. Let these emotions out, but don't dump on others unless they accept your venting. I find great ways to vent are by screaming to the ethers, passionately singing, pounding some pillows, and sighing deeply. Some of these can also be performed in the car—a perfect enclosed, private space!

Vent so that you are releasing your stress, but not to the point that you are creating more of it.

## Anxiety Tip 13: Boundaries and Breaks

Anxiety often increases with stress and exhaustion. To moderate anxiety, limit how much you take on. If you can't moderate your stress load, try to moderate your exposure to situations that trigger anxiety.

Create boundaries (limits where you say *no*) to thinking about distressing topics or ideas. At night before sleep, when hungry, or when excessively stressed, are not good times to try to resolve conflicts and distress. Choose *not* to engage in anxiety-raising topics or activities at inopportune times.

Communicating our needs and taking space to recharge create important boundaries that mitigate the stress that increases anxiety. Feel free to take a break from triggering situations and people who increase your anxiety. Do this by communicating kindly and clearly to prevent more conflict and distress.

Limiting how much we take on and postponing stressful interactions and tasks when we are already stressed or exhausted help us regulate anxiety. When we can't reduce our stress load, we can prevent it from getting worse by: controlling our reactivity, not latching onto distressing thoughts and emotions, getting enough rest to recharge, and engaging in self-care to feel more centered and level-headed.

## Anxiety Tip 14: Exclusivity

While venting anxiety can help, so can refraining. Consider *not sharing* your anxiety with certain friends/loved ones. When we're going through a tough time, most people close to us know about it. I find it helpful to have some friends I don't vent or discuss my problems with, so I can get a break and enjoy carefree and even superficial distraction time. Alternately, when needed, create boundaries with friends with whom you do usually share to create the same effect. For example, you might decide to not discuss your worries with anyone for a full afternoon.

## Anxiety Tip 15: Distraction

Our minds—like the climate—can get caught in self-reinforcing, self-perpetuating, destructive positive feedback loops. "Self" is the key word here. We can control this "self" part by breaking the loop and distracting ourselves from worries and concerns. Distractions include seeing a friend, focusing on a creative project, watching a movie, or doing anything that engrosses your attention away from your worries.

When we don't check our anxiety and break its cycle, it grows, and this can lead to sleep issues, exhaustion, and eventually to dysregulation and anxiety attacks. Distraction is a form of healthy, *temporary* denial. This is not repressing your issue, but taking time out to refresh, recharge, and give your mind and body a break. After a break, reassess and readdress any *helpful* anxiety.

## Anxiety Tip 16: Routine

Following a daily routine, whether for work, chores, or other pursuits, is another form of healthy distraction. It helps us maintain a rhythm that counters anxiety's dysrhythmia. Attending to grounded, in-the-moment, hands-on engagement is meditation in action, especially when we're mindful to avoid ruminating over anxious thoughts and to let them go, if only temporarily, when they arise.

## Anxiety Tip 17: Excitement and Angst

Anxiety is just on the other side of excitement. These are two sides of the same coin. You might have noticed that things we are excited about can also make us anxious. Being unable to sleep in anticipation of seeing a good friend or going on a vacation are excitements that bleed into the positive anxiety of anticipation.

While it's tough to turn fear into excitement, noticing the "activating" energy common to both excitement and anxiety can help us channel our anxious energy into exciting projects and purposes. Sometimes we can tap the excitement in the fear that change brings, or in the new opportunities for change and growth that otherwise cause us to be afraid.

## Anxiety Tip 18: Grief and Anxiety

The possibility of impending loss (anticipated grief) can make us anxious. We can be anxious about grief, just as we can become anxious about being anxious. Learning to make friends with the sadness of grief can be an antidote to anxiety, for grief calms and settles us down. For the same reason, anxiety can interfere with experiencing grief.

When we don't embrace loss, we can become excessively anxious about experiencing sadness. When we are fighting to hold on to what we love, which is normal and healthy, it can be tough to also let go. Again, we can hold a tension of opposites: holding loss in one hand and the fight to hold on in the other, leaning more into either as appropriate.

## Anxiety Tip 19: Nighttime and Anxious Insomnia

Nighttime seems to be a time we are more anxious. Perhaps this is because at night we are tired and less resilient in mind and body. Evolutionarily, it also makes sense because long ago (and to a degree even now), we were most vulnerable in the wee hours of the night and had to protect ourselves against invaders and wild animals intent on eating us. It's altogether possible we still carry this hardwired disposition after the sun sets. Whatever the reasons, nighttime seems to highlight our worries more than daylight hours, especially after midnight.

Psychologist Michael Breus has this to say about nighttime anxiety: "It's the first time of the day when no one is asking you any questions or you're trying to complete a task. It's when you're first alone with your thoughts, and the entire day's worth of thoughts come into your mind, which causes a level of anxiety."[88]

Because night is a Yin time of the daily cycle, it cues us to cycle down after the active, Yang phase of activity. Heeding this natural Yin-Yang cycle, in conjunction with nighttime being a more anxious time generally for many, encourages us to exercise appropriate boundaries and limit nighttime engagements to more enjoyable and relaxing activities.

In the same vein, it's best not to believe random, scary or distressing thoughts that pop into our heads in the wee hours, especially if we can't fall asleep. Creating and upholding psychic boundaries by not feeding worrisome thoughts or engaging in disputes, as well as connecting enjoyably with others during compromised times, is a powerful tool that was particularly helpful for me when I experienced insomnia with anxiety.

## Anxiety Tip 20: Meditation and Mindfulness

I mention this obvious tip to offer a different perspective. First, mindfulness is not synonymous with meditation. Mindfulness is a consciously aware, focused state of mind that can be applied to most forms of meditation or other activities.

Practicing sitting meditation with eyes closed works for some but not others during acute anxiety. Mindfulness meditation has been shown to reduce anxiety and to help heal the brain, but I have found that positive results depend on individual proclivities and the intensity of the anxiety. For milder anxiety, I find sitting meditation invaluable. I also enjoy *The Nourish Practice*, a somatic, guided meditation and rejuvenation audio practice I developed (Resource 7: "Nourish Practice Series I"). I offer you a taste of the practice here:

---

88. Firman, "Why Does Anxiety Seem to Get Even Worse at Night?"

---

• EXERCISE •

**THE NOURISH PRACTICE ("BREATHED BY THE BREATH")**

Gently lie down and close your eyes. Take three deep, full and relaxing breaths. Then allow your breathing to return to normal. Notice the natural rhythm of your breath and when you automatically inhale. Gently slow this inhalation down, bring it into your belly, and then allow it to "breathe you" by receiving it. Say to yourself out loud or silently: "I allow myself to be breathed by the breath," and allow this to happen, so that you are not willing your breath but letting it "breathe you." You want to consciously allow yourself to receive the breath, as a nourishing and comforting gift.

Once you are comfortable with this, you can try a variation: In your mind's eye, imagine the Earth beneath you. Then feel the ground beneath you and allow your body to sink into the Earth. Say to yourself, "I allow myself to be breathed by the Earth" as you experience yourself being breathed and nourished by the Earth.

---

In the throes of intense anxiety, sitting meditation usually exacerbates my state of mind. It's too difficult for me to be that intimate with distressing thoughts and somatic agitation, and at these times I often can't exercise appropriate psychic boundaries. Healthy distraction (tip 15) has helped me through intense, acute anxiety until I reached a level where sitting felt helpful.

During stints of more intense anxiety, meditating with others is more helpful and relaxing for me than sitting alone with eyes closed. So is walking meditation (Resource 7: "Walking Meditation").

We can also be mindfully active. This can include any activity: washing the dishes, painting, talking to a friend, gardening, or writing.

Do what works for you. Mindfulness meditation has been shown to be helpful during milder cases of depression and in its prevention, and this might be true for anxiety as well.[89] Whatever the case, mindfulness and/or meditation can help distract us from exacerbating anxious thoughts and bring dysregulated physiology into balance.

---

89. MacMillan, "The Simple Habit That Can Help You Fight Depression."

## Anxiety Tip 21: Be Good to Yourself

When unhelpful anxiety is getting the better of you, say, "Be good to yourself____(fill in your name)" and try to let go of your worry and worrying thoughts. You can say this to yourself silently or out loud. Speaking out loud to yourself can be more effective because actually hearing the words creates what your brain perceives to be a sense of otherness, thus simulating the support of another person or guide.

## Anxiety Tip 22: Holistic Support

I've had good success treating anxiety and insomnia with acupuncture and herbal medicine. While it's best to see a professional to tailor a personal protocol, I have found some herbs and supplements to be broadly helpful. Western herbs, in order of efficacy, include skullcap, valerian, hops, kava, passionflower, motherwort, oatstraw (oatmeal itself is a gentle nervous system tonic), chamomile, lemon balm, and peppermint. Asian herbs include ashwagandha (especially the KSM-66 extraction), ziziphus seed (*suan zao ren*), rhodiola, ginkgo biloba, oyster shell (*mu li*), Jatamansi (Ayurvedic), Chinese date (*da zao*), and poria fungus (*fu shen*). Supplements include GABA, NAC (N-acetyl cysteine), CBD oil, and calcium/magnesium. Herbal formulas include "Sleep Formula" by Gaia Herbs, and the Chinese medicine formulas: Gan Mai Da Zao Wan, Tian Wan Bu Xin Wan ("Emperor's Tonic Pills"), An Mian Pian ("Peaceful Sleep"), and Xiao Yao Wan ("Free and Easy Wanderer").

―――――

As you try out these twenty-two tips, check in with yourself to gauge how you are doing as you learn to down regulate your nervous system and find more equilibrium. A quick and easy way to do this, especially when you notice anxiety taking control of you, is to gauge your anxiety level on a scale of zero to ten, zero being no anxiety and ten being the most. Try an activity to reduce anxiety, even something like thirty seconds of deep, slow breathing. Then, ask yourself again at what number you rate your anxiety. Note if the number has increased or decreased. Recognizing that going from an eight to a seven or lower, for example, is movement in the right direction. This helpful feedback can itself be calming. Consider keeping a written log or notes on your phone for which tips work best for you and in what circumstances. The following, chapter-end exercises will likely be helpful in this regard.

———

The next three sections in the book explore in more depth each of the three facets of our triangle of resilience. I have proposed it is the breakdown of these essential, foundational connections that is largely responsible for our current climate predicament. And most importantly, to bolster and heal these relationships will place us more firmly on the path to climate cure both inwardly and outwardly.

Section III explores our first facet of the triangle of resilience relationship: self-healing via grief work and emotional shadow work. Section IV delves into the second facet of the triangle of resilience relationship: our connection with and honoring of the natural world. Section V, comprising the third facet of our triangle, is about building community and the innumerable benefits of restoring meaningful, intimate connections with fellow human beings.

---

• EXERCISE •
CHAPTER 5 JOURNALING

Please also refer to the additional in-text exercises for this chapter. Take out your journal or notepad, place it in front of you, and enjoy creating responses to the following invitations.

1. On a clean sheet of paper write "List #1" at the top-middle and then make two columns below, to the right and left. At the top of the left column write "personal anxieties" and for the other write "climate anxieties." Beginning with the strongest, write down personal issues that cause you the most anxiety. Then, in the next column write down which climate crisis issues cause you the most anxiety.

On a second sheet of paper, write "List #2" at the top-middle and again make two columns below. At the top of the left column write "anxiety tools for personal anxieties." Atop the right column write "anxiety tools for climate anxieties." For each item in List #1 (from both columns), list any of the "Twenty-two Anxiety Tips" shared at the end of this chapter that you think would best help you cope, or that have served you previously. This creates an inventory of your anxieties and ways to best cope with them. It's also a handy guide to refer to when in distress.

2. Now that you have your lists complete, you can practice "coping ahead" (actions to help be better prepared for future distress) for any of these anxieties. You can do this for as many items as you want on List #1. For example, say that one of your items is, "I get anxious when I think about societal collapse and not having shelter or food to eat." To practice coping ahead, look at List #2 to remind yourself of the anxiety tips you listed to address this anxiety. Let's say the top Anxiety Tips you listed are 1 through 7.

The next step is to sit down, when not feeling unduly stressed, and imagine the scary future per your description of it. If you feel you need any kind of support other than the tips, please enlist it. To the degree you are comfortable, let yourself feel the anxiety that arises (if it feels too much at any point, take a break and/or enlist support). Then practice your top tips to address it. Here's a practice run-through; the numbers correspond with the "Twenty-two Anxiety Tips."

1. Exercise **awareness** to notice you are feeling anxiety and say to yourself, "I am feeling anxious."

2. Begin to **breathe deeply, slowly, and steadily.**

3. Reflect on the ways you are **grateful** for any order, ease, and food you do have now and let yourself feel this **gratitude.**

4. If it would be helpful to **take action** by stocking up on food items or building a safe shelter, consider doing so.

5. **Get with people:** talk to a friend about your concerns and ask for any helpful feedback. You might even choose to do this exercise with a friend for support.

6. **Willfully control** yourself from repeatedly thinking about the scary scenarios of not having food or shelter.

7. Engage the following thought process regarding **"bad chickens"** (Anxiety Tip #7): Say to yourself, or write down, "I don't know with certainty what the future will look like. So, I will notice these scary thoughts, appreciate their possibility, but not excessively dwell on them."

3. For more practice hacking your anxiety, refer to the "Three-Step Anxiety Strategy" and the "Seven Body-Centered, Self-Care Tips for Acute Anxiety" earlier in this chapter and practice going through their motions for any of the personal and climate anxieties you did not list above.

# Section III
# INNER HEALING
## *(Triangle of Resilience Relationship #1)*

# Chapter 6
# THE GIFT OF GRIEF

*Surrendering to your sorrow has the power to heal the deepest of wounds.*
~SOBONFU SOMÉ

Holistic medicine provides a nature-based model for assessing the health not only of individuals but of whole systems. Its theories are metaphorical and therefore apply to the parts as well as to the whole. This means the whole (nature) affects the parts (human beings) and vice versa. Consequently, the integrity of the natural world depends on our collective sanity, just as we depend on nature for our well-being and survival.

A crucial yet underappreciated aspect of wellness is being emotionally integrated, which heavily influences our beliefs, choices, and actions. Emotional integration builds integrity through the transformational process of psychological death and rebirth ("dying through our pain"), modeled by the cycle of the seasons. We can therefore learn about renewing our inner nature from the cycles of outer nature. This is the cycle of regeneration we explored in chapter 3 through the lens of Chinese medicine's foundational Five Phase poetics. Each year, the cycle of death and rebirth repeats itself, reminding us of our promise for transforming pain and difficulty into joy and beauty. Autumn's letting go (grief) into winter's dissolution (death) is followed by spring's resurgence (renewal) unto summer's ease and flourishing (joy).

The more we model our psyches after nature, the more regenerative and able we are to fertilize the world with goodness, and this benefits us in return. By enacting this reciprocity of mutual care, we evolve ourselves while stewarding the climate. That we can injure the world so profoundly speaks to how comprehensively we can heal it. Ancient wisdom becomes common sense when we more fully become part of nature, so we can care for it rather than kill it.

## Tending Wilderness

Grief work is a process of transformational emotional healing through which we profoundly engage with the cycle of the seasons from decline and death unto rebirth and flourishing. To remind, we have defined grief as how we feel the pain of current or future loss, while *grief work* is how we feel unprocessed historical pain from loss—especially our core love wounds from childhood.

Grief work is a bona fide initiation into greater integrity, as it uncovers our body-centered locus for courage and creativity, inspiration and care. These inner jewels enrich us and lead us to wiser outward action. They enable us to thrive in ways that revere the natural world because our newly-renewed hearts can care more about nature's many gifts and the ways we can desist from injuring them. *Refraining from harmful acts and doing less can be as sustainable as engaging positive acts and doing more.* As we heal the personal hurts that have damaged the innocent "wilderness" of our hearts, we become more empathically equipped to address the wounds we inflict on the wilderness outside us— to the vulnerable forests and oceans, mountains and rivers. Just as our tender hearts have been at the behest of violent others who didn't own and heal their pain, the voiceless and essentially defenseless natural world is vulnerable to the projections and displacements of our current unreckoned pain.

Our emotions are the heart of our inner wilderness. We must learn to live *with* our emotions, and to appropriately manage them while preserving the wisdom inherent to their wildness (Resource 3: Weber, "Wild Inside"). This is best achieved through what we could call "inner permaculture"[90] principles, as we work *with* our inner nature and refrain from dominating it as we have the wilderness outside us, which has led to the latter's demise. Rewilding our inner lives—by way of clearing our pain and reviving our finer jewels of being human—fosters a fertile outer wilderness.

---

90. In essence, permaculture is a regenerative design system for restoring the land and local ecosystem while producing food and a thriving habitat for humans.

Inner activism fulfills its mission when emotional healing places us in a sustainable relationship with the world. This is to "become medicine for our times" by becoming the healing change we want to see in reality. Radical inner work, then, frees us to transform our relationship with the natural world we depend upon to thrive. Clearing enough of our emotional pain sets in motion the cycle of death and rebirth so that renewal can happen both inwardly and outwardly.

———

Any body-centered, emotional healing worth its salt puts us on a path of paradox: working through dark and light. Such integration yields surprises and unbidden "miracles" that can't be foreseen or linearly achieved. The magic we secretly seek is not in other dimensions, false hope, or the latest addiction craze; it's buried within the pain of our very own hearts. The self-compassion to unearth and release it births new eyes to see, new breadth to feel, and new ways to connect.

A "selfish" healing focus on ourselves, when it leads to greater vitality, wisdom, and right action, can generously be passed on to others with a depth and breadth not previously possible. I describe this process as "selfishness done right becomes selflessness." While those who have not done much inner work can reduce their carbon footprint, others who have embodied their grief and holy outrage seem more passionate about making sacrifices to not fly or drive, and generally consume less. I find this to be true for myself and among fellow climate activists whose hearts have been genuinely broken open by climate crisis.

The results of inner work are not only *quantitative* but *qualitative*. The deeper we go to heal, the more integrity we build and the more deeply we are able to touch others and infuse our actions with passion and meaning. While we may not always be able to measure these results, their impact is felt and substantively affects the world. When we don't do this inner work, we remain too numb and closed, self-absorbed, and compromised by our hidden love wounds. The paradox of metaphorically dying to live more fully undoes the cruel irony of perpetuating death as a result of denying our own and the world's pain. This inner-outer, Yin-Yang cooperation initiates us into treating the world more compassionately via both our actions and the love we share through them.

# Healing through Heartache

During my mid-twenties, I intensely worked through the pain of my core love wounds via somatic psychotherapy. I felt into the places in my body that harbored pain from not being seen and regarded by my parents (in addition to all the good they provided). These body-centered experiences included a variety of images, stories, emotions, and sensations. Sometimes these inner landscapes felt like an empty void, other times like a dense black hole, or even just a hazy discomfort. My process was to make contact, get to know, and allow these places to express the feelings they never could. They did so primarily through poetry and journaling, and released their grief-hurt through my tears for the love they lacked. During this time, I remember feeling as though I was literally pregnant—that new life was gestating in my belly. Paradoxically, I also described myself as a "walking cemetery," as I was dying to my old self and a newly integrated *me* was being born.

It's not surprising that our knee-jerk responses to emotional pain mirror our reactions to physical pain, as our brains interpret both physical and emotional pain through the same neurocircuitry. This is why Tylenol can help ease a broken heart. [91] Thus, we react to the heartache of emotional pain *as though it will literally kill us*. We must learn to act counterintuitively when we hurt emotionally, to *be with* our heartache, instead of resisting it as we do physical pain. To this end, we can:

1. Notice when we are afraid of feeling a painful emotion ("primary emotion").
2. Not give in to the fear by retreating from the original, primary emotion.
3. Allow ourselves to experience the primary emotion.

Even if you experience a primary emotion for five seconds, this is a start to build upon. For example, say you're feeling sadness, and you notice you're afraid to feel it. First, as step one, you can name the emotion and say to yourself, "I am feeling sad." For step two, you can say, "Just allow the fear to go for now, you can come back to it later if you need to." Then, as step three, allow yourself to feel the sadness. It's important not to force yourself to feel the sad-

---

91. Fogel, "Emotional and Physical Pain Activate Similar Brain Regions."

ness. Just allow yourself to encounter whatever naturally comes, even if it's only a taste of what you sense is inside, and even if it doesn't come at all. Mindful practice makes progress.

When we embrace emotional pain and the grief that dissolves it, we affirm a faithful *yes* to the hidden gifts inside our ache. Acceptance allows us to become pain's emissaries for healing. This paradoxical path generates inner richness by revealing our finer jewels of being human, among them our compassion and empathy, our courage and sense of belonging. When we don't do this sacred work, we often try to mimic its inner rewards with addictions and surrogate outer riches: fame, too many things, and opulence. The result is we excessively perpetuate consumerism, rapacious capitalism, and thereby, ecocide.

Perhaps you know someone who worships money and things, and who is arrogant, unfulfilled, and constantly needing more to compensate for feeling empty inside. An example of such a person might be US Treasury Secretary Steve Mnuchin, evidenced in his shortsighted, heartless, and ultimately avoidant response when asked if Greta Thunberg's demand for reducing fossil fuel investments would threaten US economic growth. His answer: "Is she the chief economist, or who is she? I'm confused … After she goes and studies economics in college she can come back and explain that to us."[92]

---

## • EXERCISE •
### TRANSFORMATION AFFIRMATION

Put down this book for a moment and reflect on the last time you successfully worked through a disagreement or argument with someone. Can you viscerally feel the refreshment and deep joy, the sense of wholeness, and renewed connection that resulted from compassionately working through that challenge? Take a few deep breaths to acknowledge this realization. Then, briefly journal about this experience; even a few lines is fine.

Now imagine engaging this resolution process in relation to your own pain. Imagine how life would be if you didn't have this pain. Journal about how it might look and feel. Then imagine that the pain is

---

92. Taft, "Treasury Secretary Just Stated Obvious About Teen Environmental Oracle Greta Thunberg & the Left Is Melting Down."

gone and you have an increased sense of comfort in your own skin: more passion, meaning, belonging, and creativity. These are just some of the benefits of grief work. Finally, take a deep breath and affirm that relief can indeed come from being with and working through the pain of your past love wounds and / or present heartache.

In his book, *When the Past is Present*, Jungian psychotherapist and author David Richo alludes to the finer jewels of being human as they are excavated and nourished through the unconditional presence a therapist can offer. Dr. Richo writes, "Therapy affirms how each of our feelings or attitudes, no matter how negative, can evoke compassion and lead to transformation. We then joyfully realize how every negative experience has positive, growth-fostering potential, how every liability is a resource, how every shadow trait has a kernel of value, how every disturbance or mistake can deepen our spiritual consciousness ... there is an energy of light frozen in our confusion, a luminosity we can release, if only we do not give up our mining."[93] Note, we can realize similar benefit when we affirm these qualities for ourselves through self-reflection and cathartic expression.

––––––

When our hearts break, two primary paths emerge: we shut down our feelings, or we stay open through the pain. The first path is sometimes the best we can do. But shutting or closing down—whereby we disconnect from ourselves and become numb to our feelings—without opening up again when we are able, turns us into curmudgeons, denies our creativity and our ability to love and be loved, and dulls our vitality. Shutting down in the face of heartbreak without processing our pain buries our grief, often fueling addiction, ruthless ideologies, spiritual bypassing, and unnecessary suffering—all of which drive disconnection from our triangle of resilience relationships and, eventually, climate breakdown.

The second path breaks our hearts open—sometimes what feels like as wide as the world—and delivers the rewards of renewal. We heal through this

––––––

93. Richo, *When the Past Is Present: Healing the Emotional Wounds that Sabotage our Relationship*, 12.

heartbreak by grieving. Reconciled grief humbles and softens us, turns pain into compassion, and dissolves our fear of being with what's difficult. It liberates our best humanity, the sustainable humanness many of us know can save ourselves and the world. Grief excavates and polishes our souls. It tips our balance into goodness by illuminating the clusters of darkness that, unrealized, keep our love hostage to our negative shadow.

This advent of light is the blessing of regeneration, a victory *through* psychological death that forges new life by honoring fertile darkness. It is a hero's journey, a dark night of the soul, similar to the proverbial transformation of a caterpillar into a butterfly. But before becoming a butterfly, the caterpillar dissolves into a black goo. This primordial state represents death and total dissolution, similar to how our psyches temporarily fall apart and dissolve when we die to our pain through grief work and rebirth our more brilliant selves from the fertile darkness of our old love wounds. Such regenerative dissolution uncovers and polishes our finer jewels of being human, creating the foundation from which to create a sane world. It is a holy struggle to prevent the ignored, and thereby infertile and lethal, darkness of our shadow from swallowing up all we love.

Seeking therapy for grieving our historical wounds, or our current grief, is not a weakness. Rather, it is one of the best forms of self-care, as important as going to the doctor to tend to a broken bone, or getting your teeth cleaned. I recommend working with a good depth psychotherapist, preferably one who has undertaken the journey and who is thus a living example possessing the wisdom and presence to shepherd you through the discovery and release of this stowaway heartache. Again, there is also much grief work we can do on our own via self-therapy, such as journaling, other expressive arts and self-inquiry, as well as in support groups and workshops, such as grief rituals.

Below is a self-guided grief work practice you can engage to help you contact and release emotional pain and increase your capacity for healing. It is adapted from *The Nourish Practice*, which doubles as a template for healing our core love wounds. Series II of the practice (Resource 7: Weber, "Nourish Practice Series II") describes in more depth my healing journey via grief work and offers more detailed suggestions and context for undertaking the journey. You can also employ this practice for current grief.

Bear in mind, this exercise is just one example of many for how to engage. Grief work is a radically creative process, and there is no fixed prescription for how to proceed. This said, guidance and a template can both be helpful. What's most important is to follow your intuition and engage all your faculties. Tune in to your body's wisdom, the meaning it conveys, and where it guides you one step to the next.

## • EXERCISE •
### INNER IMAGES

### Preparation

Before beginning this exercise, please read it through and see if the process seems comfortable or doable for you. If it doesn't, ask an emotionally intelligent, trusted other, such as a psychotherapist, for support. If you are uncomfortable at any point during the exercise, feel free to stop and disengage.

Wait for a time when you are in a calm, relatively relaxed state and have at least twenty minutes to dedicate to the exercise. Then, gently close your eyes and take about ten relaxed breaths as deeply and as slowly as you can, pausing briefly in between breaths. While breathing, allow your awareness to sink down into your body, similarly to how you did during the Body Survey exercise in chapter 2. Don't focus on any single part of your body, but allow your awareness to be present to your whole body. Alternatively, you can prepare by doing the Nourish Practice exercise from chapter 5, which unites all the above aspects: breath work, gentle awareness, deep body attunement, and relaxation.

### Engagement

Allow yourself to become aware of any pain in your body, physical or emotional. It doesn't matter if you know the cause or source of this pain, and it may or may not become evident even after you complete the exercise. If nowhere in your body speaks to you or you don't know where to begin, consider feeling into places that are most likely to carry this kind of ache, such as your heart center, jaw, or belly. Let your intuition guide you. Areas that are chronically tight are usually good places to start.

Now, while feeling into the pain, allow your inner imagination to present to you, one at a time, two images that represent the general sense of this pain you carry inside. These are what we call your "hurting images." For example, you might be presented with an image from the natural world, such as an animal or plant, or a meaningful object. Allow yourself to feel into your choice for hurting images for as long as it takes, even days. Once you've settled on your hurting images, close your eyes and settle on two images that represent your capacity to endure and/or heal the difficulty and pain; these are your "healing images." These might present as a power animal, a tool or weapon, a person you admire, or another healing/protective force. Hurting and healing images can be anything at all.

The next step is to give the first hurting image a voice. Allow it to speak of the pain you carry. Try to let it speak through your voice and avoid intellectualizing the transmission. Transcribe what the image conveys through its voice, intention, and imagined gestures; be patient and don't try to control it. You may want to hang out with, feel into, and get to know the image and what it might have to say before recording its message. When you have finished, take a break, if needed, and then do the same for the second hurting image.

Next, allow the first healing image to address any aspect of the hurt just expressed by either hurting image. You can do this in any form you like: the healing image can speak to the hurt, it can gesture to it, or it might perform an action or ritual to help heal the hurt. Allow yourself to sit with the healing image until it spontaneously expresses itself. Again, don't force or judge it, and don't think about it too much. Let your intuition guide you. Watch, feel, or write down what transpires. Next, do the same for the second healing image, letting it offer its healing balm, in any way it chooses, to whatever aspect of hurt was expressed by the hurting images. Address as much of the hurting images' pain as you like.

When this process is complete, when both hurting images and healing images have expressed themselves, rest in the outcome. Let it be and
take a break. You can continue this practice at any time. Sharing the
experience with a friend, or writing about it, can help to bring more
revelation, especially of nuanced messages you didn't consciously recognize during the process.

Because images are symbolic and lend themselves to creativity, you might
consider expressing your experience through art. For example, you could paint,
sing, or dance your experience. You might also craft a poem from your reve-
lations. You don't have to produce "good" art for this to be effective. What's
important is to genuinely and vulnerably express your feelings by embodying
in real time the healing experience that transpired. Just let it flow, giving yourself total freedom of expression that no one has to see … except you.

I find it especially helpful to recall the images and sensations that show up
in my grief work because they poignantly remind me of essential aspects of
my healing. Feeling the presence of these hurting and healing images in my
body-mind keeps the process current and alive. To this day, I remember and
call upon some of these image-forces. Commemorating the images and their
meanings in a poem further helps keep them, and me, flowing and growing.
Below is an example from my collection of grief-work poems, *Nature of the
Heart*, inspired by an image of thorns. The poem helped me feel not only the
way thorns can cut but also their use in coronation. This image also helped
me to connect my own hurt and recovery with the natural world. If creating
poetry appeals to you, I offer a "Healing Poem-Making" exercise in chapter 11.

### Fall

*About to fall*
*Through a bed of thorns*
*To the rest of my soul*
*I am afraid*
*To die*
*To the lie*
*As a child I learned*

*To hide*
*A bigger life*
*For little love.*
*Now I cannot*
*Live another day*
*Away, uncrowned.*

## Grief Work

The goal of emotional healing is the diametric opposite of perennial self-involvement and narcissism. Successful self-transformation via grief work frees our hearts so we can foster goodness toward others and the natural world. Not focusing on ourselves to heal results in more self-obsession (often while damaging others), greed, superficiality, and addictive consumerism. When we don't prune and grow ourselves via this self-healing (think: a robust, well-tended orchard tree) this promotes rampant, unregulated overgrowth (think: an unchecked, spindly, and unfruitful tree). Such has been the rampant growth of climate chaos, fueled by unrestrained capitalism.

As I progressed through my grief work, my pain and its stories and expressions eventually coalesced into a distinct personality representing a younger version of myself, and this inner child had loads to express! I allowed him to express himself until there was no more pain left to share. When I emerged on the other side of this dark night of the soul, I found that I cared more for my triangle of resilience relationships. These relationships became closer, more meaningful, and deeper, and I was able to give more to them. I also discovered a passion for forging justice in the world, fueled by healing through my own pain from injustice. This translated into a new abundance of care for disadvantaged others and the voiceless Earth—an empathic, natural commitment to activism.

Inner-child work is another powerful way to get in touch with our core love wounds. The previous Healing Images exercise can inform and nicely segue with inner-child work. Emotional healing of this kind is not about finding logistical solutions (fixing) as much as about being heard (by our own witnessing presence and by trusted others), embodying and expressing backlogged emotions, discovering what really happened to us once ago by assembling an accurate and truthful narrative (story) of our pasts, and making choices in the present that support our newfound integrity.

To help you initiate or further your grief work, I offer an inner-child practice below. This is also adapted from Series II of *The Nourish Practice*. Notice, the preparation phase is the same as for the previous grief-work exercise. This is because both are somatically oriented, simultaneously engaging mind, body, and emotion for holistic benefit.

---

### • EXERCISE •
### MEETING YOUR INNER CHILD

#### Preparation

Before beginning this exercise, please read it through and see if the process seems comfortable or doable for you. If it doesn't, ask an emotionally intelligent, trusted other such as a psychotherapist for support. If you are uncomfortable at any point during the exercise, feel free to stop and disengage.

Wait for a time when you are in a calm, relatively relaxed state and have at least twenty minutes to dedicate to the exercise. Then, gently close your eyes and take about ten relaxed breaths as deeply and as slowly as you can, pausing briefly in between breaths. While breathing, allow your awareness to sink down into your body, similarly to how you did during the Body Survey exercise in chapter 2. Don't focus on any single part of your body, but allow your awareness to be present to your whole body. Alternatively, you can prepare by doing the Nourish Practice exercise from chapter 5, which unites all the above aspects: breath work, gentle awareness, deep body attunement, and relaxation.

#### Engagement

Notice if there's anywhere—physically, emotionally, or energetically—that has felt chronically pained, agitated, or separated from your awareness. Allow your awareness to rest on any place you feel this discomfort.

Then, connect with this part of yourself and see if there is a story attached to its ache. Maybe it's a painful memory, story, or event from the past? Nothing has to be connected to this place, and it's best not to force any memory, feeling, or image. If an image, memory, sensation, emotion—or any or all of these—arises, rest in this experience for a bit. Just as you waited for the hurting and healing images from the previous exercise to express themselves, be patient here too for any messages or meaning to be conveyed to your awareness.

As a general rule, the most meaningful images and messages—what I call "salient" material—are those that *feel* most impactful and powerful and register as important, even if they are tender and small. For instance, you might contact a sensation of sinking emptiness (perhaps corresponding with the image of a hole in the ground, for example), and it might help you get in touch with feeling how your energy has been sucked out of you. In contrast, you might contact a bold, empowered sensation (perhaps accompanied by the image of a glimmering diamond). The message of this sensation and attendant image might be to show you the intact facets of your diamond-like strength and resilience to withstand and heal from being hurt. Please note, an image need not be a thing of the world; it is a kind of *qualia*—an inward, subjective experience. Quale (plural) need not be visual, but can also occur via other sensory faculties. An inwardly experienced fragrance, melody, flavor, or tactile sensation, for example, could be equally salient as an image.

Remember, not all feelings, images, stories, and sensations are equally salient; explore those that strike you as significant. As you elaborate their message, verify if this message *feels* true by noticing if your body responds with more of a resonant *yes* or an ambivalent *no*. Don't think about it too much! I call this somatic wisdom our *body-truth*. Pausing as needed to tune into your body-truth helps you stay on the path of what's personally true for you. You also want to corroborate your body-truth with logistical truth. If your body-truth conveys something is true but logistically you know it's impossible or highly unlikely, explore further to sort out what's most likely true. For example, if your body-truth communicates that you were not heard by your father, but your logistical mind only remembers him listening attentively to you, you'll have to reconcile this disparity via more exploration.

While working with these aspects of your inner child, notice any emotions you feel and name them. How did it feel to be you at that time in your history? How old were you? What were your facial expressions? What were you wearing? What were your surroundings? Who else was present? Rest in this awareness for a minute, or as long as needed.

For the next step you have a choice. Whichever option you choose, stay connected with the most salient aspect of any image, sensation, emotion, or story you've contacted. At any point—and most likely after you practice this for a time—you might have a palpable, integrated, mental-emotional sense of your inner child whom you can communicate with, listen to, be present with, and comfort.

**Option 1:** The first option is to simply continue resting in your inner experience and allow it to progress and unfold in your body and mind. For example, if you contact sadness with your inner child, allow yourself to embody this emotion and rest in it. You may also want to listen to anything your inner child has to "say" or "show" you. If a salient qualia arises, allow it to express itself to you; does it represent anything for you and does it have any message to share with you that is emblematic of your hurt and/or your recovery? Allow the image to express itself to you rather than trying to analyze it. If a story is most salient, let the story tell itself and unfold inside you as you pay attention to and learn from it.

**Option 2:** Another way to engage this process is to take out your journal and begin to elaborate on your experience. For example, if it's anger you feel most strongly, give your anger a voice and let it speak. See if you can write *from* your anger as much as, or more than, you do *about* it. If an image is associated with your anger, expand upon what the image means to you, what it represents, what message it might have to share with you that is emblematic of your hurt and/or your recovery. If it's a story that is most prominent, let the story tell itself as you transcribe it.

I find option 1 helpful for staying connected to my body's immediate experience as it unfolds inside me. Option 2 I find most helpful for furthering my expression and reckoning of these inner experiences.

Experiment and see what works for you. Options 1 and 2 work well together, and often occur simultaneously. After some practice, you might find yourself engaging them in tandem: writing from, or expressing, your inner experience from direct somatic awareness. I frequently pause during such expressive writing to breathe, to connect with my body-truth, and to keep my outward expression consistent with what's unfolding inside me.

Each time you sit to practice, try to come to the practice anew, with a beginner's mind, allowing space for what wants to express itself today, in *this* moment, and in its unique way. Some days you may need to rant about what happened to you that day, while other times you may be immediately immersed in the grief of heartbreak. Sometimes the two coincide: what triggers you today has historical origins. When this is the case, you get to see how the past influences your present experience. Alternatively, you can dance, draw, paint, sculpt, or sing your experience to mobilize and move through old pain. If you've identified and followed your body-truth, all paths eventually and ideally lead to:

1. Finding your way into foundational, underlying emotions.
2. Learning the true story of your past.
3. Helping you to release backlogged emotion.
4. Undoing limiting, or false, beliefs (see discussion and exercise just ahead).
5. Gaining wisdom for moving forward and making new choices.

For my own grief work, it was helpful to give my inner child a name. Actually, his name just came to me one day. Relating with my inner child by name made the process more intimate, real, and meaningful. Again, if you are at the point in your healing where the pained aspects of you develop a defined sense of self, you may want to connect with your inner child by name and let him or her express directly to you. Consider taking the process slowly at first and see what works for you.

Inner-child work is sacred, potent work. Following a few guidelines can help you feel safe, positively engaged, and keep your practice vital:

1. Engage only as long as you are comfortable.

2. For intense experiences, practice titration, healthy denial, and self-care to recharge (as discussed in chapter 3) and help you pace yourself and integrate the work.

3. If you feel overwhelmed, seek support from a therapist or friend, as you see fit.

4. Lack of appetite, sleep disturbances, feeling less happy, and decreased energy can be temporary side effects of grief work. If they become problematic for you, consider giving yourself a break and/or seek professional support.

## Unwinding Limiting Beliefs

Examining and unwinding any limiting, false beliefs acquired as a result of past wounding is also part of grief work, and instrumental for liberating ourselves. Consider an example: When our opinion is constantly shut down—as children or as adults—we can develop both an emotional and a mental wound. The emotional hurt we feel from being shut down creates a somatic wound. The mental component, in the form of a limiting (or false) belief, might be that I believe my opinion is worthless, that I am a bad or stupid person, or that I can't trust myself. We clear the emotional wound by expressing our backlogged emotion and we heal any limiting beliefs by noticing and dismissing the false belief, affirming our worth, and then acting from our worth.

### • EXERCISE •
### HEALING LIMITING BELIEFS

*The Nourish Practice*, as described in anxiety tip 20 in chapter 5, can be adapted to help heal both our emotional and cognitive wounds. Let's work with the wound of low self-esteem or self-worth. In addition to allowing yourself to be "breathed by the breath," you can simultaneously imagine and feel yourself being breathed by pure love. You say, "I allow myself to be breathed by love" or "I allow myself to be breathed by pure goodness." You consolidate your healing of these wounds by acting as though you matter, by acting in ways that are opposite to your false beliefs. This might mean expressing your opinion to others, taking action that matters, or sharing unique gifts with the world. As you act differently, your doubts and wounds will often flare up! This might scare or dissuade you from forging forward. If this happens, it's important to take deep breaths, recognize what's happening, continue to love yourself, dismiss limiting beliefs, and continue to act in accord with your worth.

As you exert your self-worth, you want to be careful to do so appropriately. When this energy has been repressed, it can want to make up for being hidden for so long. Until you more fully integrate your worth, you can come across as too forceful or inappropriately egoic. Whoops! Forgive and be gentle with yourself and make any amends as you come back into balance and find your stride. With practice, and after going overboard by excessively repressing or expressing, you naturally fall into a healthier balance. Paradoxically, once you are confident in your self-worth, you may not feel a burning need to always express and exert yourself.

## Fulfillment from Fracture

Through the process of grief work, numb and empty places inside me were nonmaterially filled by working through their pain. Psychotherapist David Richo describes this as doing the inner footwork to address our wounds, then letting grace effect healing and integration. I unconditionally abided my pain. I didn't fill or numb these fractured, aching places with things, pursuits, drugs, or surrogate pleasures. The result was psycho-spiritual fulfillment via the liberation of my finer jewels of being human. With a richer inner life, I found I was able to thrive outwardly with less—less busyness, less distraction, less consumption. In fact, I was happier with less because it freed up time for more meaningful pursuits. "Outer simplicity for inner richness" is my motto. For me, this is one way the inner activism of grief work has led to outer activism, minimalism, and a reduced carbon footprint.

To clear my backlogged pain, I also practiced receiving loving attention beyond what I felt capable of accepting. I learned how to let more love in. I remember one therapy session in particular where we didn't speak a word, as I merely sat in front of my therapist, allowing her to appreciate me unconditionally through attuned presence and eye contact. I would turn away when I couldn't let any more in, and then turn back to meet her attention when I felt I could accept more. As a result of this practice, and grief work generally, I have been able to feel and give substantially more love to myself and others, including the Earth. By cultivating what I call the "love we already have in hand"—the degree to which we currently embody our finer jewels of being human—and employing it to unconditionally abide our pain, we generate more of these psycho-spiritual resources, which eventually translates to building and protecting more outer resources.

I undertook the bulk of my grief work with my therapist, and in between visits with her I journaled profusely. Journaling creates a kind of "otherness," as different aspects of our psyche communicate with our unconditional, witnessing self. It is a great way both to initiate and to see through the process of grief work. Often, merely sitting with my feelings (see option 1 of the Meeting Your Inner Child exercise), in addition to journaling and poem-making (see option 2), was enough to process my pain.

Grief work, my own self-care, and the attuned presence of others fertilized the barren ditches inside me, allowing them to blossom with richness. When we restore our inner ecosystems through symbolic death (being transformed by our pain) and rebirth (the largely effortless, graceful flourishing that results), we naturally extend the resulting richness and care to others. We create a nourishing, positive feedback loop between ourselves and the world. This is the heart of climate cure.

While we can't heal all the pain in our hearts, *any* clearing of pain can translate to a greater capacity to care for and heal the world, especially when combined with our second and third triangle of resilience relationships. I want to make clear that this is not an either-or dynamic; we *can* heal climate disruption even though we are wounded and not our fullest selves. In other words, we can do good while we heal, and the more we heal, the more good we can do. Especially because climate crisis is now so dire, it's important we act as effectively and as wisely as we can *while* we heal through our triangle of resilience relationships. We heal these relationships with the love we already have in hand, which liberates more of our capacity to care, thus increasing the amount of love we have in hand.

## Fixing vs. Being with Pain

While being initiated to the dark night of my soul via grief work, a good friend and mentor turned me on to Matthew Fox's book on radical happiness, *Original Blessing*. In the following quote, which I've held close for decades, Reverend Fox explains that by letting pain be pain (radical surrender to *what is*) we become pain's emissaries instead of its victims (holding on to and perpetuating suffering): "It is one thing to empty. It is quite another to be emptied. Pain does this. It empties us if we allow it to ... What we must ultimately do is let go of pain. Ideally, by entering into it we become able to breathe so much freedom from within the pain that the deepest letting go can truly occur. For this to happen, the naming of the pain, the letting it be pain for a while, is essential ... But if we fail to let pain be pain ... the pain will haunt us in nightmarish ways. We will become pain's victims instead of the healers we might become." [94]

Fox's description of pain as that which empties us is akin to what I mean when I say, "We don't grieve; grief does us." In this sacralized void we find fulfillment in emptiness—or better, clearing—in the place where grief dissolved our pain, thus making grief work an embodied spiritual path (Resource 2: Weber, "Embodied Spirituality"). This hidden path or back door to a sense of the divine yields a special kind of heart-light by way of blessed, fertile darkness. It is not popular in a capitalistic, modern culture conditioned on external accolades and façades. Yet, the path Fox illuminates is absolutely necessary if we are to transform ourselves and change our climate fate. I allude to this "back door to divinity" in a poem by the same name, excerpted here from my collection *Rebearth*:

*I know that beneath the winding*
*Miles of solid bone protecting*

---

94. Fox, *Original Blessing: A Primer in Creation Spirituality Presented in Four Paths, Twenty-Six Themes, and Two Questions*, 94.

*The center of our bodies*
*Flows a river rich enough*
*To resuscitate our arteries*
*And transform our eyes*
*Once we have slipped*
*Through our heart-crack*
*To infinity, the back door*
*To divinity.*

Emotional healing into spiritual initiation is paradoxical. Similar to poetry, it's not linear and literal, as physical healing is. To heal physical injury, we combat and repair it. But to heal most emotional pain we must accept and embrace it. Unfortunately, we often apply a linear strategy to heartbreak, trying to fix it when what is required is to hold, acknowledge, and accept ourselves exactly as we are. Unconditional regard for others and ourselves has the paradoxical result of easing our pain. Our pain transforms us and subsides as we surrender to and feel it.

While we can transform the bulk of our pain, some of it is never wholly resolved. We learn to *carry* it. It's our capacity to *be with* loss, to accept and embrace it, that makes such carrying possible. We learn to carry the ache as we would adjust to living with a limp, or as we must tenderly hold sentiments we aren't, or weren't, able to express to a loved one. While these perpetually "undelivered packages" impart a burden, they also confer unexpected gifts. The pain we carry becomes a portal through which our callings find us and our compassion and empathy connect with humanity and the rest of creation that also suffers. This heart connection inspires our loving actions.

Feeling safe and supported by others who can *be with us* as we are and not try to fix our sadness is the best way I know to allow grief to unfold. The attitude I eventually adopted while passing through my core grief work was to accept the possibility that my intense grief could continue for the rest of my life. I figured I would learn to carry it. Thankfully it hasn't, but this disposition was my way to allow that grief cycle to have its way with me without meddling in its genius. Since that time, grief has resurfaced numerous times, but in milder and different form.

# Receiving Grief

In Chinese medicine, the seasons of spring and summer are Yang seasons, represented by the white paisley of the Yin-Yang symbol. In contrast, the seasons of autumn and winter are Yin seasons, represented by the black paisley (figure 1). Grief corresponds with autumn, and what is called the "Po," or "corporeal soul"—referring to our physical, embodied self—and the moon cycle.

These poetic associations correlate with my experience of emotional transformation through grief work being the most Yin-building and "grounding" practice available. This said, mind-body practices such as hatha yoga, meditation, tai chi, and other holistic energetic practices are invaluable to prepare us for body-centered emotional work (Resource 2: Weber, "Beyond Yoga"). These practices ground us in our bodies, sensitize our nervous systems, and focus our attention for the next level of body-mind integration by way of grief work. Mind-body practices are also invaluable for managing the stress of climate crisis. The late Jungian psychologist and grief advocate Marion Woodman concurs, with a dash of humor: "Continuing to do pioneering sacred work in a world as crazy and painful as ours without constantly grounding yourself in a sacred practice would be like running into a forest fire dressed only in a paper tutu." [95]

We highly value personal, individual achievement and "more doing" in the West. This is part of our excess Yang derangement. Grief is the antithesis of doing and achieving; it is a fallow Yin time for undoing, corresponding with allowing the earth to rejuvenate during the fallow, compost and humus-generating period of autumn. No wonder we are a grief-starved, and therefore pain-burdened, society. Grief is a sacred Yin practice that flows in the compassionate company of others and by our own abiding presence. Grief is not something we do but an experience we *receive* and accommodate by letting it be, feeling it, and allowing it change us—*grief does us*. It is not something we willfully achieve any more than sleeping is. We merely create the conditions for both to unfold. Once we *try* to fall asleep, we fail. Similarly, we must surrender to grief. If we employ a doing, fix-it, goal-oriented approach to grief, we are bound to fail because we will get in grief's way of working on, humbling,

---

95. Woodman, "Essay: Why is True Equality Taking so Long?"

and healing us. Grief is a transformative process that ebbs and flows of its own accord when we remain emotionally honest (naming and feeling our true feelings). We may imagine it's done with us only to have it to revisit when we least expect it. We must remain open to grief if we want to remain true and vital.

When we don't allow the more-than-human-world to decline and restore itself through fallow times, we burn it out. The soil becomes arid and infertile, and the nourishment we derive from it less fulfilling and nutritious. Notice that the globe is currently besieged by forest fires, melting glaciers and permafrost, severe drought, and warming oceans. These events evidence excessive and destructive collective Yang-heating coupled with deficient Yin-cooling energies. This trend can be traced, at least in part, to our failure to grieve, a dynamic we will continue to unpack.

## Unresolved Loss

We feel pain when we lose something, either physical or intangible, such as a home, our sense of self, or love from another. Grief allows us to release our pain as we love ourselves back into wholeness, even if we have to continue carrying some of the pain. Grief is the great inner gardener, the most soul-building of the emotions.

An inability to receive grief in the face of significant loss causes our pain to backlog inside us. This repression, as we discussed in chapter 3, creates a pressure that eventually erupts from us in unsustainable ways, such as rage and violence. In her essay "Embracing Grief," African healer and workshop leader Sobonfu Somé describes how this Yin-Yang dynamic played out when she was a teenager. Her inability to release overwhelming grief when her grandmother died filled her with anger and rage.[96]

Deep grief feels like we are dying. Yet, when we do not die *to* our grief, part of us dies as a result, and it is this deadness we employ to kill what we love. We explore these dynamics further along in this chapter as *projection* and *displacement* of our pain. In contrast, embracing our sadness softens our hearts and engenders compassion, allowing us to connect with others. Grief and love are two sides of the same coin, the medallion of wholehearted, Yin-Yang loving.

---

96. Somé, "Embracing Grief: Surrendering to Your Sorrow Has the Power to Heal the Deepest of Wounds."

In Jewish tradition, for example, it's incumbent on us to find joy in life. Yet, it's considered a greater *mitzvah* (good deed) to attend a funeral and grieve with mourners than it is to attend a wedding, a usually joyous occasion. The crucial work of grieving clears our hearts from the burden of loss, the sting of pain, and the brunt of violation, renewing our sense of fulfillment and belonging.

In a discussion about healing old love wounds, a friend once said to me that life is too short to spend the time and energy to work through such heartaches. I replied that life is too short not to. Broken-open love shows up not just for good times, but especially for tough times. Grief allows us to continue to love others, and our planet, when they are ailing. In this sense, our capacity to grieve is lifesaving. Tolerance for grief—an altogether appropriate emotion in the midst of climate crisis—allows us to remain close to the problem and minister to it. Honoring grief allows us to be cracked open and transformed by it. This is the work of wounded healers, and now is our time to shine this Yin-light.

In *When the Past is Present*, David Richo discusses the importance of grief work and how unmourned losses are not truly in the past, but in fact significantly influence our lives in the present, especially intimate relationships. The ungrieved pain of loss compromises us in the same way chronic infection saps our vitality, or a cyber-virus sabotages the efficiency of a computer. As antibiotic herbs and prescription medications clear biological infection and anti-malware software helps rid our laptops of bugs, grief is our psyche's way of clearing the emotional "infections" that stymie our hearts—and our capacity to more deeply care.

The genius of grief work is also akin to beneficial soil bacteria. Both work unseen to convert seemingly fruitless overaccumulations into vitality. Soil bacteria break down "useless" organic matter into nourishing fertilizer and promote the life cycle. Like beneficial soil bacteria, grief is the great catalyst of decomposition in the Yin phase for Yang regeneration, the vital link between death and life, allowing what has expired to be upcycled and rebirthed. This excerpt of my poem "Secret Maker of Gardens" from the collection *Rebearth* communicates these hidden processes of regeneration common to both grief and the soil.

*Lie down with your pain,*
*Your grief, confusion, and despair.*
*It will make you the fertile ground*
*You fear falling into.*
*But you must trust it more*
*Than what you see,*
*For the aura around your smarting heart*
*Knows other than the compost*
*At your soles.*

*Invest in this hidden world*
*So you may one day be the roots*
*For its fruits in action,*
*Your body its passions*
*For decent progress.*

*Lie down with the soil's equivalent,*
*Your own body of woes.*
*Nourish it with the ever-present glow*
*From deep within your chest,*
*O, secret maker of gardens.*

Both the dark ways of the soil and our dark emotions pertain to the sacred feminine Yin. Both have been stigmatized and desecrated by those in power for millennia, and both are essential to the fertility of our inner and outer worlds. Through grief we reconnect with our inner earth, as soil bacteria revive the outer Earth. Reclaiming and nourishing these sacred Yin domains of inner and outer ground are facets for radical sanity, our collective triangle of resilience relationships, and comprehensive climate cure.

> ## • EXERCISE •
> ## DARK SOIL MEDITATION
> Next time you feel sadness or deep grief, as your heart breaks open and allows your awareness to sink deeper into the dark recesses of your

body, imagine yourself sinking into the Earth, into the darkness of its soil. As you imagine, or vicariously feel the soil's bacteria breaking down "useless" organic matter, rest in the awareness of grief breaking down your burdensome pain, simply by allowing yourself to feel the pain of loss.

## Freeing Grief

If we sense our grief is stuck, we can gently nudge or indirectly encourage its flow, as we might push a boulder to get it rolling on its own. We can begin by allowing the *possibility* of grief, by facing our losses and acknowledging how much we care. We can distract ourselves less and spend more time paying attention to how we feel, or in the company of those with whom we feel safe to embody our sadness. We can also stimulate our grief through empathy by watching a sad movie and letting ourselves feel what a grieving character feels. Or, we can spend time in person with others who are grieving; empathy for them can unlock our own hearts. If all else fails, notice the beauty of the woods, the stream, the wildlife around you, or those you love, vis-à-vis the science presented in appendix 1. Once we free our hearts, even more empathy is made available to us, allowing us to connect with others' grief still more, resulting in a positive feedback loop of connection and care.

Sometimes grief brings tears, sometimes not. Feeling sorrow and allowing mourning, however it chooses to express itself, is what's key. If we sense we are holding backlogged tears, we can try to "fake it till we make it." Efforts to cry can stimulate an organic crying spell—as the metaphorical boulder rolls on its own. If tears come, we can let go and can see if the grief continues to flow as we surrender to it.

• EXERCISE •
UNRESOLVED LOSS

Do you sense you hold significant ungrieved loss inside you? Does it feel stuck and separate from you? Which of the strategies mentioned just above do you feel could help let your grief flow? Write them down in order of strongest to weakest resonance. How might you incorporate these remedies into your life to aid your grieving process? List these ways alongside each strategy you have written down. Can you think of any other ways not mentioned here to help contact any unprocessed grief you might be holding onto? Also jot these down and, if ready, create a plan to enact them.

Grief takes us down into our bodies and sets the stage for something truly new to take root in us. While the grief work we engage to substantially clear our childhood love wounds is finite, grief itself is a lifelong experience, ebbing and flowing through ongoing joys and sorrows, comings and goings, good fortune and loss. Grief is slow in its work of dissolution, bringing us down when we least expect it. Meandering in and out of our lives, grief joins the future, present and past in a spiral of one becoming. In this way, it is an antidote to linear, outward progress and overdevelopment, busyness and acquisition, control and ownership—the many perpetrators of climate crisis—and therefore a hidden cure for our destruction of the world.

When we have passed through grief work, we might find ourselves more fulfilled and content with modest, wholesome pleasures. This translates to a reduced carbon footprint. Yet, because climate grief is ongoing, we may find ourselves in a constant state of mild to intense grief. This is normal and to be expected, for when the Earth hurts, so do we (or so we should if we are paying attention). Grief's gift is to help us empathize with the Earth vis-à-vis our own pain. I call this honest, embodied relationship with the collapsing state of the world "the spirituality of a broken-open heart." From this place of intellectual and emotional honesty we have a better chance to address climate crisis at its root. Joanna Macy supports this emotional honesty when she writes, "The sorrow, grief, and rage you feel is a measure of your humanity and your evolutionary maturity. As your heart breaks open, there will be room for the world to heal."[97]

Encountering climate crisis, we may find wide-ranging expressions of grief as we navigate and integrate experiences of destruction and pollution, suffering and extinction. It's imperative we feel and express this pain, especially with

97. Macy, *Greening of the Self*, 5.

the support of others, for which working through our personal grief prepares us invaluably. Grief circles and rituals can also be helpful.

## Removing Our Mask

I call unresolved pain or trauma "encrustations around our hearts." When we don't grieve this pain, we unwittingly build a compensatory persona around our hurt—an alter ego of sorts. Some call this a "false personality." This façade was included in Jung's concept of the *persona*, which he described as "a kind of mask, designed on the one hand to make a definite impression upon others, and on the other to conceal the true nature of the individual."[98]

For Jung, individuation by way of integration involved deconstructing the persona to reveal the shadow within our often pained and messy inner lives. This deconstruction, or degrowth, of our false persona (whose external corollary is economic and consumerist degrowth) includes transforming what we have been injured by—by what we essentially *are not*. Via grief work, we deconstruct what has encrusted our hearts and enslaved our minds. This uncovers our brilliance and natural kindness, as we simultaneously undo what causes us to hurt others.

When we do not dismantle our persona, we perpetuate the pain and shadow beliefs beneath it. Letting down our guard, therefore, is crucial for grief work. This can be scary at first because it exposes our old love wounds, the adverse childhood and adult experiences we have defended against our whole lives. Yet this initial act of vulnerability—which is easier to initiate with another's caring support—can bolster our authenticity and integrity.

## Projection and Displacement

Deep-seated emotional pain can feel inert or immovable, like a lump, ache, or void inside us. Yet our pain is anything but inactive. It is akin to a metaphorical cancer or radioactive blockage whose outwardly projecting "gamma rays" attack, injure, and violate others, including the Earth. Like the pain of a tumor, this pain grows when left untreated.

Limiting beliefs, self-sabotaging habits, and knee-jerk emotional reactivity resulting from unresolved or backlogged emotional pain cause us and others

---

98. "the persona," http://psikoloji.fisek.com, *http://psikoloji.fisek.com.tr/jung/persona.htm*.

more hurt, unnecessarily increasing and prolonging suffering. Without the tools or support to reckon with our pain, our suffering metastasizes to others as we displace it onto the world. We project the logistical dynamics of our pain and displace its emotional charge onto others. *We transmit what we don't transform.*

Consider an example: let's say I perceive you to be selfish or irresponsible. If I am projecting, it means I in fact am the selfish and irresponsible one, unconsciously assigning to you what I cannot accept about myself (of course, sometimes both are true). If I deliver my judgment with attack and aggression, or simply act violently toward you as a result of projecting my beliefs, this is an example of displacing my repressed emotion onto you. The more repressed and in denial we are, the more we project and displace and the more violent the delivery and our acting out.

The adage "hurt people hurt others" refers to this transmittal—or projection and displacement—of our unconscious hurt onto others. Carl Jung is famous for recognizing the pernicious dynamic of projection, which his protégé, Marion Woodman, describes this way: "Because we reject our own humanity, we reject what Jung calls the shadow side; we've pushed that down into the unconscious, and the minute we do that, we start projecting it out onto someone else so that someone else has to carry our so-called darkness."[99] People, pets, and the Earth all qualify as "someone else," and have all suffered our projections and violent, displaced pain. Through grief work, we can replace our pain-body's projected and displaced toxic *emissions* with comprehensively caring *emanations* from our finer jewels of being human.

*Hurt people hurt others* communicates the same message as the adage: *If you don't heal what hurt you, you'll bleed on those who didn't cut you.* If you've been treated violently, perhaps you've noticed yourself lash out at someone or something uninvolved in that violation. Conversely, if you've been graced by kindness, you love others as an extension of being treated well. Both lashing out from pain and reaching out in compassion are examples of displacing what's inside us onto others; one is malicious, the other compassionate.

---

99. Horváth, "Marion Woodman: Holding the Tension of the Opposites."

Spreading more unintended violence than care is at the core of our war on each other and on nature. In a wonderful essay discussing these dynamics, Eric Garza proposes that when trauma causes us to disconnect from the world, we also dissociate from nurturing relationships that make us humane. "Could human beings engage in wars against other human beings without the ability to 'other' them..." he asks.[100] By extension, we can also ponder: could human beings engage in wars against nature without the ability to "other" it?

The self-care of grief work to free our hearts radically shifts the paradigm of *hurt people hurt others* to *healed people heal others*. This grants us the deep-down care and motivation to make relatively small sacrifices now, and engage with and mitigate climate crisis for any degree of a livable future.

## Hurt People Hurt Others

Solid science supports the dynamic of hurt people hurting others, of getting them "to carry our darkness." Several years ago, Kaiser Permanente teamed up with the Centers for Disease Control and Prevention (CDC) to conduct one of the largest studies of childhood abuse and neglect as it relates to health and well-being later in life. It is called the "CDC-Kaiser ACE Study."[101]

An Adverse Childhood Experience, known as an "ACE," is defined as a developmental trauma "beyond the typical, everyday challenges of growing up."[102] Evidence shows those with a history of overt abuse and neglect are at risk for delinquency and violent criminal behavior.[103] Both parental neglect (a form of passive abuse) and overt abuse create love wounds, or lasting trauma to our figurative hearts.[104] Out of this pain, we cause pain to others. When we are neglected, we learn to neglect others. We extend this violence not only to humans close to us but to another intimate: the Earth. In contrast, embodied love and healing through these hurts via grief work generate empathy and care for ourselves and others.

---

100. Garza, "Awakening to the Traumacene."

101. Centers for Disease Control and Prevention, "About the CDC-Kaiser ACE Study."

102. Nakazawa, "7 Ways Childhood Adversity Changes a Child's Brain."

103. Watson, *Child Neglect: Literature Review*; The National Academies Press, *Understanding Child Abuse and Neglect*.

104. Systemic racism and living in an ecocidal society inflicts similar trauma.

Author, psychologist, and trauma specialist Dr. Karyl McBride shines a light on this traumatic "chain of custody": "Ignoring or neglecting a child's needs can create many symptoms and ultimately mental health problems, which then can affect the rest of his or her life. How, for example, can a child grow up knowing how to provide empathy and nurturing if they were never taught? If children are loved and treated well, they don't grow up wanting to hurt others; they grow up wanting to help and respect others, and with the ability to provide empathy."[105]

Childhood emotional wounds are developmental traumas that need not be as extreme as the adverse childhood experiences (ACEs) of sexual abuse, chronic and violent humiliation and shaming, or physical violence. The gradations in trauma severity are sometimes referred to as large "T" and small "t" trauma. ACE traumas are generally of the large "T" variety, while milder traumas, that include many of our developmental love wounds, are small "t." Importantly, small "t" traumas are still significant. In her article "Different Types of Trauma," psychologist Dr. Elyssa Barbash writes: "A person does not have to undergo an overtly distressing event for it to affect them. An accumulation of smaller 'everyday' or less pronounced events can still be traumatic, but in the small 't' form."[106]

Barbash cites a few examples of small "t" traumas: conflict with significant others and children, infidelity, legal trouble, and conflict at work. Developmental and relational small "t" traumas—or significant love wounds—also include not being acknowledged for our opinion or genuine feelings, being shamed for our perceived shortcomings and failures, being ignored or yelled at when we need help, not being supported in our aspirations and exuberance, not having our creative gifts recognized and supported, or being covertly co-opted to bear our parents' pain and stress. Some may even feel these injuries as large "T" traumas.

Each of us has a unique perception and experience of hurt in response to adverse experiences. Pain sustained by emotional injuries, and widely variant individual responses to similar wounds, are difficult to quantify. I might sustain more hurt by being yelled at than someone else, for example. When these

---

105. McBride, "The Long-Term Impact of Neglectful Parents."
106. Barbash, "Different Types of Trauma: Small 't' versus Large 'T'."

love wounds accumulate unaddressed, their traumatic impact grows, creating a backlog of pain-pressure, as we recently explored. This backlogged pain can manifest as isolation and an inability to connect meaningfully with others and to care for them. It can also show up as rage, sociopathy, addiction, and cutthroat avarice. When we don't receive love and healing to quench our basic emotional needs, we may collapse into apathy and depression, turn to various addictions to numb the pain, or aggressively try to get (take, steal, coerce, possess) this love by violating others.

Marriage and family therapist Neil Rosenthal speaks to the dynamics of displacing emotional pain in his article "Relationships: Hurt People Hurt Others." He writes, "Hurt people tend to mistreat or act harshly toward others—especially those close to them—because those are the people they feel the safest and most secure around."[107] We hurt those closest to us because those *familiar* to us remind us of those that are *familial*. Since the beginning of our evolution, nothing has been more familiar and familial to us than the Earth and our fellow humans.

In my own work with patients, I've observed those who don't take care of their body, heart, and mind tend not to take care of the body of the Earth. Many cigarette smokers who recklessly pollute their own bodies seem to think nothing of polluting the street with butts. Smokers also report that smoking helps to numb their feelings. A healthy diet, exercise, and not excessively polluting our own bodies (all when we have the privilege to choose not to) seem to correlate with caring more about the body of the Earth and other human beings. Self-neglect and self-loathing can foster apathy, resulting in unnecessary pollution. Extreme self-hate, as a result of harboring too much pain, can become a death wish for ourselves and others. Grief and grief work help dissolve this burden.

Journalist and co-author with Donald Trump of *The Art of the Deal*, Tony Schwartz, who had extensive personal contact with the president, writes, "Beneath his bluff exterior, I always sensed a hurt, incredibly vulnerable little boy who just wanted to be loved."[108] When such love wounds are coupled with

---

107. Rosenthal, "Relationships: Hurt People Hurt Others."

108. Schwartz, "I Wrote 'The Art of the Deal' with Trump. His Self-Sabotage is Rooted in his Past."

far-reaching power, global neglect and ecocide can result. This is evidenced in the president's corruption, which extends beyond dismantling the Environmental Protection Agency, opening national heritage sites to fracking and logging, building large carbon footprint walls while destroying sacred indigenous lands, and enabling other despots like Jair Bolsonaro of Brazil to plunder the Amazon rainforest.

If Schwartz is right, these love-wound dynamics describe a deterioration of self-esteem and integrity, the breakdown of supportive interpersonal relations, a pernicious division between self and environment, and crimes against humanity and the Earth. Herein lies our climate change crisis, perpetuated by generational emotional trauma and deteriorating intimacy with the Earth and human community—our triangle of resilience relationships in decay.

We therefore must *become* compassion, not just try to muster it. We effect this by liberating care from our pain, especially via grief work. Otherwise, we can't truly *be the change*. Until we do this inner work, we will ultimately create too much destruction, no matter what palliative fixes for climate crisis we invent. Our developmental love wounds are not our fault, but they are our sacred responsibility—our opportunity—to heal. This way we pay love, not malice, forward.

## Eco-Grief

Personal grief work prepares us for grieving environmental loss, what is known as *eco-grief*. The reverse is also true: grieving the demise of nature can help us grieve our personal losses. In fact, either can catalyze the other, as personal and environmental loss intertwine in our hearts. We engage with the destruction of what we love by allowing our hearts to break, sharing our sorrow with others, allowing the poignancy that results, and when ready, mobilizing ourselves with a greater love and fiercer resolve gained from the process. With greater resiliency and more of our finer jewels available to us as a result of grief work, we are more psycho-emotionally resilient to face turbulent times. Our sadness, outrage, despair, and fear are all on our side when it comes to climate cure. The same emotions we encounter through personal grief work can help us face, endure, and engage with healing (through) climate crisis.

Because climate crisis originates inside us and is not separate from us, "fighting" it misses the mark. We are therefore destined to fall short if we try only to fix it. In contrast, when we embrace and work to heal the crisis, we cease to objectify and demonize nature; acknowledge our involvement in the damage; invoke regenerative solutions rather than palliative Band-Aids; and encourage acceptance, understanding, and cooperative relationships for comprehensive cure. We must engage the inner work (Yin) to heal its root causes and follow through with the outer action (Yang) of climate activism to change its course.

Because our climate is an ongoing, unmitigated disaster projected to worsen until further notice, we can practice carrying its hurt as we persist in its crucible of heartbreak. Again, this is best undertaken together and why gathering in community to grapple with loss is so important. Yet, most of us walk around feeling alone, and the conversations—much less an openly-acknowledged communal carrying of the crisis—scarcely happen. Climate breakdown is a global, communal issue for which holding its pain together is the needed, commensurate response. The climate change discussion and support group I created has gone a long way toward filling this need (Resource 5: "Climate Change Café"). Meeting together in person helps us "hold" and heal through the impact of the crisis in a way none of us could alone.

## Doing Without

Grief schools us in doing without by temporarily stripping us of vitality, cherished beliefs, productivity, and progress. Sojourns through psychic minimalism train us to do without material excesses. In this radical simplicity, we learn not only to survive, but to experience more of our humble humanness. Grief primes us for sustainability in all facets of life because we experience that with less we can truly fare better. This is core inner activism for the outer activism of degrowth—divesting from the consumerist heat engine driving climate crisis (Resource 2: Weber, "Lockdown").

While the great philosopher Nietzsche believed that all pain is birth pain, some pain is less remunerative and can feel overwhelming and insurmountable. The heartache of climate crisis is a prime example. In light of this ongoing breakdown, I find my own baseline of happiness to be lower than it used to be. Amid the devastation of our world, I am more melancholy and irritable in the face of our predicament. Opportunities to grieve give me relief.

Recently I've been grieving my previous life, the more carefree and exhilarating years on my farm in Hawaii prior to climate crisis thundering onto the public stage. Simultaneously, I've been grieving the promising and secure future I was expecting. I also grieve for my nieces, whom I madly love, in light of the precarious future they inherit. It's not possible for me to remain in denial about climate crisis—honestly apprehending *what is* takes priority over pursuing perpetual happiness that can't accommodate distressing news. While this honesty is tougher to bear, it breeds integrity and the kind of tough-love, minimalism-engendering climate sanity we need.

We can't deny the bulk of our pain and difficulty if we want to live and love as fully as possible for the long term. Paradoxically, reconnecting with our care involves feeling some pain and making sacrifices. Remaining honest and feeling our grief helps us process pain as it rises, a practice of emotional housecleaning I call "keeping our hearts clean." This way, we don't hoard transformable pain inside us, and this inner freedom helps us stay vitally engaged with climate action. In climate crisis, I grieve to stay afloat while doing what I can to move the chains.

## Healing Through Climate Trauma

Almost half the children in the United States have experienced at least one childhood trauma (ACE) and "nearly a third of United States youth aged twelve to seventeen have experienced two or more types of childhood adversity that are likely to affect their physical and mental health as adults."[109] Added to small "t" traumas, this amounts to a collective tsunami of trauma and potential for displacing our hurt.

Generational trauma is a process by which love wounds are passed down from one generation to the next via the dynamic *hurt people hurt others*. Because untended, generational love wounds result in mistreating others, they are a primary, invisible cause of climate crisis. Grief work to help heal our childhood

---

109. Stevens, "Nearly 35 Million U.S. Children Have Experienced One or More Types of Childhood Trauma."

love pain is therefore a core and sorely missing modern-day initiation rite into responsible adulthood, a process I call *sacred permission*, discussed further in chapter 8. As we unearth and grow our finer jewels of being human—as the results of grief work—we treat others (social justice) and the Earth (environmental justice) more compassionately, and are less likely to unduly contribute to climate disruption.

We cannot ultimately separate our personal and collective pain from the Earth's suffering, nor the Earth's desecration from our personal woes. We're killing the planet because we've tried to kill, rather than heal, our personal pain—the same abuses projected and displaced among *familials* and *familiars*, generation to generation.

When we make peace with our deeper hearts, with this "ground zero" inside us, we make peace with difficult reality and can begin to comprehensively heal our physical bodies and their corollary, the body of the Earth. Such inner practice confers a fortitude to face other difficult emotions, such as those that arise in the face of climate change, that are often buried beneath the surface of our lives. The next chapter will help you to further identify and express these hidden, shadow dynamics of your heart to become a more potent, wounded healer as medicine for our times.

———

Without reckoning with our personal traumas, we will have a tough time facing what Colorado psychotherapist Benjamin White describes as "the greatest trauma on the grandest scale."[110] Ongoing climate trauma is arguably more ominous and overwhelming than many of our personal traumas. How can we hold disturbing climate science news and cope with the real-life impacts of climate disaster if our hearts are already too burdened with unresolved personal trauma?

Climate crisis appears to be distinct from our thoughts and emotions. But in reality, it is a result of our collective inner and relational crises. Climate cure lies at the intersection of inner healing and transforming the outer world. Yet many of us—like sponges saturated from personal trauma—can't absorb enough of the severity of climate crisis to mobilize enough for it. We must,

---

110. White, "States of Emergency: Trauma and Climate Change."

to a greater degree, resolve our personal hearts to contend more effectively with climate crisis and its traumatic effects. For this, broad-spectrum emotional intelligence is essential. It's crucial to clear our hearts as much as we can so we have both the space for, and the resiliency to tend to, climate crisis and its grand-scale, exponential effects.

Many of us may unconsciously cower from climate awareness to defend against both the present devastating climate news and our own unresolved, personal traumas that climate crisis triggers in us. The corollary, of course, is we can begin to face *either or both* personal and climate trauma to initiate healing—a holistic transformation that is at once personal, interpersonal, and inter-ecological. "Thus the knowledge of an ever-present, ever-growing threat to the biosphere is serving as a kind of universal catalyst to bring the unresolved trauma buried in every individual, culture and society to the surface," writes Matthew Green in his insightful article, "Extinction Rebellion: Inside the New Climate Resistance."[111]

———

As our climate predicament worsens, grief may be harder to come by. And while I agree that curtailing our grief might be necessary at times, there are several problems with this approach. One, it presumes we have control over grief. Two, it fails to recognize that avoiding or suppressing grief makes us toxic to ourselves and others. Three, it doesn't appreciate that grief is a portal to deeper love and community, and for many, a path to activism. Four, avoiding grief sows anger and violence. Finally, a grief-denying perspective doesn't appreciate the deep grounding and Earth-connection that grief bestows, essential for wise climate warriorhood and treating the Earth with care by allowing it to lay fallow, as we wisely "do without" through our own cycles of grief.

Being transformed by grief occurs in both the short- and long-term. As conditions worsen, the window for benefiting from longer-term grief initiation may close. We would then be forced to acutely, and less comprehensively,

---

111. Green, "Extinction Rebellion: Inside the New Resistance."

address climate crisis. This juncture would mark an unfortunate (and ironically, sad) lost opportunity for inside-out climate cure, which is why grief work and other triangle of resilience work is desperately needed now.

---

### • EXERCISE •
### CHAPTER 6 JOURNALING

Please also refer to the additional in-text exercises for this chapter.

Take out your journal or notepad, place it in front of you, and write out your responses to the following prompts.

1. List the five most significant personal losses and/or traumas you have experienced. On a scale from zero to ten, with ten being the greatest, how alive are these losses for you today? Have you given yourself time to grieve them, to feel your sadness and longing for them?

2. Gently close your eyes and allow an honest answer to surface to the following inquiry: Do you notice yourself acting out on others—people, the natural world, or things—as a result of your own frustrations, anger, or helplessness? List the ways you do this and what you think the underlying causes of these actions might be. Would you like to resolve any of these underlying causes, and how capable do you feel doing so? How willing are you to seek support—via therapy, a support group, self-therapy and personal resolve—to convert this displacement of pain into compassionate service?

3. What is the mask you wear that you don't want anyone to know you are wearing? What is underneath it? What do you imagine would happen if you let go of this mask and exposed your true self? Note: Our psyche has its own way of creating what we need to evolve once we're aware of it, and especially if we work with it.

4. What are the ways you distract yourself from healing your heart? Name up to three addictions—mild, medium, or severe—you engage

in and rate them on a scale from zero to ten for how much they detract from what your heart of hearts would like to be doing. What changes would you like to make in your choices?

5. Which difficult emotions—sadness, anxiety, guilt or remorse, fear, anger, helplessness, hopelessness, for example—do you experience most frequently? Distress Tolerance action: Allow yourself to feel these emotions in your body and to be with them without trying to fix them. Make a time each day to sit with these feelings. For each emotion, do this for five seconds once a day. Try increasing by five seconds each subsequent time. Feel free to disengage at any point if you feel too uncomfortable.

6. What aspect(s) of grief or grief work described in this chapter spoke most saliently to you? Why do you think this is so? How do you think this information and/or your resulting realizations can benefit you? If you are unsure of the answer to any of these questions, can you commit to sitting with these questions and seeking outside support to explore them if you need it?

# Chapter 7
# EMOTIONAL SHADOW WORK

*To confront a person with his shadow is to show him his own light.*[112]

~C.G. JUNG

In previous chapters we learned that experiencing all our emotions is key to becoming an integrated and therefore regenerative person. This integrity translates to how wisely we act and how we treat others and the natural world. Additionally, to heal from past love wounds—our small "t" and large "T" traumas—and face current climate trauma, we must be able to tolerate and be transformed by a broad range of emotions. If we cannot contact and embody all our emotions, we can't mitigate their harm or reap their boons. To summarize, befriending and embodying all our emotions, especially our difficult ones, allow us to:

1. Heal through our past love wounds.
2. Cease displacing so much of our pain onto the world and exacerbating climate crisis.
3. Better cope with the pain arising from the breakdown of our world.
4. Increase our fear-mark so we can interface with climate crisis and work for its cure.

---

112. Jung, "Good and Evil in Analytical Psychology," 872.

To this end, we must identify both pleasurable and difficult emotions that are repressed and underrepresented in us and strive to skillfully experience and express them. This form of emotional intelligence is what I call "positive and negative emotional shadow work." This chapter therefore is about uncovering our shadow emotions so we can embody the emotions we need for full-spectrum emotional intelligence and to offer a more holistic contribution to climate cure.

In traditional depth psychology, the *shadow* refers to unconscious aspects of our personality with which we do not identify. Shadow may also refer to the entire contents of our unconscious—everything of which we are not fully aware. Shadow is the unknown side of ourselves, the parts to which we say, faithfully but mistakenly, "that's not me." While these hidden aspects, or blind spots, usually refer to tendencies, motivations, or qualities, in this chapter we primarily explore our shadow emotions—those emotions trapped inside us we have rejected as "not me." My experience is that these hidden emotions often strongly influence, or indeed govern, our motivations, beliefs, and actions. We will also explore why it's imperative to acknowledge and integrate these powerful, dormant forces.

## Half Full *and* Half Empty

As we've learned, emotional transformation and subsequent integration are the path to "becoming the change we want to see in the world" and "changing our consciousness." There's much more to these phrases than is commonly gleaned, which is why our world has not transformed and is crumbling. The rub for our failure to be this change in consciousness rests in the difference between an embodied (Earth-oriented, black-*and*-white, emotionally intelligent) and a disembodied (imagination-oriented, black-*and*-white, emotion-denying) orientation. Shadow work, from which we birth comprehensive kindness by working through darkness for the light, is key to an Earth-centric life because it helps us to transform our pain into service…rather than weaponize our pain.

Shadow emotions are those we have difficulty accepting not only in ourselves but in others. Some of our "positive" and enjoyable shadow emotions include joy, ecstasy, inspiration, empathy, and pleasure. "Negative" or challenging shadow emotions include grief, anger, fear, worry, and despair. Reclaiming both our positive and negative neglected shadow emotions helps deepen our finer jewels of being human. I place the polarities of "positive" and "negative" in quotation marks because, remember, these are relative states and perceptions, not concrete value judgments.

While we have learned the importance of befriending our negative emotions, liberating our positive shadow is also essential, true to Yin-Yang wisdom. Embracing sustainable, non-addictive, pleasurable emotion is just as important as embracing difficult emotions. Our capacity for pleasant psychospiritual states keeps our love of life and our will to live alive. Our cultural norm is to repress and marginalize negative shadow emotions and to celebrate and encourage positive emotion. We generally deny our grief, fear, anger, and despair more than we do more enjoyable states. For this reason, here we focus on integrating our "negative" shadow emotions.

Jung believed that shadow is our link to more primitive instincts, which we override with our conscious minds during childhood. In this sense, our emotional shadows often result from traumas big and small, as we discussed in the previous chapter. We may find it just as difficult to feel pleasure as we do grief, for example. Without joy, we become cynical and quickly descend into nihilism and apathy. This extreme can lead to unrealistic, pessimistic perspectives based on emotional reasoning. It can also lead to black-and-white thinking and catastrophizing—seeing an empty glass even if it's half or a quarter full. When we can hold our dark and light sides hand in hand, we see a half-filled glass as part full *and* part empty, not only part full *or* part empty.

When pessimism divorced from reality overtakes us, we have little incentive to work toward a better version of ourselves and the world. Such negativity becomes the weakest link in our ability to be part of climate cure. For this reason, it's important to have some positive emotion already in hand before we dedicate ourselves to the not-so-fun and temporarily distressing self-work of confronting what's painful. This reservoir of positive regard is what's called being "well resourced." Being well resourced also includes self-care and support from others, including the natural world. Experiencing the Yang of pleasure, fun, and happiness helps to integrate the Yin counterparts of grief, anger, despair, and fear. Unsustainable living arises when we excessively cling to positivity or negativity. Modern Western culture is guilty of the former: we collectively cling to too much positivity while our unconscious negative shadow emotions run the show of violence and destruction. This denial of our shadow leads to climate bypassing. To remind, climate bypassing means to deny difficult emotions that arise in relation to climate crisis, which leads to our ignoring climate crisis and prevents us from wholeheartedly engaging with it.

## Befriending Our Shadow

Each of us has a unique preponderance of emotional tendencies. Noticing which emotions we have difficulty expressing, or being present with in others, can be a portal into our emotional shadow. We may, for example, find ourselves unable to celebrate another's joy or success. We may be uncomfortable around or unable to tolerate another's anger, fear, or sadness. Noticing this, we can choose to practice welcoming and expressing these emotions. A first step into emotional shadow work is naming the emotion. "Oh, that's sadness I'm feeling" or "Wow, I'm angry!" We also can practice hanging out with these emotions in others to integrate our shadow. At first this might be uncomfortable, so we need to practice tolerating the discomfort.

Emotions we are uncomfortable with often lead us to our hidden love wounds. Why is this? Two reasons are: *learning* and *mirroring*. We grow up around others who don't share or tolerate certain emotions and we learn to abandon or repress the same in ourselves. We also mirror the emotions of our elders, embodying those they express. Or, if we recognize their shadow, we knee-jerk to the opposite extreme to "not be like them." Either polarity separates us from our wholeness, because the extremes neglect the positive aspects of the shadow we reject. For example, we may gravitate to kindness and softness in reaction to a caretaker who abusively expresses anger. As a result, our own anger—along with assertiveness, boundary-setting, and protection—becomes repressed under a façade of gentleness. A more holistic solution is not only to seek out kindness, but also to embrace the anger and all other emotions that arise in us (emotional honesty) and process the pain the abusive anger caused us. This way we protect ourselves and retain the core benefit in anger and any other emotions.

If we cannot express our emotions in the face of hurt, they become locked inside us, repressed in our shadow. When we encounter these hidden emotions, such as we did with grief in the previous chapter, they are linked to the story of that heartbreak. Memories and images of a painful past may surface as these emotions are released. Working through shadow emotion that results from fractioned learning or unhealthy mirroring is best done in therapy, aided by our own self-care resources such as journaling, peer support, and nature connection.

There is no shame in harboring shadow emotions. Everyone I know is heartbroken to some degree. It's our soulful responsibility—for sacred permission—to reckon with this hurt. In the process, we become more experienced with and integrate aspects of our vitality, which then become part of a fuller psychic palette. If I don't express or feel much anger, for example, this can be a clue that I'm harboring substantial hidden anger. Releasing repressed anger, while uncomfortable and unwieldy at first, liberates the visionary and exuberant energy trapped inside it. This creative mobilization of anger can also act as a powerful antidepressant, as it did not only for Greta Thunberg but also for youth activist Mary Annaise Heglar. Author Ellie Hansen writes, "Heglar's depression only subsided, she says, when she channeled her despair into anger and passion for climate activism."[113]

## Shadow Gifts

Shadow emotion, creativity, and passion are intimately linked. In her essay on the shadow, psychologist Carolyn Kaufman shares Jung's view on the connection between our shadow and creativity: "…in spite of its function as a reservoir for human darkness—or perhaps because of this—the shadow is the seat of creativity."[114]

Repressed anger, as just discussed, mutes our passion (creativity + vitality) and can lead to physical health problems related to what we call in Chinese medicine "excess heat" syndromes. Anger, we recall, pertains to the Yang-natured Wood Phase, which corresponds with heat and creativity. The healthy expression of Wood Phase energy is creativity, which emerges in part from healing through and integrating anger's positive and negative aspects. Anger's hot, rising, creative energy needs to mobilize its vitality (sustainably engaged

---

113. Hansen, "Our Climate Change Inaction: Is 'Climate Trauma' the Missing Link?"
114. Kaufman, "Three-Dimensional Villains – Finding Your Character's Shadow."

and expressed heat). The creative, expressive gifts inherent in anger are both vital capacities for climate mobilization. The courage for rebellion, the inspiration and creativity for engaging in regenerative solutions to carbon-heavy activities, and the willpower for making personal changes and "sacrifices," are all fueled by anger.

When anger's creative energy is stymied, excess heat accumulates inside us, which can lead to insomnia, irritability, apathy, and volatile rage. Repressed heat and creativity also lead to impulsivity, needless busyness, and compulsive activity. In this light, "excess heat" is actually "misused or misdirected heat." This agitating, misused heat translates to more outward heat as aimless, fleeting, and frivolous activity—often in the form of "fun" and entertainment—resulting in needless greenhouse gas emissions. Here we see how internal (personal) warming affects outer (climate) warming.

In addition to anger, all our challenging emotions impart hidden gifts. I discuss these dynamics in my article, "Dark Jewels: Mining the Gifts of Eight Difficult Emotions," which I summarize here:

1. **Guilt** returns us to our values, morality, and care.

2. **Fear,** as the "helpful" variety discussed in chapter 4, alerts us to our limits and boundaries for self-protection, thereby guiding us to right action, and therefore to care.

3. **Remorse** signals that we have made a mistake, caused harm, or could have done better. Remorse, like guilt, informs an appropriate apology and remedy.

4. **Despair** can help us face and grapple with the truth, let go of worry, anxiety, and unnecessary control, as well as reveal inner strength we didn't know we possessed.

5. **Worry and Anxiety,** when realistic, can show us what we care about and prompt us to helpful action.

6. **Grief** shows us what we love, clears our pain, and slows us down. Grief curbs anger, can alleviate anxiety, and helps us empathize and connect with others in pain.

7. **Envy and Jealousy** reveal what we aspire to, pointing us to our greater potential and fulfillment, as well as what matters to us and what we want to protect.

8. **Anger or Rage** alerts us to where we have been hurt (which we can also grieve), what we care about, where our boundaries lie, what we want to protect, and provides the fuel for right action.

---

### • EXERCISE •
### EIGHT DIFFICULT EMOTIONS REFLECTION

For each of the above eight difficult emotions, describe an event or issue in your life which has elicited that emotion. Allow yourself to express that emotion by feeling it and/or journaling about it, or by any other expressive means. After you've expressed yourself, identify any of the hidden gifts this emotion might bestow upon you and how this new dynamic might affect your life.

---

A patient named Dana recently came to my practice. She felt stuck, frustration (a form of anger), and struggled for a sense of purpose. Feeling stagnant and frustrated are symptoms of a Wood phase imbalance in Chinese medicine.[115] Dana also was dealing with painful, inflamed acne, a clear sign in Chinese medicine of excess heat.

To address Dana's complaints, I first used acupuncture and herbs to address the excess heat in her liver and heart organ networks.[116] Simultaneously, I helped Dana identify the places in her body where she felt "stuck," by asking her where she felt chronically tight, dissociated, and bothered. As she felt into these places, she encountered feelings of anger and frustration in her throat, chest, and abdomen. Because she liked to write, I invited Dana to journal

---

115. Note, Chinese medicine acknowledges imbalance more so than pathology, per se, because within pain and dysfunction are hidden joy and functionality, true to the interdependence of Yin and Yang. This is consistent with Jung's positive and negative shadow being relative states, and not inherently bad or good.

116. Remember, they are called "organ networks" or "organ systems" because they relate to a constellation of mind-body qualities, as discussed in chapter 3.

what these angry and frustrated feelings wanted to communicate to her. What emerged was remarkable.

As Dana's emotional repression and heat were mobilized and cleared both through treatment and therapeutic journaling, she rediscovered her voice and a heartfelt calling: to do creative writing work with children, a passion she had abandoned years earlier. In my experience, a dormant creative longing often lies hidden behind repressed liver and heart heat. The liver and heart organ systems in Chinese medicine are intimately related. They collaborate to help us galvanize our passion into action. After more treatment and soul-searching, Dana resolved to pursue her revived calling. Her frustration and, eventually, her acne also eased.

Although the acne was not the root of Dana's complaint, this symptom helped lead her to the core of her dis-ease. She understood her painful break-outs as a disguised, maladaptive expression of her pain caused by not following her desires. Trapped within her repressed anger were her finer jewels of inspiration and creativity, meaning, and purpose. Through holistic treatment, she transformed her unused, and therefore misdirected, heat into passionate service. It took courage for Dana to acknowledge and embody her anger. She is an example of how we can all use the goodness we have in hand (her original courage) to create more goodness (her renewed, amplified courage). Leaving her frustration, irritability, and physical symptoms unaddressed, Dana's vitality and calling would have remained buried in the shadow, depriving herself and others of her gifts.

It's worth highlighting the difference between this deeply regenerative form of treatment and the typical, corresponding Western medicine protocol of pain killers, sedatives, and topical acne cream. The latter treats presenting symptoms with medicines that carry deleterious side effects, and ignores the psychological drivers of the soul's desires that, once revealed, contribute to a more beautiful world. Western medicine's linear treatment of disease misses the poetry, meaning, and messages in our symptoms and the deeper causes of distress, which can arise spontaneously in holistic treatment or with a little digging, as they did for Dana. Allopathic treatment focuses on fixing the physical manifestations of disease, which is sometimes what is needed. Holistic treatment facilitates the symptoms of pathology into gifts, while curbing their harmful effects.

Not all medical symptoms have hidden meanings, but often there is more to our diseases than meets the eye. An example from my own life is when I tore the medial meniscus in my knee at age twenty-five (which I eventually healed with natural medicine). The pain was excruciating and my tears flowed abundantly. But after about thirty minutes, something surprising yet providential and beautiful occurred: I realized I was crying not because of my knee pain but over my parents' recent divorce. My femur represented my father and my tibia my mother, and I (represented by my meniscus) was in between them, torn and aching. This experience propelled me into psychotherapy, where I did the bulk of my grief work that transformed my life.

When we address the physical, emotional, and relational aspects of disease, we join our inner genius with a world that needs and benefits from these gifts. When medicine embraces our dark, shadow emotions—in Dana's case, her pain, frustration, and longing, and for me my hidden grief—instead of viewing them only linearly and pathologically, we create integrated, holistic cures and human beings more able to minister to and steward a thriving world.

Experiencing and wisely working with all our emotions re-wilds, regenerates, and creates a thriving "jungle" inside us. A vibrant inner ecology translates to a vibrant outer ecology. When we ignore this inner-outer holism, we ignore beauty and create horrors inside and out. The problems of our world, such as climate collapse, are rooted in our failure to engage with our best-kept, most healing resources—the treasure trove of difficult emotions in our deep hearts from which emerge our finer jewels of being human, to augment the goodness we already have in hand, with which we create sustainable thriving.

---

### • EXERCISE •
### EMOTION IN ILLNESS REFLECTION

Can you recall any illness or physical injury that revealed your hidden desires or emotions? Did their release help ease your physical discomfort? Did the discovery of these positive or negative shadow emotions enhance your life? If so, how? Feel free to journal about any other aspects of your experience and realizations.

# Catharsis

Unprocessed grief (a Yin emotion), as we've learned, often manifests as depression, and apathy. It also contributes to symptoms of imbalance in its counterpart emotion of anger (a Yang emotion), which often manifests as violence and unsustainable destruction. For Dana, it manifested as a loss of meaning and purpose. Additionally, the degree to which we are uncomfortable with another's grief can indicate the degree of core grieving we have to do.

Recall that grief is the emotion of the Metal Phase. The lung and large intestine are its corresponding Yin-Yang organs. Challenges with expressing grief often show up in this pair of organ networks. They also show up in the heart, since grief and love are two sides of the same coin. Acupuncture helps to facilitate the embodiment and expression of grief. Patients have teared up and outright sobbed while receiving acupuncture on the meridians (called "channels" nowadays) corresponding with these organ networks. And not because of any pain from the needles! As a result, blockages of unprocessed sadness, as well as other symptoms pertaining to the lung and large intestine organ systems, can be mobilized from the body-mind. Patients often appear and express feeling renewed after releasing grief this way.

Holistic medicine is beautiful because it works on all aspects of our humanness simultaneously. We can access emotion via the physiology and organ system body maps, and vice versa, all within the cogent and time-tested paradigm of the Five Phases. Please don't worry if you don't fully grasp the Chinese medicine terms discussed here. The takeaway is that this holistic medicine's integrative paradigm can help us release under-expressed shadow emotion and curb compensatory, over-expressed emotion (as in Dana's case). In the same way our mind, body, and emotions are inextricably interconnected, the metaphorical framework of Yin-Yang and the Five Phases helps us understand our interdependence with, and mutual effects on, the biosphere and the planet.

Befriending our own difficult emotions and purging our pain ultimately translate to better overall health. So does accepting, and even rejoicing in, these emotions in others. Greater emotional breadth and depth augments our compassion and empathy, helping us build more intimate and resilient community networks. Holistic healing via the web of organ networks translates to more robust social and ecological webs of connection. We create relationships with more common ground, the way Pema Chödrön, one modern champion for our humanness, describes so aptly in her book, *Comfortable with Uncertainty*: "Compassion is not a relationship between the healer and the wounded. It's a relationship between equals. Only when we know our own darkness well can we be present with the darkness of others. Compassion becomes real when we recognize our shared humanity." [117]

## Pathos

Another way to get in touch with under-represented shadow emotions is to notice which emotions arise in us, or fail to, during provocative moments. We might notice these most poignantly when watching a movie, listening to music, reading a poem … or an article about climate change. In ancient Greece, such elicitations in oratory and theater were the function of pathos: an appeal to the emotions of the audience to evoke feelings lying dormant in them. Because of its power to heal, such catharsis was an early form of psychotherapy.

In pathos we identify with certain characters and themes to release or simply notice unexpressed or under-expressed emotions. Our emotional reaction to a sad song or scene might range from feeling completely unmoved, to choking back tears, to feeling the welling up of tears that do not spill, to weeping uncontrollably. These instances show us which emotions we have difficulty expressing or are most prominent for us. Being open to feel these emotions and allowing them to see the light of day, if only gradually, and being with any triggered memories of past or current loss that are still "alive" for us, can help us process backlogged pain and free our hearts.

None of this suggests we should indulge any emotion at any time. Yet, when we can feel and appropriately express a wide range of emotion in skillful measure, we embody and flesh out the full Yin-Yang symbol of our heart-minds and become more regenerative people. When we have difficulty experiencing any of the Five Phase emotions (anger, joy, worry, sadness, and fear), we can overidentify with a world event, become excessively angry or sad, afraid or excited about it. This too creates a shadow, resulting in misaligned

---

117. Chödrön, *Comfortable with Uncertainty: 108 Teachings on Cultivating Fearlessness and Compassion*.

relationship with reality. As a result, we may displace our personal, backlogged pathos onto global issues. Accurate assessment, measured concern, and wise resolve get lost in the projection of catharsis. Yet, because they purge us, such projection and displacement are ultimately helpful, *as long as we realize we are doing it.* We are dealing with real life, after all, not a theater performance or movie. I've observed this dynamic frequently—which, ironically, saddens and upsets me—when discussing activist issues on social media: lots of drama, little measured discussion, and even less resolve to take action.

When we need to vent, we can *mindfully* allow our overreactions. Shadow emotions we make contact with will often emerge from us in extreme form. This extreme usually modulates over time, once the emotion is processed and the issue surrounding it is metabolized. A key to being skillful when this occurs is to be aware of the overreaction…and allow it to happen, in private. For example, when I contact rage (old or new) I find it most helpful to journal it, scream it, or otherwise share it with a trusted friend or therapist—not express the bulk of it publicly in the moment. Releasing the rage helps unburden me so I can levelheadedly revisit the issue and adjust any misperception of reality I assumed during the upheaval. This way, I honor myself by releasing what has been trapped inside, and remain cognizant of reality by not allowing emotional backlog to unreasonably skew my view of objective facts. This also helps prevent emotional reasoning and unhelpful knee-jerk reactions. All this is true integrative healing: working with head and heart to better ourselves while being fair and kind to the world around us. With skill and attention, we can release extreme emotion and keep our heads on straight—or mostly so!

• EXERCISE •
PATHOS REFLECTION

Reflect on any movie, play, speech, performance, poem, or other piece of art that has elicited strong emotion from you. Which emotions were most strongly stirred for you? Briefly describe the eliciting event and your experience of the emotion/s that emerged from you, including how the experience has helped and changed you. Which emotions do you feel might currently be "stuck" inside you and need more expression? What form of pathos (external, eliciting event) do you sense could help you release them?

# The Costs of Avoidance

In his powerful essay on racial justice titled, "What Kind of People Are We Becoming?," Umair Haque writes, "We look away from the things we must look at, because they frighten us with the knowledge of ourselves."[118] When we displace shadow emotions and simultaneously overidentify with the emotions we are more comfortable with, we might avoid dealing with crucial issues altogether because we can't handle the shadow emotions triggered in us. In other words, we avoid exposing ourselves to difficult reality because we fear how it makes us feel. This is the dynamic of our "fear-mark" as discussed in chapter 4.

Fear of feeling dark emotion compromises us, for example, when we hide from climate awareness and persist uninformed, or when we hide from having a difficult talk with someone we care about. An artist I know is unable to discuss important issues because he becomes defensively angry when someone challenges his beliefs. When triggered like this, he perceives he is wrong and shames himself. "I am bad, wrong, stupid, and worthless," he tells himself, when self-correction is all that's called for. He could replace his self-shaming with, "I misspoke or made a mistake or didn't realize something; I am not a bad person." He experiences his triggered emotional reaction but fails to inquire into the inaccurate conclusions informing his reaction. As a result, he needlessly retreats in fear of being upset, when the cause for his upset is misperceived, via emotional reasoning, to begin with.

Perpetually perturbed, my friend avoids engaging in such discussions, concluding, "I'd rather be happy and just do my art." This way, he conceals his wound, disengages from further edification, mistakes the facts, perpetuates defensiveness, and remains wounded and in hiding, a victim of his own lack of reckoning. If he were able to work with his anger and the feelings of worthlessness and shame that arise when he is wrong, he could bolster his emotional intelligence, see beyond his emotional reasoning, unburden his heart, create more valuable relationships, and experience more joy. He might also discover more passion and fulfillment than he does by merely "doing his own thing." Overcoming shame indeed helps us welcome goodness and become happier, more engaged, and more effective.

---

118. Haque, "What Kind of People Are We Becoming?"

When we compromise our emotional healing, we shrink away from what begs for our participation. Noticing our emotional discomfort zones and reckoning with our shadow and backlogged love wounds reduces this maladaptive tendency. As we learn to handle the feelings that difficult issues stir, we knee-jerk less, think more realistically, become more equipped to face troubling external issues, and speak up in the name of justice. This is why emotional intelligence and its attendant critical thinking have everything to do with contributing to climate cure. We see now how truly difficult—if not impossible—it is to act consistently wisely and compassionately enough without shadow work. Our global predicament originates inside us.

Our capacity for pain, horror, and empathy are limited, and chronic overexposure can shut us down. Constant media streams of traumatic events desensitize and cause us to avoid learning about important issues. We respond less to news of the hundredth mass shooting or species extinction than we do to the first few. We become inured and can no longer take even terrible tragedies to heart for too long anymore. We must unconsciously filter out overwhelming information just to remain functional. Learning to filter information more consciously, however—similarly to how we extend awareness to what feel like overwhelming emotional triggers and extremes—enables us to selectively take note of information that is crucial *not* to ignore.

Another reason we don't care as much as we could is that we relate to bad news as another reality show or movie, when it's not. This is another pathological form of normalization. We unconsciously assume, *if it's on TV, it's entertainment and must not be real.* The parents and peers of mass shooting victims and survivors from any of the recent massive hurricanes or floods can assure you the horrors are real. After enduring two massive evacuations—first from the Thomas Fire in southern California and then from Kilauea volcano's lava eruption on the Big Island of Hawaii—I also assure you these events have severe impacts beyond our mere imagination of them.

## Inner and Outer Collapse

It's arguably more important to prepare psychologically and spiritually for further climate breakdown than it is to prepare physically. One way is to begin a process of conscious personal collapse that simultaneously renews you. To use a metaphor from current climate change events, this self-initiated collapse can serve like a controlled burn for a wildfire: a little pain now to help mitigate greater devastation later.

Personal breakdown is preparation for climate breakdown, and vice versa. You can begin such a process of relatively controlled chaos by feeling all your feelings, exposing yourself to climate change news, critically thinking through any unrealistic rosy or catastrophic assumptions you have, and addressing any major, unresolved grief in your heart. These practices increase psycho-spiritual resiliency by helping you to acknowledge and meet reality while wholeheartedly facing challenging experiences.

With support from others, this kind of emotional shadow work will free up your vitality, creativity, and sensitivity, and prepare you well for difficult news, climate activism, and tougher times ahead. Another incentive for engaging these initiatives now is to take advantage of the relative calm and regulation present in yourself and in your community before times get tougher.

Climate change aside, this is the work of a lifetime to rejuvenate and awaken your life. Climate crisis included, it's even more important. Case in point: at several junctures while healing from my losses to the lava in Hawaii, I realized the inner resiliency I had cultivated prior—in particular through anxiety management, grief work, and clawing my way out of depression—allowed me to endure the moment-to-moment unknowing and eventual loss of my home and farm without going mad and falling apart.

---

• EXERCISE •
## COLLAPSE REFLECTION

Reflect on any instances in your life when you have fallen apart: had a nervous breakdown, fallen *seriously* ill, or suffered significant physical injury. For each instance, describe how it changed you and made you more resilient. Then, pick out key words from your writing that capture the ways you overcame or grew stronger and wiser *through these experiences*. For each word you choose, describe how that quality or aptitude might help you cope with climate stress.

## Our Climate Shadow

Climate disease is human-made; it originates from us. If its cure were as simple as changing our behavior, we would already have done so. Indeed, climate crisis results from deep psychological processes that propel us to act persistently against our survival despite the overabundance of foreboding evidence. Climate cataclysm therefore reflects our collective inner crisis. We heal this inner crisis via shadow work, in particular emotional shadow work.

To become one with climate breakdown is to recognize it as part of who we are. This allows us to take radical responsibility for it. When we recognize climate crisis is our unresolved darkness descending upon us, we begin to heal it by owning our shadow. Because climate crisis is arguably the greatest darkness ever to befall humanity (and true to Yin-Yang and depth psychological wisdom), it also holds the seeds for our greatest light, which is to create a sane and equitable life for all. Transforming our inner darkness transforms climate darkness because it changes the nature of the emotions that propel our actions, and therefore the effects of these actions. Instead of hurt people hurting others, we become healed people healing others. We change infertile, denied shadow into fertile, integrated shadow. The latter bears sustainable light; the former remains a death wish.

To become climate-aware and climate-engaged in the most holistic sense is to become able to act wisely in all domains of life and to continue acting and adjusting wisely in relation to external cues. Our emotions, when we are attentive to them and they are regulated, alert us to these cues. Our difficult emotions in particular alert us to when our wellness is in jeopardy; this is why our dark emotions are adaptive and secretly at the helm of saving the planet and ourselves.

Because we collectively deny our shadow, radical climate cure is a steep learning curve. But since we have to become shadow-aware to save ourselves, emotional shadow work is crucial to this end. The most potent way to engage this is to position ourselves so our dark emotions—especially those that arise from climate crisis—can transform us. An example is the grief work described in the previous chapter. This orientation requires humility, honesty, and courage. In this sense, pain is our guru, not our enemy. Our shadow pain can save us. But if we act on our fear of avoiding it, it will destroy us.

> ### • EXERCISE •
> ### CLIMATE SHADOW EXPRESSION
>
> Which climate-related emotions, that you don't readily feel or express, do you sense might be lurking inside you? Jot them down. Then, allow yourself to journal freely about them, or otherwise creatively express these emotions. See if you can write *from* instead of *about* your emotion. An example of writing about anxiety is: *Stronger wildfires are predicted in the future and this scares me.* In contrast, writing from your anxiety is: *I feel afraid about future wildfires.* Beginning with the words "I feel" can help you stay embodied in the emotion and write from it.

## Integrating Shadow

We never wholly vanquish our malevolent shadow. We integrate what we can by learning to make our unconscious conscious *enough*, tend to its pain, notice when it hides or acts out, and appropriately encourage or moderate its expression. We also get better at noticing our triggers and managing our reactions to them, which translates to compassion and preventing harm. Such mindfulness and emotional work allow renewal to outweigh malevolence.

One way to address our sadness and anger is to cry or yell out from the pain these emotions cause us. Bursts of raw emotion renew us in the act of breaking us open. It's important we also understand when to willfully curb these emotions, especially when we are powerfully tempted to direct them outward at other people or the natural world, especially before learning the facts. Another way is to work mindfully with both fear and anxiety, as discussed in depth in chapters 4 and 5. This kind of inner activism does not render us perfect, but better—better enough to stay within a functional range of death and rebirth, inner work and outer action, humility and boldness, Yin and Yang.

Because both our dark and light (positive and negative) shadows sequester our finer jewels for being human, ignoring or eradicating them would be akin to throwing the prized baby out with the apparently only dirty bathwater. This is why Jung believed that, "To confront a person with his shadow is to show him his light."[119] We engage shadow work *via negativa* style (paradoxically), by fully

---

119. Jung, "Good and Evil in Analytical Psychology," 872.

allowing our under-experienced shadow emotions to emerge and change us, so beauty and light can emerge unbidden from suffering and darkness. Radical emotional acceptance creates nonlinear change and exponentially regenerative actions. In stark contrast, physical healing often requires we actively fend off, manipulate, and try to fix what hurts. We are reminded: different domains of healing require different approaches.

Recognizing and remembering this Yin-Yang dichotomy of linear versus nonlinear healing is pivotal for how we engage with what hurts at different levels of our being. It is also emblematic of the linear and rational versus circular and regenerative models of global progress and transformation. Our overdependence on linear perspectives for personal and global systems creates more derangement than we can sustain. Regenerating biological systems, such as rebuilding the soil, planting new forests and reviving old ones, as well as undamming streams and rivers, are ultimately superior to adding synthetic fertilizers and pesticides, clear-cutting, and blocking the free-flowing arteries of the planet.

Similarly, holistic medicine regenerates our wellness more over the long term, while allopathic medicine helps best in emergencies and when natural means are insufficient. Degrowth and mitigating greenhouse gas emissions by consuming and driving less and regreening the planet are more holistic, sane ways of challenging climate crisis than geoengineering the skies and scrubbing the atmosphere of $CO_2$ with massive machines. But unless we can act preventively—akin to visiting the doctor soon enough—drastic palliative measures akin to global chemotherapy will likely be used.

In addition to a lack of education about climate disruption, our underlying resistance to embodying our shadow emotions drives both the degree to which we confront climate crisis and our response-in-action to it. We must be comfortable with feeling bad enough to welcome Yin (dark and difficult) as well as Yang (light and easy), so we can embody and employ fertile, sustainable darkness to serve goodness. The more we cozy up to shadow, the more we can cozy up to inconvenient truths and effect real change. That's the rub. We can't enjoy the light without welcoming its counterpart, and we accomplish this through shadow work. I do not know a greater, more tragic irony than to believe otherwise.

Jung believed that everyone possesses a shadow, and the less one is aware of it, the darker and more entrenched it becomes. If we become aware of our blind spots, we can reconcile them, but if they remain unconscious, we can't integrate them. For too long we have unconsciously denied the dark, as well as the power of our emotions to shape our fate. Consciously uncovering and working through our positive and negative shadow emotions allow us to change both our personal and planetary destinies.

---

• EXERCISE •

CHAPTER 7 JOURNALING

Please also refer to the additional in-text exercises for this chapter.

Take out your journal or notepad, place it in front of you, and enjoy creating your responses to the following:

1. While reading this chapter, did you overhear any part of yourself speaking to the rest of you, and if so, what did it say? Write this down, along with any more you learned about your shadow from this chapter.

2. Which emotions are you most uncomfortable feeling, expressing, and being with in others? Honestly journal about why you think this is so. Can you identify any past insults, injuries, or insufficient mirroring from others that dissuaded you from any of these emotions?

3. Write down three names of others you have treated poorly. How have any of the positive or negative shadow emotions you identified in #2 influenced you to treat others poorly?

4. When others act out and "dump" onto you or the ones you love, how do you both protect yourself and your loved ones? What would it take for you to "hold space" for the ones who "dump" (such as practicing "not taking it personally") by responding with compassion and understanding (when appropriate), rather than merely perpetuating more blame and violence?

# Section IV
# NATURE CONNECTION

*(Triangle of Resilience Relationship #2)*

# Chapter 8
# BECOMING NATURE

*I only went out for a walk and finally concluded to stay out till sundown,*
*for going out, I found, was really going in.*[120]
~JOHN MUIR

Before settlers arrived, the land where I currently live in southern California had been stewarded by native Chumash peoples for over ten thousand years. At a city council meeting in late summer of 2019, Julie Tumamait-Stenslie, a Chumash elder in my community, spoke about the festival called Hutash (also the name for Mother Earth), which was underway. Hutash coincides with the transition from summer into autumn and is the Chumash time of thanksgiving, during which they appreciate the Earth and animals through song and dance. Elders are reminded to honor the children and children to remember their elders. As Mrs. Tumamait-Stenslie shared, I sat in my seat realizing how sane such a festival is compared to the business-as-usual dealings at typical city council meetings, and the bloody heritage Americans celebrate during Thanksgiving.[121]

Insulated in cities, picking fruits and vegetables from supermarket shelves instead of from trees and vines, turning on the river from the tap at our sinks, and never having to set foot on rocky ground unless we choose to—modernity affords a dazzling array of dangerously seductive conveniences. While these

---

120. Wood, "Quotations from John Muir."
121. Cain, "The True Story Behind Thanksgiving Is a Bloody Struggle That Decimated the Population and Ended with a Head on a Stick."

luxuries arguably increase our "quality of life," they deny us a direct connection with the source from which our lives derive and are sustained. Without an integral bond with the natural world, we embody less of the ineffable simplicity we need to truly thrive. We walk through life essentially impoverished, with an attenuated capacity to respect and preserve the natural world.

Cities contain and represent what is most imbalanced about us. They reflect back to us the contents of our own minds, trapping us in our neuroses. In contrast, being in nature fills us with primordial images and information we have evolved with for millennia, including the bounty of other life forms with which we share the planet, and need to survive. The disconnected soul and anti-Earth worldview of modern living is another hidden, root cause of climate crisis. Add social media and technological addiction, and we brew a perfect storm for continued disease-making. On a recent walk, I suddenly realized the liability of living in a modern city during these relatively early stages of climate collapse. Being dependent on ease and convenience is not how I've lived for the last twenty years. But it is now, and it doesn't seem to be good preparation for harder times.

## Raiding the Pantry

Enlightenment zealots such as Harvard professor Steven Pinker laud how well-off we are now compared to our supposed "brutal savage" past,[122] while seeming to ignore the technological arc that has destroyed so much (in but a nanosecond in planetary history) at the expense of the vastness of all other life. As Pulitzer Prize-winning journalist Chris Hedges astutely observes, "What are demagogues like Donald Trump and Boris Johnson, positive psychologists and Candide-like prognosticators such as Steven Pinker, other than charlatans who insist the problem facing us is not real?"[123] We would be wise to instead abide Jung's prescient warning: "Coming generations will have to take account of this momentous transformation if humanity is not to destroy itself through the might of its own technology and science."[124] Indeed, we have mined and looted the Earth for temporary abundance. The honeymoon is over.

---

122. Survival International, "Survival Condemns Steven Pinker's 'Brutal Savage' Myth."
123. Hedges, "The Last Act of the Human Comedy."
124. Jung, *The Undiscovered Self*, 110.

Raiding the kitchen pantry for a feast might look like prosperity. But how much is left in the cupboard for future meals? At first blush, even as we've pushed much of our pollution out of sight, it would seem we're succeeding—until we wake up and look around. No glory attained by burning fossil fuels is worth catalyzing the sixth mass extinction and driving our own species to the same brink. Welcome to the age of climate chaos, of hubristically plundering the pantry for excess outer abundance and inner, psycho-spiritual poverty.

When progress leads us to the cliff's edge, we must question the worth of our innovations. Digital devices and apps, for example, are purposefully engineered to hack our brains, colonize our attention, and endlessly trigger our neurological reward centers to crave more.[125] As engines of addiction and distraction, they are therefore not morally neutral. In their thrall, we become ever less able to attune to the needs and conditions of our surroundings and refrain from consuming and polluting. To heal this rift, we must return to the wisdom of our bodies, and sensitize ourselves to the natural world and to intimate, in-person relationships. This way, we access and enact our deeper, innate caring that lies buried beneath pain and addiction.

Body-centered, Earth-based wisdom is an amalgam of knowledge and passion born of heart and mind in vital union. Unfortunately, this practice, and sensitizing to nature, are disparaged by popular culture. To address the disease of our times we must tap our deepest medicine: the repudiation of superfluous distraction in favor of dedicating ourselves to cultivating a rich inner life and restoring the biosphere. This isn't as easy as it might seem because, in addition to making "sacrifices" to free up time, degrowth requires feeling and facing our fears and pain. Resisting the commodification of our hearts is essential because when our hearts are owned by corruption—whether by old hurts causing us to hurt others, or too many gadgets distracting us from nourishing relationships—we quickly and pervasively corrupt the world.

We must resist modernity's excesses and ensuing apathy, and be able to choose *we* instead of *me*. A sense of *we* mitigates our propensity for greed and for acting on irrational fears of separation (as we will explore in the next section). This requires emotional humility, often forged in earnest via

---

125. 60 Minutes, "Brain Hacking: Silicon Valley Is Engineering Your Phone, Apps and Social Media to Get You Hooked, Says a Former Google Product Manager."

heartbreak and an embodied connection to nature. I'm not proposing a return to hunter-gatherer ways, but enough contact with nature to keep this relationship vital, to fuel our efforts to care enough for the natural world and each other's hearts, and thereby curtail the climate changes we've caused.

## A Famous Backpacking Trip

In a poem titled, "The City of My Mountain," I write: "Yet, there is no law/ that requires the people/ to visit the mountain/ even once a week/ nor should there be." A requirement to visit the mountain would diminish inspiration gained from the journey, the original purpose for the sojourn. If we were more nature-centric, we would be motivated by an innate, soulful pull to visit the mountains and other sacred nature spots. Such in vivo relationships have informed indigenous peoples' bonds with nature for millennia. They remind us of our simple affinity with the more-than-human world, and require no religion or superstition.

Regular pilgrimages into nature are a vital component of global health and healing our climate crisis. It would be of incalculable benefit to require such immersions of presidents, legislators, and corporate leaders! Imagine a backpacking trip during which our politicians could sleep and dream with the Earth, sparking epiphanies for sensible regulation and business practices that honor an enlightened sense of *we* to include the Earth—if only! When I shared this uncanny idea with a friend, she told me, to my surprise, that such an escapade in fact took place.

In 1903, renowned naturalist John Muir took then-United States president Theodore Roosevelt on a three-day trek through Yosemite National Park, a place Muir had grown to love over decades. The beauty of Yosemite inspired Roosevelt to unprecedented political action to protect it, along with many other natural treasures. Following this epic jaunt, the president went on "to sign into existence five more national parks, eighteen national monuments, fifty-five national bird sanctuaries and wildlife refuges and one hundred fifty national forests."[126] Nature itself, and the passion of a man in love with her,

---

126. MacGillivray, "The Camping Trip that Changed the Nation."

changed the heart and mind of a president whom we can thank for much of the protected wilderness we have today.

Industrialization disease perpetuates our separation from nature. In contrast, wilderness provides us with ineffable sanctuary for the Earth-centered, embodied spirituality we need to deliver us from our commodification of everything so we might survive into the future. To this end, in *Our National Parks*, Muir wrote: "Thousands of tired, nerve-shaken, over-civilized people are beginning to find out that going to the mountains is going home; that wildness is a necessity; and that mountain parks and reservations are useful not only as fountains of timber and irrigating rivers, but as fountains of life. Awakening from the stupefying effects of the vice of over-industry and the deadly apathy of luxury, they are trying as best they can to mix and enrich their own little ongoings with those of Nature, and to get rid of rust and disease."[127]

## Ecocide: Deeper than Greed

Climate crisis is part of our larger war on nature. This ecocide includes pandemic polluting, objectifying and "resourcing" nature, factory farming, incessantly noxious machine noise, and cementing over the Earth. Many consider greed to be the root of this ecocide, yet I invite us to look deeper.

As our harbored emotional pain and disconnection from the natural world increase, so do our insulation and greed. The greedier we become, the more we destroy the biosphere. Greed is therefore a branch symptom of deeper relationship dynamics (with self and nature) that also becomes malicious in its own right. The less we experience nature, the more we divorce from the web of life and the richness of original beauty. Such fracture further increases our isolation, compulsive anthropocentricity, and greed. This self-reinforcing, downward spiral is a positive feedback loop that exponentially breeds disease as we persist in trying to fulfill our need for meaning and belonging in disastrous ways that cannot succeed—especially via excess consumerism.

Living apart from the natural world is akin to not having friends. In contrast, creating a relationship with nature enhances our lives and fortifies all three of our triangle of resilience relationships: not only the obvious connection with

---

127. Wood, "Quotations from John Muir."

nature, but also our inner healing and our sense of community. Wilderness reminds us of reciprocity and the interdependence of death and rebirth, give and take, and our humble place amongst all things—the antithesis of greed and self-obsession. It places us directly in touch with the essentials for our survival and the sacredness of all life. Such encounters with nature leave us humbly awestruck and open our hearts to the marvel of creation and our place in the cosmos (Resource 3: "National Geographic"). The more we participate in this Earth-based spirituality, the more kindly we treat the world, and this in turn enhances our own lives, creating a healing positive feedback loop.

Perverse greed is a form of addiction that leads to ecocide. Depth psychologist Marion Woodman offers us insight into this dynamic: "I think we are acting like addicts. We have all this wonderful life, but we cannot believe we can lose it. That is too horrible a thought. So the fear is expressed in adding more and more stuff, stealing more and more from the Earth, and acting more and more irresponsible."[128]

Woodman also says, "In my work with addicts, I see again and again that the addict is trying to escape his own or her own humanity. It hates what it is to be human … wants to escape into some kind of transcendent reality."[129] Like other addictions, greed is an attempt to rise above our humanness, to buffer and bypass its inherent pain. More than simply a vice, greed is better understood as a form of escape, a transcendence, which denies us a compassionate, embodied union with one another and the Earth. Working wisely with our emotional pain ushers us into our full humanity; succumbing to greed is a doomed strategy to fill our love-voids that result from a deficiency of human-to-human caring and humble belonging in the world. How can we feel fulfilled when pain blocks our hearts and the invisible ways of the natural world cannot fill us with awe and reverie?

## Sacred Permission

Earning the right to significantly affect the world is the capstone to a threefold rite of passage I call *sacred permission*: its essence is engaging inner activism for inner sustainability and a rewilding that leads to outer regeneration and thriv-

128. "The Addicted World" clip from *"Marion Woodman: Dancing in the Flames."*
129. Horváth, "Marion Woodman: Holding the Tension of the Opposites."

ing. One facet of sacred permission is to substantially heal our core love wounds, as described in chapter 6. Sacred permission is fleshed out, integrated, and expanded by establishing intimate connection with the natural world and with human community. All three processes can happen simultaneously and interdependently. In essence, sacred permission is the process of becoming an elder.

Of course, emotional healing does not exist in a vacuum, and requires a measure of reciprocity with nature and fellow humans to support this "personal" work. Once we heal the bulk of our backlogged pain, however, we become more emotionally available to build even deeper, more meaningful relationships with others, including the Earth. This intimacy of inter-being in turn leads to more personal healing. Notice, these three facets of healing (self, nature, and our fellow humans) comprise our triangle of resilience relationships. Transformational healing via sacred permission, which moves organically from inside us into the world, is captured in the term *becoming medicine for our times.*

Traditionally, teenage rites of passage mark the leaving behind of childhood and the initiation into adulthood. They entail a sacred journey and that often includes a brush with death, during which adolescents must dig down deep and find a power and endurance they didn't know they possessed. Initiatory encounters with death typically occur in the natural world and include interactions with nonhuman beings. The rites are both physically and emotionally challenging and the participants are well-supported by the tribe. Such controlled trauma creates a bond with the internal and external forces one wrestles with and survives, thus consecrating intimacy and a sense of power. The result is adult fortitude, especially psychological resilience, wherein children cease to be nourished only by elders but learn to provide for and protect themselves and their community.

In the hunter-gatherer Dakota culture, for example, "a boy spends several days naked, vulnerable, and fasting as he awaits the arrival of animal-spirit allies who might help him to develop and actualize his understanding of the spiritual and ecological unity of nature."[130] In Vanuatu, a small island nation in the middle of the South Pacific, "young boys come of age by jumping off

---

130. Paddon, "The Earth Wisdom of Male Initiation."

of a ninety-eight-foot-tall tower with a bungee-like vine tied to their ankles, just barely preventing them from hitting the ground. The catch? Unlike a bungee cord, the vine lacks elasticity, and a slight miscalculation in vine length could lead to broken bones or even death."[131] In many traditional societies, the purpose of initiation rites was to transform the consciousness of the initiate from "an egocentric to an altruistic, ecological self-image."[132] So crucial is the result of this encounter with death for the greater good that traditional cultures mandate it. While today it's unrealistic to engage in such harrowing rites, we must find creative, even unorthodox, ways to initiate and move from human anthropocentrism to eco-centrism.

When we suffer emotional trauma in childhood, part of our psyche remains stuck at that stage of development—thus the term "developmental trauma." Most of us were not supported through this trauma as the initiates of traditional rites of passage were. We discover our initiation later in life, should we choose to revisit and work through our pain, initiate the developmentally frozen parts of us, and free ourselves to "grow up" from the inside out. This healing passage preserves our childlike nature (vitality, innocence, liberation, and care) and transforms what is childish and wounded (entitlement, false ego/persona, constant need for fun). Such healing paradoxically allows us to move into responsible adulthood, where fun is a slice of the pie, not the entire goal. Ironically, as responsible adults tending to our healing, we seem to encounter a preponderance of childish adults who condemn us for focusing on healing our tender hearts.

Grieving our core love wounds is a modern version of traditional initiation rites, a dark night of the soul during which we die to and through our pain. It is not a brush with literal death but can feel like one. It is an immersion into psychological death and eventual rebirth, a comprehensive and potent initiation into adulthood that emblazons in our heart-minds many of the core qualities needed to be responsible and caring. During this work of mourning and healing our large "T" and small "t" traumas, we transform (or better, are transformed by) what has kept us frozen in psycho-spiritual mediocrity. The

---

131. Nuñez and Pfeffer, "13 Amazing Coming of Age Traditions From Around the World."
132. Paddon, "The Earth Wisdom of Male Initiation."

qualities forged in us through sacred permission are none other than our finer jewels of being human.

Unlike in traditional rites of passage, nature connection is not absolutely essential for the modern dark night of the soul. Yet many who undertake this odyssey to heal emotional wounds, including me, find great refuge and support being in nature. This is why sacred permission is not onefold but threefold, and nurturing a relationship with the natural world and one's community—during and especially after emotional work—ensures this growth work is robust and sustainable.

We can be kind to others and work to heal the world without passing through the rite of sacred permission. But love as just a feeling or mustered compassion—as the care we already have in hand prior to dark-night-of-the-soul work—is helpful, but not enough. If it were, we would not be where we are today. We must resurrect more embodied and integrated love, mined from our pain and denial, what Jung described as making the unconscious (dark) and conscious (light). To become more deeply loving, more genuinely compassionate, more sustainably helpful and giving, we use the love we already feel and turn it toward the places that hurt inside—the places of unrequited love.

Sacred permission allows us to do much greater good, because by transforming our darkness of backlogged pain we augment the love we already have in hand. We liberate and bolster our finer jewels that have been sequestered by our shadow pain. Sacred permission is a comprehensive, integrated, embodied path for being more loving, not just for superficially mustering care. The latter is less effective because, when push comes to shove, our shadow pain raises its ugly head to sabotage our best intentions.

———

Certainly, our would-be leaders and elected officials need as much sacred permission as possible. If we required of them a modicum of emotional intelligence, nature-connection, and experience with caring community before taking office, I imagine they would think and act differently on behalf of the greater good they purportedly represent. But leaders with the green heart of Roosevelt are rare, and most who create our laws today don't care enough for us and the more-than-human world. This missing compassion is what social scientist and activist Kenneth Clark means when he suggests "people in power should all be required to take an 'empathy pill.'"[133] If only it were such a quick fix! The issue is not only greed but a lack of sacred permission.

Pain-driven, nature-divorced greed and ignorance are also exacerbated by the quick fix, "me" mentality promulgated by modern culture. Inner activism initiates us into the deep process of sacred permission, frees up our hearts, and liberates our ability to act on behalf of the greater good. Simultaneously, spending time in nature sensitizes and inspires us, supporting inner work and our connection with others. Being able to change our ways requires taking an honest look at ourselves and surrendering to be transformed by our long-held personal and generational pain with humility and honesty. Once sufficiently initiated, we can deeply extend this courage, humility, and care to the natural world and other humans. We gain the heart-mind bandwidth to treat everything more kindly and employ innovation wisely for the betterment of all. This is *being* comprehensively compassionate.

• EXERCISE •
## CHAPTER 8 JOURNALING AND FIELD TRIP

Take out your journal or notepad, place it in front of you, and write down your responses to items one, two, and four.

1. What is your favorite nature spot near you? What qualities make it special for you?

2. Can you identify a time in your life that qualified as a rite of passage into adulthood via the process of sacred permission as described in this chapter? How long did it last, or has it lasted? How did it change your relationship with yourself and with the world? What gifts and resources, if any, have you harvested from it?

3. Field Trip: Find a quiet place in nature, sit or lie down, and close your eyes. Feel the Earth beneath you. Then, one by one, and for as long as you like:

---

133. Rosin, "The End Of Empathy."

- Tune into the sounds around you. Allow them to become you, so the sounds *are* you, as one with your body, existing within or emanating from your body. Rest in this oneness.

- Tune into the scents around you. Notice the aroma of the Earth: any sand, soil, plants, water, flowers, trees, grasses, or other natural things. If pleasing to you, allow these scents to become part of you, so your being becomes infused with their scents. Rest in this oneness.

- With your eyes open, notice the elements of nature you just listened to and smelled. Notice their color, texture, distance from you, and their unique qualities. Allow yourself to be with them.

4. What part of this chapter spoke to you most poignantly and why? What internal changes or external actions does it inspire or catalyze in you?

# Chapter 9
# ECOCENTRIC

*Psychology, so dedicated to awakening the human consciousness,*
*needs to wake itself up to one of the most ancient human truths:*
*We cannot be studied or cured apart from the planet.*[134]
~JAMES HILLMAN

Immersion in the natural world benefits our mental, emotional, and spiritual wellness. It is especially important to fortify this connection as climate crisis progresses. Public health social worker and certified ecotherapist Phoenix Smith sums it up well: "We all must strengthen ourselves for what is to come as a result of climate disruption. We know that living on Earth is going to become more difficult as temperatures continue to rise, natural disasters continue to get stronger and the gaps between the rich and poor increase. Nature connection strengthens us, provides healing and restoration from trauma, can reduce symptoms of depression and anxiety, brings communities together, reducing isolation, and invokes awe and joy."[135]

I have lived close to the natural world for most of my adult life, for a good stretch directly in the wilds. Its solace provides a Yin, safe container to allow my heartaches to ease and figure themselves out. Its Yang fierceness challenges my survival skills, initiating and enriching me. Cities fill our psyches with reflections of our minds, but the natural world fills us with images and shapes, sounds and scents, from the original matrix from which we have evolved. The

---

134. Hickman, "What Psychotherapy Can Do for the Climate and Biodiversity Crises."
135. Smith, "We All Must Strengthen Ourselves."

wild world embeds us in a larger context and reminds us we are humbly dependent upon all the plants, creatures, and elements with which we share the planet. Returning to what we are intrinsically embedded in helps us care more for the more-than-human world. Yet because many of us have forgotten our connection to the natural world, we need intellectual justification to rebuild the bridge back to nature.

There is hardly an aspect of ourselves not reflected in the wild, and it in us. John Muir said, "When we try to pick out anything by itself, we find it hitched to everything else in the universe."[136] We recognize the truth of this when we try to scale down fossil fuel consumption and industrial growth (degrowth) and quickly discover all aspects of our lives affected, including the triggering of our difficult emotions. For this reason, healing through climate change is an opportunity to transform all aspects of ourselves. The natural world—especially now, in crisis—provides a metaphorical "mirror" (just like intimate human relationships do) for radical healing. We can view climate crisis as a guru, challenging and humbling us at every turn. When we learn from and adjust to it, dance rather than fight with it, we can attain a sustainable, ecocentric perspective.

Intimacy with the natural world allows us a more profound and nuanced experience of that world, which in turn helps us heal corresponding aspects of our own psyches. Tending to a struggling sapling or fitting a lame deer with a splint reminds us we too are injured, and helps us treat ourselves with compassion. These positive feedback loops of compassionate reciprocity propel us out of numb comfort and increase our self-care and kindness with one another. This uplifting dynamic is in stark contrast to the downward spiral resulting from no nature connection, not working through our heartaches, and the isolation and apathy that follow. If we can't become comfortable in and care for our own bodies, how can we care for the body of the Earth?

## The Science of Common Sense

Mental health disorders have increased in proportion to urbanization and disconnection from the natural world. Those living in the city have a 20 percent higher anxiety risk and a 40 percent higher risk of mood disorders than those

---

136. Muir, *My First Summer in the Sierra.*

living in rural areas. And those born and raised in cities have a twofold likelihood of developing schizophrenia.[137] A study from Stanford University shows that time spent in nature helps to reduce symptoms of depression. Researchers found that a ninety-minute walk in nature helps reduce rumination (repetitive negative thinking associated with increased risk for mental illness) compared with walking for the same amount of time in an urban environment. It also suggests that easier access to nature spaces in urban settings could be imperative for improving mental health in a quickly-urbanizing world.[138]

One factor in depression is our lack of contact with the earth itself—with soil. Recently it was discovered that soil bacteria activate neurons in our brains that release the neurotransmitter serotonin into the prefrontal cortex, an area of our brains associated with mood regulation.[139] A lack of serotonin is associated with depressive symptoms. Certain soil bacteria confer benefits similar to those attributed to antidepressant medications.[140] It makes adaptive sense that we'd be rewarded with feel-good neurochemistry by digging in the dirt, since the activity increases our chances of planting food to feed ourselves and survive. Gardening and growing food, for example, not only expose us to micro-critters that help us feel better, but also reconnect us to nature's rhythms.

Scientists also have discovered an anti-inflammatory fat in soil bacteria that boosts our health. They discovered that when soil bacteria are taken in by our immune cells, they release a special fatty acid that inhibits cascading inflammatory reactions. Inflammation can be a major contributor to many diseases, from depression to cancer and from arthritis to coronary artery disease. Injection of the inflammation-reducing soil bacteria into mice has demonstrated that these symbiotic microorganisms could prevent a PTSD-like syndrome and decrease the animals' anxiety under stress in the future.[141] Senior author of the study, Christopher Lowry, even envisions a "stress-vaccine" to inoculate against

---

137. Jordan, "Stanford Researchers Find Mental Health Prescription: Nature."

138. Bratman, Hamilton, Hahn, Daily, and Gross, "Nature Experience Reduces Rumination and Subgenual Prefrontal Cortex Activation."

139. Than, "Depressed? Go Play in the Dirt."

140. University of Colorado at Boulder, "Healthy, Stress-Busting Fat Found Hidden in Dirt."

141. Ibid.

high-stress situations.[142] Perhaps we could simply play in the soil to derive similar immunity.

Note the tragic irony here: our disconnect from nature and the land increases depression. When we're depressed we're more likely to disregard nature. Neglecting nature exacerbates climate change, which increases anxiety and depression.[143] We've come full circle in another positive feedback loop yielding negative results. The exponential effect of many such climate-disrupting positive feedback loops—especially those that occur partly inside us—makes it difficult for climate models to predict, or for us to truly grasp, our climate future.

## Positive Feedback Loops and the Exponential Effect

"The greatest failure of the human race," said the late physicist Albert Bartlett, "is our inability to understand the exponential function."[144] With regard to climate change, the exponential function refers to disturbances to the climate building upon one another in a nonlinear, exponential, way—such as how two squared yields four, but four squared yields sixteen, and so on. The exponential function explains how climate crisis has gained on us so quickly. Professor of journalism and best-selling author K.C. Cole explains it this way: "Climate change was able to creep up on most of us with cat feet because it snowballs in the same way, well, as snowballs snowball. Each subsequent change builds on the change before. The bigger it gets, the faster it grows. Just as our brains have limits grappling with numbers, our senses have limits grasping sizes much beyond our personal, human-sized, scale, where different laws of nature dominate."[145]

Just as no one knows the precise, cumulative and exponential effects climate disruption will continue to have, no one yet knows the cumulative and exponential effects of the remedies we will enact. These remedies are coming fast and furious now. As massive amounts of funds are being allocated to climate solutions, large tree planting projects have begun, renewables are at an

---

142. Ibid.

143. American Psychological Association, "Climate Change's Toll on Mental Health."

144. Bartlett, "Arithmetic, Population and Energy - a Talk by Al Bartlett."

145. Cole, "Why You Didn't See It Coming."

all-time high, and their production is projected to outpace all other forms of energy generation. However, if fossil fuel use increases into the near future, as it is projected to, this could outweigh many of solar energy's benefits.[146] While there are shortcomings and limitations to these strategies, they pose more net gain than loss.

Conversely, one example of an environmental positive feedback loop leading to exponential negative change pertains to Arctic ice. Arctic ice depleted by melting from global warming reflects less light back into space. This loss of albedo (reflection of light) from the ice causes the oceans to absorb more heat, which in turn melts more of the ice, resulting in more heat absorption, on and on in a vicious cycle. Another example is drought that has led to a proliferation of bark beetles in Washington state. Drought worsened by climate change weakens the trees, which makes them susceptible to infestation by the beetles. The beetles kill the trees, creating more tinder for wildfires, which exacerbate drought, resiliency, and the biodiversity of the local environment, and climate change globally.

The IPCC, the world authority for the most accurate and comprehensive climate science (with its shortcomings, discussed in appendix I), excludes discussion of such positive feedback loops in its reporting, and some scientists claim this omission is one reason to consider its projections conservative. Because the IPCC models don't consider all the recently updated positive feedback loops that lead to dangerous tipping points, their reports underestimate the rate of climate collapse.[147] Other reasons for IPCC conservatism (also comprehensively discussed in the appendix I) include the IPCC's failure to consider the impact from the majority of methane emissions and the fact that carbon capture and sequestration (CCS)[148] technologies have not been substantially implemented despite IPCC projections assuming their contribution to reducing greenhouse gases. Cofounder and United States program director for the popular climate change group 350, Jamie Henn, tweeted, "This is the scariest

---

146. Monbiot, "For the Sake of Life on Earth, We Must Put a Limit on Wealth."

147. Queally, "What's Not in the Latest Terrifying IPCC Report? The 'Much, Much, Much More Terrifying' New Research on Climate Tipping Points." Watts, "Risks Of 'Domino Effect' of Tipping Points Greater than Thought, Study Says."

148. A term broadly referring to the removal of massive amounts of $CO_2$ from the atmosphere and safely storing it. See Appendix I: "The Science of Climate Crisis" for more.

thing about the IPCC Report—it's the watered down, consensus version. The latest science is much, much, much more terrifying."

The human-environmental positive feedback loops just mentioned (such as depression and lack of care for nature) and the more strictly environmental loops (such as albedo loss and rising ocean temperatures) overlap and exacerbate each other. When any one positive feedback loop collides with another, their effects magnify exponentially, causing us to feel exponentially worse. As a result, we may feel more helpless and less proactive to tackle the original stressor of climate crisis. For example, environmental disaster in one sector of the biosphere affects other aspects of the environment, leading to exponential decline, which exponentially exacerbates how we feel. The worse we feel inside, the worse we treat each other and the planet, while the resulting environmental impoverishment causes us more angst and despair, usually leading to more environmental neglect. It is therefore more imperative than ever to fortify our triangle of resilience relationships.

Climate disruption also triggers our historical love wounds. Per the exponential formula—and if we don't intervene with a curative response—we can quickly spiral into the same despondency and neglect as when the positive feedback loops just mentioned collide. The way out of this seeming catch-22 is first to change perspective by using emotional triggering as an opportunity for growth and greater care. We do this by consciously working with our emotional responses, finding (even simple) ways to care for the natural world, and taking action in the world with others—engaging with all our triangle of resilience relationships.

Multiple, interacting positive feedback loops can be visualized as many infinity signs joined at their centers—like a mobile, with all of their loops intersecting with and feeding the others. We can also understand these exponential effects as the Yin-Yang circle in dysregulation without a regenerative balance of dark (healthy destruction and minimizing) and light (sustainable growth and progress), resulting in a downward emotional-biological spiral and collapse. Identifying the anatomy of eco-human positive feedback loops can help us unwind this insidious holistic disease process. We can reverse these vicious cycles and create exponential good by turning the downward trend upward.

Climate crisis has become a battleground between good and evil, sanity and ignorance. It is *Star Wars* on the world stage: the best, most life-affirming human values versus the most evil, death-affirming vices. Even though climate cure remains a huge uphill task, we must try. On the dark side is unreckoned pain, our imbalanced domination over nature, and isolation—our three triangle of resilience relationships in disrepair. Fueling the side of good are our finer jewels of being human, cultivated via our triangle of resilience relationships and the regenerative solutions we create. These are the fundamental drivers behind a love and respect for all forms of life and the healing of climate crisis.

## Nature, for Its Own Sake

Some children, and even adults, have never left the city. Whether due to habit, obligation, poverty, or other restraints, the reasons are many. But there is abundant scientific evidence for the benefits of natural environments on our mental health. So, we should do the best we can to get out.

Not only does nature have a positive effect on us, cities negatively affect us. Scientists have recently found "the childhood experience of green space can actually predict mental health in later life."[149] Other studies show that city noise pollution damages our health, reduces quality of life, and predisposes us to serious stress-related diseases such as heart disease, cancer, sleep problems, brain aberrations, and respiratory issues.[150] It is especially damaging to children. In 2014, the World Health Organization (WHO) declared noise pollution second only to air pollution as the biggest threat to public health.[151] Another study suggests "exposure to residential road traffic noise increases the risk of depressive symptoms."[152]

Machine noise that fills the urban soundscape is highly abrasive and causes us to stressfully retreat into ourselves and tune out, breeding isolation and psychic distress. In contrast, it's pleasurable and relaxing to tune into the sounds of nature. They invite us in, promoting openness and union.

---

149. Betuel, "Scientists Discover a Major Lasting Benefit of Growing Up Outside the City."

150. Bartz, "How City Noise is Slowly Killing You,"

151. Hänninen, et al., "Environmental Burden of Disease in Europe: Assessing Nine Risk Factors in Six Countries."

152. Orban et al., "Residential Road Traffic Noise and High Depressive Symptoms after Five Years of Follow-up: Results from the Heinz Nixdorf Recall Study."

We delight when a soft chorus of birds' wings alights on a tree, its leaves shimmering in the sunlight. Or how the ever-changing, constant melody of a stream eases us to sleep. We are reminded of everything to which we belong. When we garden, we become more aware of the soil and rain, sun and shade, decay and renewal we depend upon to survive and thrive. All this increases our care for the natural world, boosting our capacity for climate cure. Connecting with nature not only boosts our overall wellness, it decreases the time we spend in health-eroding city environments.

Doctors in Scotland have even begun writing "nature prescriptions" for their patients (something I have done for decades with my patients, along with poetry prescriptions).[153] While it's great that medical professionals are recognizing the primal healing power of nature, it's also sad we have dissociated so much from the natural world that we need doctors to prescribe what was once common sense. Hitherto, nature was once a remedy we didn't have to search for and in fact couldn't avoid. Though helpful in the short-term, framing nature's benefits as "medication" could ultimately do harm by relegating the natural world to a human-centric realm of consumerism. This skewed perspective is also problematic because once we think something (or someone) doesn't immediately benefit us, we tend to stop caring for it and abandon it. This perpetuates the *me* of humanity at the expense of *we* with the natural world. For this reason, appreciating the sacredness of the natural world—for its equal right to thrive, and beyond its utility to us—is a decisive change of perspective for healing through climate disease.

Viewing the more-than-human world of nature primarily as a collection of "resources" also exemplifies our self-serving position and our entitlement to destroy it for our "benefit." Author and journalist Ben Ehrenreich writes, "There is no way out of this [climate change] but to cease to view the Earth, and its populations, as an endless sink of resources from which wealth can be extracted."[154] We must recognize that without a thriving wilderness, we imperil our well-being in ways we are just now discovering. This is one more reason why respecting the natural world as sacred, even absent any knowledge of its benefits to us, is imperative.

---

153. Housman, "Scottish Doctors Are Now Issuing Prescriptions to Go Hiking."
154. Ehrenreich, "To Those Who Think We Can Reform Our Way Out of the Climate Crisis."

A more equitable perspective sees us as equals with nature or, more wisely, as subordinate and at its mercy. The practice of Shinrin-Yoku, a Japanese term for forest bathing, can help cultivate a sense of communion and humility with the natural world. This description from the Association of Nature and Forest Therapy shares some of its core relational qualities: "Forest Therapy is not an extractive process, where we treat forests as a 'resource' from which we extract well-being for humans. Instead, it is a deeply relational practice, characterized by a sense of loving and tender connection. This connection leads naturally to an ethic of tenderness and reciprocity." Forest therapy is about creating relationships between humans and the more-than-human world, in which the relationship itself becomes a field of healing and a source of joyful well-being.[155]

---

It is undeniable that humans possess a selfish, egocentric side. If we could only revere the natural world as much as we do ourselves, our selfishness could help preserve the biosphere. Many ecocentric, indigenous cultures seem to have solved this conundrum. Native American and Amazonian peoples, for example, believe that all things share a common "spirit," meaning every aspect of the natural world, including humans, is part of an integral whole. This worldview is ingrained in children from a young age, allowing them to treat the more-than-human world with the same importance as themselves. Such perspective helps allay the selfish, harmful aspect of human nature on the environment.

Until we deeply grasp that we must safeguard nature for its own sake, we will continue to commodify and destroy what is irreplaceably beautiful and exponentially inspiring. This foundational ethos also applies to averting pandemics worse than COVID-19.[156] The biosphere is an integral part of who we are on every level, impervious to summing-up in mathematical equations or positive feedback loops. We may never be able to discover all its benefits or describe them. Nor should we. We can rest in the humble intuition and self-evident truth that we need it to thrive. In a saner world, we shouldn't be forced

155. Association of Nature and Forest Therapy, "The Practice of Forest Therapy."
156. National History Museum, "Scientists Say We Will Face Worse Pandemics Than COVID-19 Unless We Protect Nature."

to visit the mountains. Yet, because not everyone feels an intuitive call to the mountains, nature-positive science reports can help some get into the outdoors more often.

## The Evidence for Belonging

In-person connection with nature engenders an enduring emotional bond with the natural world and, therefore, caring for the environment as we do others we love. A nationwide poll by the Nature Conservancy shows: "Exposing kids to nature is a crucial step to getting kids to care about environmental issues, the poll finds. Those with personal, positive experiences with nature were twice as likely to view themselves as strong environmentalists and were significantly more likely to express concern about water issues, air pollution, climate change and the overall condition of the environment."[157]

More support comes from the Greater Good Science Center at UC Berkeley, discussing the impact of nature on children: "When a problem [referring to climate change] seems distant or abstract, it can easily be pushed aside by more pressing, immediate concerns, like schoolwork or relationship worries. But scientists have learned that there is a way to overcome these deterrents: developing a compassionate relationship with the natural world. Research suggests that the desire to conserve is intricately tied to our *connection to nature*— or the degree to which we enjoy spending time in nature, empathize with our fellow creatures, and feel a sense of oneness with nature. That emotional connection increases our sense of personal responsibility toward nature and makes us want to do more to preserve it."[158]

A *Washington Post* article titled "The Radical Political Implications of Spending Time Outdoors" asks, "But could spending time in natural scenery also have larger implications for how we behave politically, or how we treat one another?" The study suggests the answer is yes: "there's a link between actually experiencing the natural world, and behaving in a sustainable way."[159] This finding is supported by a more recent, large-scale study in England demonstrating the link between exposure to nature and eco-friendly behavior;

---

157. The Nature Conservancy, "Poll Suggests Kids Need to Get Outdoors and Play!"
158. Suttie, "How to Raise an Environmentalist."
159. Mooney, "The Radical Political Implications of Spending Time Outdoors."

the study also found that those not exposed to green spaces were less inclined to act green.[160] So, if you can't make the switch to an electric car and know you can do more than recycle, try getting out to the wilds more often and see what happens as a result.

The common denominator in all these studies is *emotional connection*. Intimacy with nature is fostered most robustly by being in nature, not learning about it. When we develop a relationship with nature—as we do with one another and with animals we love—we bond with and care for it. We tend not to care as much about animals and places with which we don't have a personal relationship (Resource 3: Harvey).

Simple common sense suggests that reconnecting with the environment would have profound implications for everything alive, in more ways than can be immediately identified. Unfortunately, common sense is no longer common knowledge. A connection with nature that improves cognitive function and positively influences our emotions is a good recipe for bequeathing to our children a world transformed by the best version of ourselves. This contributes to the upward-spiraling positive feedback loops we so desperately need.

If you want to help mitigate climate crisis, connect with nature and take your children with you. It's good for your mental health and good for the planet.

## Denying Climate Disease

For decades I have witnessed how patients deal with illness. Many aren't proactive enough until they have no choice, and even then they have a hard time changing habits that contribute to their illness. Others don't want to admit they are sick at all, which is why honesty is the first step to healing.

A similar honesty is needed to address climate crisis. Denying the severity of the climate crisis (evidenced by the climate science in appendix I) delays the first step toward healing through it. Admitting what's true relies on our emotional capacity to bear the truth. Per our fear-mark, we are selectively aware of

---

160. Ian Alcock et al., "Associations between Pro-Environmental Behaviour and Neighbourhood Nature, Nature Visit Frequency and Nature Appreciation: Evidence from a Nationally Representative Survey in England."

what we consciously or unconsciously assume we can emotionally handle, and we ignore what scares us too much.

To truly grasp difficult issues and take meaningful action, we need emotional willingness—the courage—to be impacted by what *seems* larger or more powerful than we are. Courage, from the Latin *cour,* is heart-centered. Poet and elder Maya Angelou refers to courage as the most important of all virtues.[161] But the impetus to let go into what *seems* like it will destroy us feels counterintuitive. Surrendering to and growing through the fear of what we think we can't handle (but often can) confers more courage. It is a leap of faith to being blessedly broken open by more difficult challenges.

When we experience that good can come from temporarily feeling bad, we grow. We develop the courage, maybe even excitement, to allow in the dark night when it knocks on our heart-door. A common, milder example of such healing paradox is successfully having a difficult conversation with another to clear up misunderstandings and hurt feelings. After, we feel better about the relationship. Embracing and skillfully working with difficulty benefits us in the longer term.

The denial we exhibit during personal illness or emotional challenge is the same we apply to climate crisis, a potential terminal illness for most everything alive. One evening, a man with stage IV cancer attended my local climate change discussion and support group. He shared that he won't be alive next year and that knowing he is going to die soon has radically changed his appreciation for life and being in the moment. But the point he drove home is that climate crisis is equally a terminal diagnosis, and to ignore it because it might not kill us today or tomorrow is akin to knowingly having cancer and not confronting it. Just as tending early to personal illness helps our prognosis, addressing climate crisis now improves our chances of surviving it.

Similarly to how cancer or blood loss to a limb reaches a tipping point beyond which we can't reverse it, our planet is approaching such a tipping point, if we haven't in fact already reached it.[162] Our capacity for wholesale denial of this crisis saddens me deeply, for it's going to take many more of us coming together to get through the challenging years ahead. I am not referring

---

161. Ju, "Courage Is the Most Important Virtue, Says Writer and Civil Rights Activist Maya Angelou at Convocation."

162. Harvey, "Tipping points' could exacerbate climate crisis, scientists fear."

to saving the planet or our species, per se, as much as I am to staying afloat through the predicted changes to come—if we don't radically take this to heart and to the streets, now.

We must muster the courage to reverse our denialist and complacent track record and address climate chaos as seriously as is required before we are in its terminal stages. Marion Woodman said, "Most of us have to crash into the wall before we can wake up."[163] Arriving at this desperate point, we might be forced to treat our feverish, cancer-ridden planet chemo-style, via geoengineering or some other pervasively toxic means.

## Visiting the Climate Doctor

*Geoengineering* refers to a collection of technological interventions designed to mitigate climatic warming. One such method is called solar radiation management (SRM), which is the spraying of aerosols into the atmosphere to reflect the sun's warming rays, thus cooling the Earth. SRM mimics the sun-dimming particles a volcanic eruption spews into space. Depending on what substances are used, SRM could in effect "pharmaceutically medicate" our atmosphere, a kind of celestial chemotherapy. SRM also carries large risks such as increased droughts, hurricanes, and biodiversity loss.[164] [165]

Worse, SRM is not a one-time deal; it would require endless repeat applications. To quote a National Center for Biotechnology Information (NCBI) study: "Importantly, SRM approaches to managing climate change require initial and ongoing addition of aerosols to the atmosphere, with increasingly greater additions as emissions of greenhouse gases (GHGs) rise, given the risk of sudden and potentially catastrophic warming if aerosol levels are not maintained."[166]

Harvard scientists are preparing to test geoengineering the stratosphere as we near the desperate threshold that will require this kind of emergency

---

163. Horváth, "Marion Woodman: Holding the Tension of the Opposites."

164. Dunne, "Unregulated Solar Geoengineering Could Spark Droughts and Hurricanes, Study Warns."

165. Christopher H. Trisos et al., "Potentially Dangerous Consequences for Biodiversity of Solar Geoengineering Implementation and Termination."

166. Utibe Effiong and Neitzel, "Assessing the Direct Occupational and Public Health Impacts of Solar Radiation Management with Stratospheric Aerosols."

room-style plan to cool the planet.[167] The potential side effects seem as unimaginable as spraying a vegetable garden or school playground with the carcinogen glyphosate, found in the herbicide Roundup. While the Harvard team is testing with calcium carbonate, a relatively benign substance, another preferred SRM substance is sulfur dioxide, a known carcinogen.[168]

Climate crisis is similar to metastatic cancer, in that both are characterized by rampant overgrowth. In the lexicon of Chinese medicine, this is an expansive, consumptive Yang disorder. Is it any wonder that along with human lung cancer, (the second most common form of cancer behind female breast cancer), we have also caused cancer in the air space *outside* our lungs? And how, along with the increasing prevalence of lung cancer in women,[169] climate change is also rapidly spreading through the sacred feminine, mother Earth? The poetry is consistent: destructive Yang energy is out of control at the expense of nurturing Yin.

Holistic medicine advocates implementing lifestyle changes prior to taking medicine to cure disease. Geoengineering is being tested because we have neither mandated nor made the changes required to mitigate environmental crisis. Geoengineering is a late-stage treatment for attacking climate illness, just as chemotherapy is for fighting cancer. Both are allopathic, warlike efforts. Environmental journalist Jonathan Watts says of our polluted planet: "The take-home message is that we should have gone to the doctor sooner."[170] Better late than never: we can make that appointment now.

## GMOs and Climate Crisis

Genetically modified organism (GMO) "farming" is a form of monoculture, industrial-style agriculture that depends on toxic pesticides and artificial, petroleum-based fertilizers. Peer-reviewed research demonstrates that this

---

167. Tollefson, "First Sun-Dimming Experiment Will Test a Way to Cool Earth."

168. Effiong and Neitzel, "Assessing the Direct Occupational and Public Health Impacts of Solar Radiation Management with Stratospheric Aerosols."

169. Elster, "Lung Cancer Is Commonly Associated with Smoking. But Rates of the Disease among Non-smokers – and Women – Are Rising."

170. Johnson, "'Ominous' UN Report Warns Human Activity Has Pushed One Million Plant and Animal Species to Brink of Extinction."

method of farming—especially because it causes habitat loss and is reliant on pesticides—is the primary cause of the current, global insect apocalypse,[171] which is both accelerating climate change and is in turn exacerbated by it. "If insect species losses cannot be halted, this will have catastrophic consequences for both the planet's ecosystems and for the survival of mankind," said Francisco Sánchez-Bayo, the study's lead scientist.

The mainstay of GMO farming is what's called "Roundup Ready" crops. These are genetically altered plants, such as corn and soy, that are resistant to the toxic herbicide Roundup. Thus, the spraying of Roundup kills weeds without killing food crops. Whether or not GMO foods are just as healthy as organic foods is an important issue, yet ultimately too anthropocentric. A larger, less appreciated, eco-human problem is that GMO farming methods necessitate large amounts of pesticides, which injure everything and everyone. Glyphosate, the active ingredient in Roundup, is a probable carcinogen[172] that also degrades the soil, injures earthworms, and in formulation, negatively impacts beneficial fungi.[173] The poison remains on the plants, which humans and animals then consume; glyphosate is also potentially harmful to farm workers.[174]

A decade ago, I founded GMO Eradication Movement (GEM)[175] to empower citizens like you and me to resist buying GMO products, because I realized our government was not going to limit, properly label, or oversee the proliferation of GMOs into our food chain. I therefore created a three-tiered, eleven-step process to identify, resist, and spread the good word about bad GMOs (see appendix II).[176] The goal has been to create a citizen-based empowerment movement that would achieve the same ends as a top-down, government-issued ban.

---

171. Sanchez-Bayo and Wyckhuys, "Worldwide Decline of the Entomofauna: a Review of its Drivers," 232.

172. Kogevinas, "Probable Carcinogenicity of Glyphosate."

173. The Soil Association, "The Impact of Glyphosate on Soil Health: the Evidence to Date,"

174. Pesticide Action Network North America, "Farmworkers Represent the Backbone and Marrow of Our Agricultural Economy. Yet This Group Is One of the Least Protected from on-the-Job Harms—Including Exposure to Pesticides."

175. GMO Eradication Movement ("GEM"), "60 Minutes Australia: Roundup and Cancer," video.

176. GMO Eradication Movement, "11 Steps for GMO Eradication."

Organic gardening and farming provide us with better-quality and safer food, as well as foster beneficial insects and healthy soil that support biodiversity and preserve the foundation of our food chain. Add permaculture techniques to the organic mix, and this form of growing food becomes regenerative, boosting inherent natural processes and sequestering vast amounts of carbon to mitigate climate change. Yes, humans can actually enhance nature by maximizing its inherent design.

GMO Eradication Movement's resistance to GMOs is the kind of grassroots climate resistance movement we need to exert against the fossil fuel industry, especially since the mandate to desist from carbon polluting is not coming from the top down, as it should.[177] Many complain about our government's tyranny over us, but we invite it by our failure to unite and rebel, grassroots-style, to drastically reduce our emissions and lifestyles. It seems we require a "nanny state" government to impose the strict regulations we need to save ourselves from carbon emissions and self-extermination. The Green New Deal—a congressional resolution that lays out an overarching plan for significantly addressing climate crisis—and any other version of life-saving sanity, is in our hands, if only we could tolerate initiating degrowth on our own by downscaling our lives.

Switching from a commercial corn or soy product to an organic or even commercial non-GMO variety is often more expensive, but doable, because a similar, easy enough substitution exists. Most of us, however, can't do without our combustion engine cars or at least occasionally flying in airplanes because the alternatives aren't so convenient. To keep our emissions in check, we can travel by train, ride-share, use public transport, or best, ride a bicycle or walk.

---

177. Byskov, "Climate Change: Focusing on How Individuals Can Help Is Very Convenient for Corporations."

The more we do, the better we feel about ourselves. The more we set an example and spread the word, the more we benefit everything else.

---

### • EXERCISE •
### BEING WITH NATURE

1. Nature, unplugged: Clear some time (as much as you see fit) so you don't "have" to be on your phone or computer (or iPad, iPod, or gaming device) for important calls. Let anyone who might wonder or worry about you know that you'll be unplugged. Also consider letting them know where you will be in case of emergency. Go into nature without any of these devices and enjoy.

2. If you can't spend a whole day in nature, begin by taking as much time as you can and increase from there. Notice how you feel when you disconnect from social media. Use the empty space to connect with yourself and the natural world. If you can't go out into nature without any devices, try not taking any pictures, so the preoccupation with "capturing the moment" does not impede your immediate experience, which can result in losing the moment! You can also practice being silent for stints, such as going on a hike with a friend and agreeing not to talk. Behold and be held by the natural world.

3. To honor your relationship with the natural world, choose three activities (more if you like) from this list to honor the many obvious and unobvious ways connecting with nature helps you:

    • Hike or walk: Choose a place to do this two times a week for at least twenty minutes (or what you can) in a natural environment, preferably as devoid as possible of cars and city noise. Instead of listening to music on your hike, tune into the natural sounds around you: your feet on the Earth, the wind, animals, water. Give yourself the gift to enjoy direct, unimpeded connection with the outdoors.

- Start a vegetable garden. This is on many people's bucket list and too often stays at the bottom. Starting a garden not only connects you to the Earth, it feeds your stomach and your brain. If you don't want to grow food, consider starting an herb garden. If you don't have existing earth, consider: pots, raised beds, wall gardens (Resource 2: "Real Simple"), or contribute to a community garden. If gardening daunts you, start small.

- Next time you meet a friend, organize a meeting, or engage in a hobby, consider doing it outdoors in a natural setting!

- Next time you see an insect and have the time, spend five to ten minutes hanging out with it, or them. You might choose to watch the nuanced machinations of a praying mantis, marvel at the organized chaos of an anthill, or the undulating topsy-turvy flight of a butterfly or moth.

# Section V
# BUILDING
# COMMUNITY
*(Triangle of Resilience Relationship #3)*

# Chapter 10
# WE NEED EACH OTHER

*We relate, therefore we are.*[178]

~HARBEEN ARORA

Our deep kinship and interdependence with one another are illuminated by celebrated neuropsychiatrist and best-selling author Dr. Dan Siegel. Dr. Siegel is also Clinical Professor of Psychiatry at the UCLA School of Medicine, codirector of the Mindful Awareness Research Center, and director of the Mindsight Institute. His innovative, relational theory of mind-body wellness includes a third element: our relationships. This way, each individual becomes what Siegel calls "more than me, but a part of we."[179]

According to Siegel, everyone we relate with is part of our extended nervous system. "The brain is the social organ of the body, where one hundred billion neurons reach out to other neurons," he says.[180] Tom Oliver, author of *The Self Delusion*, corroborates this, writing that the new science of social networks shows we are all so interconnected it's unclear where one person's mind ends and another's begins.[181] I am part of you, and you are part of me. Our minds and bodies are therefore not entirely our own; their very integrity relies on others. We need meaningful relationships for healthy minds, healthy bodies, and a

---

178. Arora, "We Relate, Therefore We Are," 63.
179. Siegel, *Pocket Guide to Interpersonal Neurobiology: an Integrative Handbook of the Mind*, 42–7.
180. de Llosa, "The Neurobiology of 'We.'"
181. Oliver, "The Age of the Individual Must End – Our World Depends on It."

healthy world. We can't be whole without each other. The profound effect on and need we have for each other also speaks to the vital importance of healing our hearts, so we can treat each other more kindly.

## A Plural Self

Dr. Siegel includes our relationship with the natural world in his plural definition of the self, which forms what he collectively terms a "neurobiology of we."[182] In addition to our relationship with other humans, we experience nature as an intrinsic part of who we are. This makes sense, since we have evolved as intimately with the natural world as we have with each other. Oneness with nature and its rhythms, which occurs outside as well as inside us, is also fundamental to holistic medicine's founding tenets and a plural sense of self. According to Siegel, nurturing this interdependence makes us less likely to destroy the planet. He says:

> If I say the self is defined as this body, then I can just use up all the resources on the planet and why would I give a hoot? In fact, we know that when you have a sense of self that's separate, what do you do? If you know there are limited resources, you gather them up for you and your family as much as you can because you don't know when they are going to run out. You don't actually try to help out the bigger picture.
>
> If the self is defined as a singular noun, the planet is cooked. But if we can be really creative, collectively, and find a way to develop in this generation, and absolutely the next generation that takes over stewardship of the planet, that [sic] the self is in fact a plural verb, so that we can allow kids to be raised to know that "I" am more than "me," and I am connected to you, but I am a member of "we" ... we'll have a different outcome, because then caring for the planet is not something you have to scare people into doing.[183]

---

182. de Llosa, "The Neurobiology of We."

183. Siegel, "The Neurological Basis of Behavior, the Mind, the Brain and Human Relationships."

Highlighting Dr. Siegel's views, the American Psychological Association (APA) has reported an increase in mental illness attributed to climate trauma, and simultaneously recommended robust interpersonal ties for climate change resilience.[184] After all, humans have evolved for millennia in tightly-knit communities of support and accountability. Modern, capitalistic culture, with its emphasis on the individual and our resultant collective isolation, has eroded the integral support networks that Siegel says support the health of our nervous systems and a sustainable sense of self and ecology. Nurturing a fertile "neurobiology of we" with one another and the natural world, along with healing through emotional trauma, comprises a robust triangle of resilience.

## Yin-Yang Consciousness

Dr. Siegel's interpersonal notion of the self parallels the holistic worldview of Chinese medicine. We can apply the dialectical model of Yin and Yang to understand Dr. Siegel's discussion in an overarching, integrative context. His pejorative description of the self as just a "body" correlates with the excessively Yang qualities of individuality, narrow-mindedness, unreasonable selfishness, isolation, and unhelpful fear. At times, perhaps we've all felt disconnected, self-obsessed, trapped in our own skin, and unable to connect and share. Some of this is reasonable and adaptive, but not when it becomes our unconscious default. A more Yin sense of self, on the other hand, is represented by open-mindedness, sharing, connection, and trust. These capacities also require collective maturity and responsibility consecrated by sacred permission; otherwise corruption prevails. Yin and Yang support one another when a sustainable *me* feeds a regenerative *we*, and when *we* feeds back into *me*.

According to Chinese medicine, healing results from the mutual support of Yin and Yang. This model of interdependence is inherently paradoxical because it holds a dynamic tension of opposites in wholeness. In fact, Yin-Yang theory says that wholeness can exist *only* when we integrate relative opposites. Consider a romantic partnership. A healthy sense of self (individuation) contributes to an integrous and empowering relationship. Reciprocally, a robust

---

184. Sliwa, "Climate Change's Toll on Mental Health."

relationship further supports both partners' individuation and sharing of their unique gifts.

Yin and Yang attributes are not inherently wrong or right, good or bad; all are valuable when appropriately expressed. They become problematic when excessive and unchecked. This nonbinary, both-and, black *and* white relationship—in contrast with a non-regenerative black *or* white separation—is imperative to practice in thought, feeling, and action. Western individualism represents excessive Yang snuffing out regenerative and cooperative Yin. Some everyday examples might provide more clarity:

1. Individuality, a Yang attribute, is a strength when balanced with contributing to community, a Yin attribute. Individuality cultivates uniqueness and specialization, with which we contribute novelty to the whole. In turn, the whole (say, in the form of others' help, viewpoints, comfort, and attention) enriches our individuality, which again enhances our contribution to the whole.

2. Narrow-mindedness and determination, both Yang qualities, are important for focus and progress. Open-mindedness and an appreciation of what's around us, both Yin qualities, help better inform our worldview so we can discern and be wise in our focus. The result: outdated, unhelpful ideas fall away (Yin) while new ones take root and proliferate (Yang). Yang focus informed by Yin collaboration effects sustainable progress and collective justice.

3. Joy and fear also share reciprocity. Joy, a Yang emotion pertaining to the Fire phase, is arguably a goal—the flower—of life. But joy must be sustainable to safeguard the welfare of everything around it. Otherwise, joy becomes overly exuberant, too selfish and mindless, and can exhaust itself. Fear, a Yin emotion pertaining to the Water phase, aids joy by keeping joy in check and aware of its surroundings and limits. Fear alerts us to *what* threatens our welfare and generates the care of protection (aided by the energy of anger), while wisdom informs us *how* to act in order to preserve ourselves and ecological balance. But too much fear paralyzes and destroys our aliveness. Joy keeps fear in check by curbing fear's

tendency to shrink and diminish. Together, joy and fear create a balance of expansion and contraction, carefreeness and caution, that promotes thriving.

These ontological dialectics are examples of helpful positive feedback loops. They represent Yin and Yang transforming into one another, promoting the cycle of interdependence and revolution—our lives in harmony with the world around us, represented by the clockwise turning of the Yin-Yang symbol from Yin to Yang and Yang to Yin, ad infinitum. We foster this model when we are at once individually empowered and growing with others. Unhelpful, excessive behaviors are curbed while cooperative ones proliferate, modeling the death (decline) and rebirth (prolificity) process of regenerative relationships. This contrasts with the damaging, unchecked, linear, positive feedback loops of Yang-progress and consumption that are tearing down our world today—exponential adverse change arising from unsustainable obsession by individuals *and* organizations—that jeopardize the Yin of eco-human wellness. In this scenario Yin and Yang separate and no longer interrelate with one another, leading to unnecessary decay and demise.

While Yin-Yang reciprocity applies to human dynamics, it originated in the natural world. Today, in a forest or garden, what dies fertilizes new growth, which in turn dies and becomes compost to nourish more new growth. Round and round, this is the endless cycle of death and rebirth for which both light and dark rely on one another to curb and enhance the other. Thus is born the *middle path*, the integrated result of embracing the natural flow of highs and lows, excesses and deficiencies, and everything in between.

When we consciously participate in this process, we contribute to the greater good by cultivating depth and inclusivity, creativity and flourishing. Cultivating our personal gifts (Yang) to directly benefit the world (Yin) is paramount during climate crisis. A dangerous imbalance of global Yang dynamics has precipitated climate chaos and we must ensure our Yang endeavors—our work, creations, and consumption—directly help mitigate emissions and enhance the biosphere. How might you apply the core aspects of your own work and leverage your talents and privilege to help heal climate breakdown?

Excessively self-absorbed individuals view life as a personal indulgence project, as opposed to a compassion-based transformation process. This manifests in a failure to initiate via sacred permission, and fosters an ontology informed primarily by impulsive Yang principles with little input from the more difficult, wisdom-rich, and collective-oriented Yin. We have swung too far to the archetypal masculine Yang for far too long, and a compensatory, judicious swing to the feminine Yin is called for on all fronts.

Yin-generating endeavors include creating community, building fertile soil with organic amendments, growing food without poisons or excessive machine pollution, minding and caring for our bodies, emotional healing, conservation of all kinds, and embodied experience generally. Healthy Yang acts such as resistance, rebellion, and bold activism to halt fossil fuel expansion and promote social and environmental justice must accompany these Yin endeavors.

## An Unlikely Patient

As a holistic medicine practitioner, my remedies derive from the Earth. One day, several years ago, it struck me: if the Earth is not well, the foods and herbs I use to heal can't do their best job. Also, when we pollute the environment, we simultaneously embed illness in ourselves. This means we are banging our heads against the wall trying to become healthy. And our medicine, to a degree, is but a Band-Aid. Medicine, and any measure of holistic wellness, must include *and foster* the integrity of the natural world and the welfare of all humans—all of which affect our own well-being. Earth justice and social justice—vying for a true, thriving community of *we*—are therefore powerful medicine for climate cure. Since Chinese medicine seeks root cures for disease, I have had to step outside the traditional purview of even this "alternative" medicine to practice the radical medicine to which I am called. To this end, my healing practice over the last decade has increasingly taken the form of environmental activism: focusing more on climate cure than individual cure. While this change has resulted in a big pay cut and personal sacrifices, it has been a rewarding calling to live in alignment with our times.

The passion of embodied care mirrored in the Yin-Yang symbol as the integration of light and dark fuels my activism. Such passion is distinct from the unilaterally light-bearing, growth-obsessed, dysregulated and patriarchal Yang version that is excessively addicted, needlessly distracted, and unreasonably self-centered. This misuse of passion has contributed to our planetary crisis by ignoring its dark-revering, compost-making, sacred feminine Yin aspect, which curbs maniacal growth in favor of renewal.

When both women and men tend to the feminine (Yin) aspect, we begin to rebalance deranged masculine energy (in each of us) run amok. Recognizing we all possess both masculine and feminine qualities can help us ease perennial gender wars and begin to cooperate more wisely and efficiently. Instead of forever pointing fingers at the opposite gender, we can work toward integrating what Jung called the *animus* and *anima*. Animus is the masculine aspect of a woman's psyche and anima the feminine aspect of a man's. This respective Yang-within-Yin and Yin-within-Yang provides a window into identifying hidden shadow dynamics (explored in chapter 7) so we can recognize our brothers and sisters in every living being and stop endlessly blaming one another and ourselves. This approach could help us uphold women's rights and generate a more compassionate and integral global community from the inside out.

In addition to the Yin-generating practices mentioned just previously, less obvious Yin-nourishing activities include developing genuine and intimate relationships, communicating deeply and clearly, doing what we love that also serves the whole, and embracing our failures and shortcomings. When we bolster healthy Yin, we buffer the distorted and perverse passion of Yang, informing its excesses with wisdom. Thus, Yang is appropriately humbled (*humble* shares the same etymology as *humus*) by Yin. This leads to a more responsible, sustainably aligned, dark-informed Yang-light, with an enhanced ability to nurture and respect life rather than to burn up the planet.

Taking to heart the unconscious dynamics that lead to careless and destructive behaviors against the Earth has transformed my environmental activism into sharing more about inner activism and building community. This is a path for becoming *able* (never mind *wanting* to) create a healthier world from the ground up.

## Regenerative Psyche

Dr. Siegel's relationship model of the plural self encourages more community (Yin) to balance the destructive, excessive individualism (Yang) of Western culture. His holistic sense of *we* embraces a "trialectic" of self in relationship with both human and nonhuman community, which in turn creates an intimately connected biosphere. When we come into fertile relationship with ourselves by recycling pain into beauty, we forge a regenerative psyche and lifestyle that fertilizes the world with Yin-Yang care in action.

At the same time we provide for ourselves and our immediate family, we are caretakers for the natural world and our extended communities well into the future. This aligns with an ethos common to that of many indigenous Americans: that our actions must benefit the next seven generations. Wilma Mankiller, the first female Chief of the Cherokee Nation, said, "…Leaders are encouraged to remember seven generations in the past and consider seven generations in the future when making decisions that affect the people."[185] A similar eco-psychological view is shared by best-selling author and psychologist Jordan Peterson: "I think that truth is the highest value, although it has to be embedded in love. What I mean by that is that truth should serve the highest good imaginable. For me, that is what is best for each individual, in the manner that is simultaneously best for the family, and the state, and nature itself."[186]

Notice the balance of Yin and Yang from both these integral thinkers: In Mankiller's, the past is Yin and the future is Yang; for Peterson, personal gain is Yang, which he says must be balanced by the Yin of love and goodness for others. By example, applying this wisdom to procuring food means choosing food with a small carbon footprint that is also organic, whole, pesticide-free, and produced by fair-trade standards with minimal packaging and waste. This way, what nourishes and pleases us equally benefits the land, air, and those who produced it.

As a mindful ritual, we can remember what we procure for personal gain relies on the effort of others, including the Earth. In my early twenties, before eating, I would acknowledge and thank the Earth for the food on my plate, as well as trace the path of as many ingredients as I could and all the helping hands that brought it to my plate. This prayer could easily take half an hour, for which I simultaneously practiced great patience! Eventually, I shortened the blessing as I embodied and integrated its care. It was illuminating to entrain

---

185. Minthorn and Chávez, *Indigenous Leadership in Higher Education,* 88.

186. Peterson, quoted on Instagram September 18, 2019.

myself to the life story of wholesome, nourishing food (Yin) so easily taken for granted in our overly-processed (Yang) culture.

Operating from a sense of *we* requires the ability to see beyond our primitive survival fears, our entitled egos, and our proclivity to gather up resources only for ourselves and family (pingback to Dr. Siegel). For this to happen, we need more than a conceptual understanding of *we*. We must embody heartfelt connection with other members of our plural self—other humans, the natural world, and our abandoned inner selves.

Our capacity to develop sustained intimacy requires emotional depth. Emotional depth requires clearing our pain so we can connect more deeply. Connecting more deeply with both ourselves and others relies on good communication, which we develop from our triangle of resilience relationships. We initiate more intimate connections by reaching out for support and connection and letting ourselves receive the qualities of *acceptance, attention, appreciation, affection,* and *allowing.* These qualities of embodied loving are what Dr. David Richo calls the "Five As."[187] Because effective communication depends upon thinking critically, the latter is also essential for building community. In her article in *The New Yorker*, best-selling climate change author Elizabeth Kolbert corroborates: "Reason developed not to enable us to solve abstract, logical problems or even to help us draw conclusions from unfamiliar data; rather, it developed to resolve the problems posed by living in collaborative groups."[188]

When you and I feel supported and connected with others, we can more easily work through and let go of our heartaches. Conversely, when we go within to clear our hearts of personal pain (Yin), we can more easily open up to others (Yang) and experience life-sustaining connection. This inward-outward reciprocity creates an upward spiral, a positive feedback loop of deepening integrity between *me* and *we*. The more we let go, the more deeply we can connect; the more we connect, the more comprehensively we can heal our hearts. The result is a web of caring for our world. I've been fortunate to experience this kind of enriching connection living in community with others, in support groups and group therapy, in intimate relationships, in activist groups, and in growing food with friends.

---

187. Richo, *How to Be an Adult in Relationships: The Five Keys to Mindful Relationships.*
188. Kolbert, "Why Facts Don't Change Our Minds."

Tending to our emotional wellness by working through the pain of our adverse childhood experiences and smaller "t" traumas is largely an inner, Yin affair. So is intimately connecting with nature and one another. Beyond personal satisfaction, the goal of inner work is to create justice and compassion for others. All these endeavors require and build essential Yin and Yang capacities. Each facet of resilience enhances the other, true to Yin-Yang's guiding principle of the interdependence of apparent opposites. Inner work affects the quality of our actions, while the effects of our actions impact our inner lives. When implemented with wisdom, each continuously informs the other. Back and forth, inward and outward, we turn and grow, just as the seasons transform into one another year after year and the invisible, global Yin-Yang symbol smiles and thrives. This is the deep transformation we need to holistically heal all our relationships to both weather and curb climate catastrophe.

## • EXERCISE •
## CHAPTER 10 JOURNALING

Take out your journal or notepad, place it in front of you, and write out your responses to the following prompts.

### Reflection

1. Do you have a strong network of climate-aware friends whom you feel seen, accepted, and nourished by? Do you want more people like this in your life? If so, does anything stand in the way of developing more intimate connections?

### Action

2. If you desire more climate-aware community, in which of the following ways might you bolster community support? Which of these suggestions do you want to enact?

    • Join or create a climate change support group in your area (Resource 5: "Climate Change Café").

    • Join a Facebook climate change discussion/support group.

    • Begin opening up to friends you think might be amenable to discussing climate crisis.

- Join an environmental justice group, like Extinction Rebellion, or other strike group in your area to make friends and join the cause.
- Spend time in nature with friends and loved ones. If you don't have time in your regular schedule, plan your next vacation to be in nature with others in a low carbon footprint way, such as camping.
- Post on social media or in a group email to friends that you want more community, especially around climate change issues.

## Visualization/Journal

3. Sit quietly and let your awareness sink down into your body. How does your heart want to connect with others? What does it look like, what does it feel like, what key elements need to be included for it to be great? Register the image: maybe draw and/or journal about its qualities and meaningful elements.

# Chapter 11
# COMMUNITY AS GURU

*Whatever it is that you're drawn to do in the Great Turning*
*[a shift from an industrial to a sustainable society],*
*don't even think of doing it alone.*[189]
~JOANNA MACY

Intimate human support networks are crucial for climate resiliency and will become increasingly valuable as the crisis worsens and we become less secure and more reliant on one another. Being part of a caring community also keeps our hearts open and the love flowing, as we manage the best we can through this predicament.

"Being socially connected is our brain's lifelong passion,"[190] says Matthew Lieberman, professor of psychiatry and biobehavioral science at UCLA's Semel Institute for Neuroscience and Human Behavior. Interpersonal connection has been "baked into our operating system for tens of millions of years," he says, and this need is as basic as our need for food, water, and shelter.[191]

In other words, we are hardwired to be together and to depend on one another across all aspects of our lives. Even today, we depend entirely on one another; it's just less obvious so it seems like we don't. Smaller tribal networks of the past had more *direct* mutual accountability because disappearing from

---

189. Macy, *Stories of the Great Turning*, 8.
190. Wolpert, "UCLA Neuroscientist's Book Explains Why Social Connection Is as Important as Food and Shelter."
191. Ibid.

view (as we do nowadays) was not an option. Saying to another, "I owe you nothing" was unthinkable. Everyone performed a discrete vital function, and the breakdown of any single function caused immediate consequences felt by all. Each individual was essential to the whole, held in a net of belonging with friends, extended family, and the more-than-human natural world.

Extreme individualism is a modern disease that goes against being richly human. We still live in connected networks, but technology and our massive population have made it possible, and in many ways forced us, to live with less immediacy and accountability. Because economic channels are so diverse and divorced from our actual survival needs, we often don't even know whom we depend upon. This primal disconnection has allowed us to believe we owe each other nothing. It's part of our throwaway culture. If we can't honor all life, at the very least we could treat friends and those close to us as non-disposable, even when they have nothing to offer us.

Yet we carry cellular memory of our history, and this might be one reason why, for example, we revel in handmade crafts and antiques, especially those made from natural materials. These evoke our roots in the natural world, the luxury of time to craft things we need, and the intimacy of sharing them in person with neighbors.

Today I don't know the people who made my furniture, shoes, or shovel, or the canned soup I grab off the market shelf, much less who grew the vegetables in that soup. Our capitalistic system allows us to reap the fruits of everyone's labor impersonally, using currency instead of our relating directly with the producers of goods. Less in-person contact among members of our greater community means fewer of the social interactions we require for wellness, thriving, and—if we believe Lieberman—our very survival. This weak link in our resiliency adds to our isolation. We can consciously mend it by building closer ties with others and expanding our day-to-day interactions with a wider circle in our local communities. Shopping—or just socializing—at local farmers markets and craft shows are good places to start.

## Don't Be a Rock

Rugged individualism and the belief we don't need others is disempowerment in disguise. Ironically, we flaunt it as empowerment with an underlying belief that *the more independent and entitled I am, the more people I don't have to care about, and the more important I feel.* But this thinking is often just a defense against underlying insecurity. We can't deny the inalienable truth of our interdependence, nor the implicit vulnerability embedded within it. Autonomy is essential for togetherness, yet too much independence can leave us helpless when we truly need help. Beyond just succor, our mental health and longevity require the support of close social ties.

We need a balance of togetherness and aloneness. While boundaries are crucial for healthy living, they can also become separatist ego games. Equally, desperately clinging to each other for fear of being alone must be reconciled with self-reliance. Balance is required. Sometimes we isolate to heal, especially from love's wounds, and this is natural and normal. Yet fear can cause us to resist interpersonal connection and prevent us from accepting support when we most need it. Simon and Garfunkel's sang "I Am a Rock" to remind us that we cause ourselves more suffering when we isolate from love's inevitable pain. After a certain point, we suffer more persisting in our cocoon when we are indeed ready to become butterflies.

Because relying on one another is deeply ingrained in our DNA, it's natural, if not healthy, to become upset when people let us down. Grief and skillful expressions of anger help us get through such disappointments. Of course, nowadays we have the luxury to disconnect from those who disappoint us. Yet, it's easy to overexercise this privilege and never engage in deep problem-solving with others. This strategy backfires when we don't have the luxury to discard others. Building the muscle to work through difficulty is infinitely more valuable than easy, heartless ghosting. And it will prove to be indispensable through worsening climate chaos. Just ahead in the section pertaining to Extinction Rebellion, for example, I discuss persevering through challenges with others to achieve a larger goals.

Maintaining intimate connection with those who do show up for us, yet occasionally fail us, is more meaningful than no connection. We can abide Alfred Tennyson's poetic wisdom that it's better to love and lose than not to love at all. Inner work, our first triangle of resilience relationship, is key to help us love and keep on loving in an imperfect world.

# Cyber ... Reality?

At no other time in history have we been able to be in touch with so many people we don't know. Our ability to communicate and interact with complete strangers on Facebook and other social media platforms has obvious benefits. But there are downfalls to investing time and energy in relationships that don't manifest in person. Virtual friends in distant places can provide only so much, especially when we really need help and support. A virtual hug will never feel the same as a real one; a laughter emoji cannot invigorate us as a real laugh does.

Cyber reality not only fails to fulfill many of us as much as real life does, it can also diminish the quality of our in-person relationships, according to Drs. Jim Taylor and Susan Greenfield.[192] Chronic engagement with the virtual world progressively robs us of our patience, increases distraction, and compromises our ability to be focused and relaxed in the company of others. We're all familiar with the constant checking of cell phones. This lack of attunement with one another affects the quality of our shared neurobiology. Practicing being together, paying attention, and slowing down are good medicine for this modern disease. Fulfilling our human need for quality, in-person contact creates the milieu of belonging for which our nervous systems have evolved to thrive.

Too often, we abuse technology's innovations. This abuse isn't exactly our fault, because much of it has been designed expressly to addict us, as described previously. We would do better to swing the pendulum back to more intimate and localized, simpler ways of interacting. And not inwardly simple, but outwardly. For this, we can choose ways to cull our virtual realities and move away from artificiality while engaging in more traditional ways of being with each other and the natural world. Ironically, however, technology is indispensable for cleaning up the pollution we've created. While we minimize unnecessary enmeshment with more technology, we must continue to support technological efforts to mitigate climate crisis (fighting fire with some fire), spread both good and difficult news, and valiantly tend to suffering.

---

192. Taylor, "Technology: Virtual vs. Real Life: You Choose."

## Nondualism and Healthy Attachment

We can also examine so-called spiritual beliefs about our autonomy to see if these truly serve us. The concepts of "letting go" and "detachment" have their place in an embodied (reality-based) spirituality, but are problematic when misunderstood and used as defenses against admitting our fears of closeness and acknowledging our dependence on one another. This can promulgate disenfranchised social networks unless we make the effort to emotionally bond with one another and the world. Such aloofness, especially concomitant with a lack of critical thinking and a humble embrace of our humanness, easily leads to isolation, less care, and diminished passion for environmentalism.

Many of us fear intimacy for the pain of heartbreak. So, to protect from pain, we might distance ourselves and try to transcend or detach from the Earth, everyday problems, and one another. But, because we need each other, it seems we are damned if we get close and damned if we don't. If there were a cure for the pain of heartache, we could break this bind, reap the benefits of intimacy, and have a strategy for dealing with unavoidable heartbreak. The answer to this is grief, our biologically-inherited ally for letting go and processing the pain of loss. We accept this dark side of love just as we accept its light, feel-good side. Grief is an essential tool on the journey into more intimate community. And remember, grief is not *only* painful. It births our finer jewels of being human for a rich and meaningful life. In sum, grief helps us enjoy being close with one another, deal with the pain of being close, heal through trauma, and gifts us a rich inner life.

Honest sadness helps revive a heritage of connectedness that might seem strange to the sensibility of modern efficiency. Yet, as we discussed in chapter 6, it is actually a means for degrowth, a cure for our dysregulated progress. Our relationship with grief is also a measure of our ability to practically and generously love. It is a courageous path to accept the sadness that comes with such connected community while admitting and embodying how much we truly need one another.

## Showing Up

"Commitment" is a curse word for many. We're so burdened by unwanted responsibility, we cringe at the thought of more. Unfortunately, many of our responsibilities, such as working nine-to-five for money, often promote more bad stress than wellness. Interpersonally, many of us have control and fear of intimacy issues that prevent us from committing, and therefore showing up.

Showing up for one another might seem easy, but apparently it's not. Most of us can count as many or more people who *don't* show up enough for us as those who do. Showing up requires a degree of wellness and the time to do so. Yet, many seem to have the time, just not the will, and thereby justify absence on being too busy. Being there for others requires selflessness, which requires emotional maturity, which develops not only with age but especially through inner work. It takes emotional work to show up and to commit.

Difficulty and struggle are part of relating. Making friends with difficulty by developing compassion, good communication, and empathic listening skills, is invaluable for building sustained, deeper relationships and more intimate community. A narrow focus on easy-fix, feel-good-now means to happiness works against nourishing ties that *truly* make us happier, which is to feel fulfilled. For my part, I happily commit to building bonds that last, and I show up for my friends and family. Sometimes, when I feel too busy or overwhelmed with this or that to show up, I try to take a look at what's really going on, and commit to showing up anew.

Part of healing is adapting to changing times. In light of climate change, scientist Susanne Moser says, "... Yeah, we're going to get a lesson in dependence and interdependence like you haven't seen. Well, none of us [sic] has seen."[193] I recommend we practice with friends, family, and neighbors by consciously committing to one another, with express agreements of accountability. This mimics the interrelatedness of traditional communities, of relying on one another by necessity. Such is conscious community: being available to one another not only by chance, but by choice and as a heartfelt need.

To practically adapt this model to modern life, we could adopt parameters that fit our individual needs and limitations. For example, you might be able to commit to showing up for a friend only when you're not at work, taking care of children, or otherwise genuinely unavailable. You might find the more

---

193. Mazur, "Despairing about the Climate Crisis? Read This: A Conversation with Scientist Susanne Moser about Climate Communication, the Benefits of Functional Denial, and the Varied Flavors of Hope."

you show up for others, the more they show up for you, which gives you more time.

## The New Guru

I call community *the new guru*. In truth, community is an old friend with much to teach and remind us. When we are well, we can easily forget our interwoven connectedness. When we are ill or incapacitated, we become acutely aware of how much we need others. Climate sickness is here, so now is the time to build truthful, durable relationships. As the world becomes more unstable due to environmental collapse and the unsustainable systems we rely upon for support crumble and fail us, we must build the inner and outer capacities for sustainable relationships. To sum up, these include:

1. Diligent critical thinking (examples: discerning what's more likely both subjectively and objectively true, especially before making and operating on assumptions; spotting fractioned, binary reasoning; sorting facts and good science from fake news and junk science).

2. Clear, honest, empathic, quality communication (examples: sharing from heart and mind in union, practicing intellectual and emotional honesty, giving helpful talks/presentations, creating poignant art and poetry).

3. Embracing difficulty, working with and through all our emotions, and mobilizing their benefits for regeneration (examples: grief work, finding the jewels in fear and the gifts in anger, using our privilege to create joy and ease for the underprivileged).

4. Engaging inner work and enjoying the resultant ability to show up more deeply and genuinely for others (examples: shadow work that leads to compassionate listening, sharing wisdom, helping others to heal).

5. Nurturing the inspiration and mustering the courage for outer action to create stronger support networks (examples: learning more about climate crisis and weathering the difficult awareness of it with others, planting gardens and trees together, living in community, rebelling and striking, showing up to actively participate in local government hearings).

6. Embodying the trust and courage to vulnerably expose ourselves to others (examples: humble disclosure, admitting when wrong, making amends, asking for and offering forgiveness).

7. Creating sacred space to express deeper dynamics and feelings (example: creating a climate change support group or a grief circle).

As we individually and collectively embrace inner work, love of nature, and community building, we begin to build a durable and robust alliance to heal through and address climate crisis. Inner work provides us with a baseline of the regenerative qualities (our finer jewels of being human) we need to bond and cooperate with others and to protect what we love. Connecting with the natural world allows the resiliency we gain from inner work to spread beyond human-centrism. Bonding with one another confers exponential strength and propels us to work together for personal and social, economic and environmental, justice.

The remainder of this chapter is dedicated to a discussion of how the abovementioned seven qualities have come to life in several community groups I have facilitated or been part of over the last several years. These groups include:

Community Living on the Big Island of Hawaii

Lava Flow Grief and Gratitude Circle

Climate Change Discussion and Support Group

Eco-Grief Circle

Extinction Rebellion

## Mahalo 'Aina ("Thank You, Land")

Before introducing the first group I started, I want to share a story with you, snippets of which you've already heard. For eighteen years, I cultivated a permaculture farm on the Big Island of Hawaii. Homesteading amid the harsh, yet also nurturing elements of sun, salt, wind, and rain—not to mention the mosquitoes, fire ants, and mud—was exhilarating and often defeating.

On five virgin acres of lava, I carefully cleared parts of the jungle by hand for the first garden and a simple thatched hut, which I lived in for years. I had one small solar panel for power. I dug the first holes for fruit trees in solid rock with a metal pole, called an o'o bar in Hawaiian. Each hole took weeks to dig. After that experiment, I brought in a bulldozer to break up the rock to make the ground more fertile and easier to cultivate. Over the subsequent years, I dug hundreds of holes by hand with a pickaxe and shovel. The saplings I planted needed constant amendments for the first couple years, until they were self-sustaining and could derive nutrients from the ground cover and soil that eventually formed from decaying plant matter, beneficial insects, crushed volcanic rock, and the abundant sun and rain. During the latter part of this stint, I built my home on this land. I created a thriving sanctuary, with dozens of distinct fruit varieties, yielding the tastiest organic produce in the area.

In June, 2018, lava from the Kīlauea volcano covered my permaculture farm, my home, my entire community, and all the lush, tropical surrounds for miles. Ironically, lava is part of the island's natural beauty, if not what humans need to thrive, because of the land and fertility it creates. The loss was devastating and continues to be, as I remain displaced and mourning what I'd built and the way of life that so robustly sustained me and this seaside ecology (Resource 3: "The Poetry of Predicament").

Before the lava buried my neighborhood, a 6.9 magnitude earthquake jolted my homestead and sent me dashing out from under my covered outdoor lanai (patio) to open sky. Sweating and with both knees quivering uncontrollably, I said, "That's it, I'm outta here!" I evacuated up the coast to Hamakua with my eighteen-year-old cat to a muddy, mosquito- and fire ant-infested farm. I stayed there in a tent at the invitation of my friend Melissa, who had also evacuated the lava-inundated area of lower Puna, the southeastern county of the Big Island ravaged by the flow. After a number of days at this farm, I was invited to stay with other friends at Mahalo 'Aina Farm and Retreat (Resource 6: "Mahalo 'Aina Sanctuary"). It was there, on ten acres overlooking the ocean, that I lived with a dozen other evacuees as the lava broke out from new fissures each day and meandered haphazardly across the Puna landscape some forty miles away.

About three weeks later, a fresh breakout suddenly created a new tributary of lava, which began to flow in the general direction of my community. We were all told it would likely follow the line of steepest descent, travel directly to the ocean, and bypass our homes. Instead, it flowed where no one thought it would. That same night at 10:30 p.m. I watched a livestream of the lava reaching the Kapoho coast where I lived. There it did the seemingly impossible. It ballooned out and spread south, toward our homes and farms. My heart sank, yet somehow I managed to get to sleep.

In the morning I learned that everything was gone. Eventually, the lava even took out Ahalanui Park, the geothermally-heated swimming hole where we frequently gathered. On hearing the news, I retreated to my camper van that I had used to evacuate. I lay down and began to cry, then sob, then scream out in pain. I wailed so loudly from the deepest place in my body that was one with the land I loved—the land that nourished, grew, and taught me so much for so long. I wailed and wailed all morning, writhing in grievous agony. Everything I had worked so hard for was gone, including my community and all the pristine swimming holes, natural hot ponds, and jungle nooks—all within easy walking and biking distance. The future I'd created disappeared overnight.

My pain flowed from me like lava from the earth's molten core. It burned, emptied, and eventually calmed me, leaving raw love in its wake. Such deep sobbing is vital for any of us, if we feel it, to let out the deep pain not only of personal loss, but any aspect of climate-related loss.

## Lava Flow Grief and Gratitude Circle

I'm still close with the owners (stewards) of Mahalo 'Aina, Steven and Fabi. To this day, at unexpected moments, my gratitude overflows for their taking me in, along with other lava refugees. Our tears were welcome there and, like the lava, they flowed off and on for weeks. It was at Mahalo 'Aina, among a dozen others from my decimated community, that I created a grief group for our shared loss. We sat together once a week and shared our concerns, fears, and even our joy. We recounted old stories of the area, precious memories we had of being on the land, and the magic of lower Puna.

About six of us were present during any given circle. We would welcome each other, share some words and hugs, then gather on the living room floor of the main house. We took turns sharing, council-style. Just being together helped us regulate our minds and bodies and relax. Following is the format we used, which I've transcribed verbatim from my original notes. Each numbered item (save for #5) represents a round during which we took turns sharing.

Process:

1. Brief initial introductions.

2. Name what you are grateful for.

3. Name what you have lost.

4. Describe what you need now.

5. Brief silent meditation to close.

Guidelines:

To ensure safety and trust for all, please confirm that you acknowledge and agree to the following:

1. To support unconditional space for others' sharing.

2. To not interrupt another while they are sharing.

3. To be mindful of not trying to "fix" others.

4. To ask another if they want advice or feedback before offering it.

5. That you are not obligated to share anything you don't want to.

6. That you are free to leave the group at any time for whatever reason.

Confidentiality:

Whatever is shared in the group stays in the group, unless permission is granted by the sharer.

We gathered in circle perhaps half a dozen times. Our shared experience of loss was more manageable together. We found strength in each other and in shared stories that felt too much to hold alone. All of us felt renewed after meetings. There was a sense of liberation at being able to face our fears together, embody our true feelings, and be with our broken hearts exactly as they are.

One of the most poignant moments for me was when a friend who was displaced from (but did not lose) his home, shared: "I have all I need. I have food for today, I have shelter, I have clothes, and I have friends." His simple gratitude and truth sparked a revelatory moment for me. I had lost a lot, but I too had these essentials. I was, mostly, also well... enough. This recognition didn't erase my grief, but it did help shift my perspective and ease my pain.

Simply acknowledging *Wow! I'm okay!* gave me a ground of gratitude to stand on.

After several circles, I was able to name all I had lost. This included my community, my gardens and orchards, my house, my belongings, my sense of home, all the seasons spent cultivating the land and building my home, the hard work, my place of refuge and safety, and my future security. Yet, I could feel in my body something else, yet to be named. I remember when I finally named the last loss. When I could say *my habitat*, I had a palpable sense of completion, of acknowledging my full heart of losses. I realized it took me so long to name everything because I'd lived holistically, fully intertwined with everything around me. As I moved through the acute phases of grief, I composed this poem, which helped me acknowledge the lava incident and gave me strength to endure the loss.

### The Courage of Faith

*Can we remain open long enough,*
*Muster enough courage for fear,*
*The mettle to endure feeling*
*The persistent sting of transition*
*Without knee-jerking*
*Into action, trying to recreate*
*What has left us?*
*Can we persist in the void*
*Of ache that presses*
*Against our souls*
*With the weight of a hundred mountains—*
*A downturn that is not suffering, hopelessness*
*Or self-destruction*
*But trusting*
*From our very marrow*
*That some providence we could*
*Otherwise never receive,*
*Some ivory incandescence*
*Or liminal incantation*

*Rising as a mist*
*Or thunderous whispering,*
*Could emerge from the ruins*
*Of our lives*
*With a response, a vision*
*That's been waiting as a seed*
*In the deep loam of our bodies*
*For this very moment,*
*That can only emerge*
*By resisting ease in favor of ardor,*
*To forge softness from shards,*
*For a life we never could have planned*
*Or imagined under so much hardening.*

I shared this poem in our circle, which touched one member in particular, and for obvious reasons. Sofia had to endure a slow burn. Her property
was one of the last to be incinerated. The lava had taken out nearly everything
in our neighborhood—save for some small, random islands of jungle  and
was now oozing ever-so-slowly toward her home. After weeks of agonizing
waiting, her home and farm were finally engulfed. My place had been gone
for weeks and, while I was still raw, I was a bit further along in mourning and
was able to hold space for her fresh pain. This sort of "eldership of loss" was
helpful to me before my place was taken by the lava. My friend and colleague,
Dr. Roy Lozano, lost his place early in the eruption event. He lent solace and
helpful words when I lost my home and farm a month later. The solidarity I
shared with him was healing, and I could then share that with Sofia. None of
us was alone.

Astonishingly, we also all laughed in the midst of our losses. Our joy would
erupt spontaneously—just like our tears or the magma that took out our community—often in absurd fashion. Being together made it easier to laugh. In
fact it birthed our joy, something I couldn't have mustered on my own. Our
grief was amplified and healed together, and so was our joy. After each ceremony, we felt lighter and more empowered. Our sadness was ever-present, but
so were other essential elements I hesitate to try to name. Let's just say it was

ordinary magic, sparked by our coming together, as billions of once-separate neurons intermingled in shared care.

---

• EXERCISE •

## HEALING POEM-MAKING

One of the best ways to learn how to create poetry is to read poetry, let it inspire you, and then practice writing it. This said, if poem-making is new to you, here are some tips for composing a healing song unique to your own experience and sensibilities:

1. Try not to judge any of your work. If you do judge yourself, make light of it, and try to let any judgment go. Poetry is an ever-evolving craft and, as mentioned previously, you don't have to be proficient for any poem or art you create to be healing.

2. Identify your feelings, name them, feel them, and write them down before beginning.

3. Try to write from your body as much as from your mind. Taking deep, full breaths every so often can help. As you engage these prompts and the poem itself, allow your feelings to transcribe themselves onto paper. What you write should eventually *feel* as though it is flowing out of you and in turn encourage this flow of feeling. Reserving judgment helps the flow, and you can edit later.

4. Before you begin your poem-making, consider making a list of the images, names, and/or objects germane to your experience that you can refer to for inspiration and reminders while composing.

5. Poems don't need to rhyme. So, don't worry about rhyming, just let it flow. Even if you end up writing a lyrical journal entry, any forays into thinking and feeling metaphorically exercise your poetic muscle.

---

## Climate Circle

I stayed at Mahalo ʻAina for a couple more months before deciding to leave the island for the mainland. During that time, I realized anew the importance of living in community, and specifically, the necessity of gathering in sacred space together. During latter Grief Circles at Mahalo ʻAina, as I emerged from the acute trauma of loss, one of the questions we contemplated was, "What calls you most strongly now?" My response was: a desire to create and participate in more circles for intimate sharing.

When the lava erupted, I was already three years into writing this book. As I shared in the introduction, it was an initiation into climate disaster which, uncannily, helped inform this work. So, when I arrived back on the mainland in August of 2018, I immediately started up a "Climate Change Discussion and Support Group" ("Climate Circle" for short) in Ojai, California. This is the third healing community experience I want to share with you.

At the time of this writing, I have been leading Climate Circle for over a year. We meet every other Tuesday evening from 7 to 9 p.m. I created the group believing everybody was as brokenhearted and anxious about climate crisis as I was. I imagined these residents from my new community would pour in with their hearts on their sleeves, especially since the massive Thomas Fire in December, 2017[194] had just wiped out many homes in Ojai. But this was not the case.

Those who attend Climate Circle come from all walks of life, have all different levels of climate awareness, and distinct concerns. I have found myself teaching about climate change as much as holding space for others' reflections and feelings about it. The group has therefore morphed from a "support group" to a "discussion and support group." Again, I invite you to consider starting such a group in your own community. An easy start-up template is available to help you at *climatechangecafe.org* (Resource 5: "Climate Change Café").

The venue for Climate Circle is Greater Goods, a community gathering space in town. We call Greater Goods our "community living room" and all events are by donation. It provides a tremendous service for all who wish to attend and host classes and gatherings of all shapes and sizes. Such community spaces are vital for gathering in our isolationist culture, especially in the midst of climate crisis. Greater Goods is a bit of a *swimming against the stream* venture in the best of ways, a small, precious crack in the shell of capitalistic fatalism. We need more venues like Greater Goods and more people taking the risk to

---

194. Less than five months after evacuating from the Thomas Fire, I evacuated from the Kilauea lava eruption in Hawaii.

put community before profit. So, Greater Goods is itself yet another community resilience experience I share with you!

Climate Circle has been medicine for climate crisis malady, which Chris Hedges expresses so well: "The longer we publicly deny the bleak reality before us and privately cope with our existential dread and pain, the more crippling despair becomes."[195]

––––––

We open Climate Circle with hellos and a brief, personal check-in. Each person shares what is on their heart and mind, climate change-related or not. Sometimes, especially when no time limit for sharing is specified, check-ins become a discussion springboard for the rest of the meeting. I oscillate between creating a stricter agenda for the evening and letting the conversation flow, more often favoring the latter. Sometimes we watch a video or documentary and follow this with a discussion. Other times, we discuss a piece of writing—an article or book excerpt, for example. More often, we participate in an organic group discussion. Whatever the format, participants report feeling renewed and refreshed, even (or especially) when the discussion gets heavy. Hearing what is on others' hearts and minds is comforting and emotionally regulating. There's also the sense that, regardless of what anyone shares, it's healing just being together.

Like the Lava Flow Grief and Gratitude Circle, Climate Circle is also a ceremony of sorts. We take time out from everyday life to drop into intimate sharing, which many find otherwise difficult. Carving out time for this is especially important these days—making the time to heal, build meaningful relationships, and convene over the most pressing issues of our time. Most recently, I participated in a COVID-19 pandemic support group hosted on Zoom by a friend who attended the local Climate Circle. What goes around comes around.

Another climate support group leader, Debbie Chang, says, "There's not really a space, I don't think, for people to talk about these feelings…People don't want to dwell on negative emotions, but people want to be heard and

––––––

195. Hedges, "The Messiahs of Hope Assure Us Everything Will Be OK in the End. But It Won't."

validated."[196] Anxiety, grief, hopelessness, and anger are the most frequent emotions shared in Climate Circle. Relief and resilience result from sharing these feelings together.

Several members of the Climate Circle have attended since the very first meeting. Tamara, who has lived in the Ojai Valley for forty years, gives impassioned reports about the condition of the trees in her yard and the changes she notices. For her, that's enough experience with climate crisis to drive the issue home. Chris is a talented artist and deeply sensitive person who suffers from chronic depression. She brings her art supplies to each meeting to maintain unfocused attention with us all. While coloring, sketching, and doodling, she pipes up when inspired. It's tough for her to get too embroiled in climate issues due to her depressive bouts, but she finds comfort being with others in a meaningful space. Agnes, who is in her sixties and rides a bike everywhere, seems to find relief when authentic feelings are expressed, allowing her to dip into her own, which she expresses in a tenuous and beautiful way. Molly, who formerly spent years in monastic-style Buddhist training and is now a passionate activist and mother of a wonderful five-year-old wild child, shares full-palette, authentic emotion and deep psychological insights regarding the backward system we're part of, and her passion to midwife our sick culture into a more humane way. Joseph, a Renaissance man in his seventies, lost his home to the Thomas fire in 2017, the second largest wildfire in California history. He believes in the power of community and—with the help of Habitat for Humanity—is planning to rebuild a home where more than twelve people can live together. Joseph believes the way to climate cure is to reinvent culture by changing the way we use language.

I'm constantly surprised by the depth and insights shared at Climate Circle. Hearing others' perspectives both broadens and expands my limited perspective and experience. I'll frequently overhear myself saying, "Oh yeah, that's so true." or, "Wow, I had forgotten about that." This happens with regard to ideas *and* emotions. As I hear and feel what I've not yet articulated, my heart-burden is relieved. Sometimes someone will share an experience—such as gratitude or a health challenge—that has a comprehensive healing effect that's difficult to

---

196. Arciga, "Climate Anxiety Groups Are the New Self-Care."

put into words. Exposing ourselves to different ideas changes how we think; empathizing with raw emotion in others opens our hearts. These experiences expand our sense of wholeness and connection, influencing how we act.

Similar to the Lava Flow Grief and Gratitude Circle in Hawaii, just being together in Climate Circle—even if we don't discuss and commiserate about climate change—brings relief. It's medicine without side effects. I find my sense of self shared in everyone else, bringing to life Dan Siegel's "neurobiology of we" and Matthew Lieberman's "lifelong passion" to connect.

## Eco-Grief Circle

Two additional groups have grown out of Climate Circle. The first is an Eco-Grief Circle; the other is Extinction Rebellion, which I'll share about next.

I prefer to refer to our eco-grief group as a *heart renewal circle* because renewal carries a less intimidating vibe than grief, and because participants often feel renewed by our gatherings. I also don't like calling it a *grief circle* (though I do for clarity) because I'm uncomfortable with the possibility that those coming to a grief circle will *try* to grieve. This effort, as we learned in chapter 6, can get in the way of grief, since its nature is to arise spontaneously. Here we recall from chapter 6: *grief flows in the compassionate company of others.* So, I abide *via negativa* wisdom and hold a space for us to name and share our losses and what organically comes from this.

In Eco-Grief Circle we gather in similar fashion to the Lava Flow Grief and Gratitude Circle I led in Hawaii. We practice unconditional listening while others share. Participants are gently encouraged to speak from the heart and, if it feels right, to share what feels more vulnerable and riskier than what feels safe. Everyone is given the same amount of time to share and there is allowance to go overtime. Yet, surprisingly, going overtime has never been an issue. We do two rounds of sharing: the first is to share personal losses, the second to share our sense of ecological loss (eco-grief). Participants spend about ten to fifteen minutes naming/listing their losses and then journaling about them. We then share whatever we choose to with the group. Many emotions come out in participants' sharing, not just grief. Some choose not to share, and just bear witness to others. Cross talk is not allowed and sometimes we sneak in a quick, extra round of reflection and discussion.

The best way I can describe the grief circle is *groundbreaking*. Carving out time to share our losses creates a sense of beauty and connection difficult to achieve in everyday life. Compassion and deep care blossom in the circle, which is not surprising since love and grief go hand in hand. I have noticed my heart soften in places that have become hardened over the last few years. After the ritual, I generally feel calm, even blissed out, from the quiet, attuned space of courageously sharing and being with our losses and challenges. Such courage is what I call *Yin leadership*—leading with a vulnerable, broken-open heart. Yin leadership demonstrates it's okay and healthy to cry and be brokenhearted. It bonds us, keeps love flowing, and centers us in what deeply matters. It's public propaganda for emotional honesty and renewal—a form of climate activism because it reifies the crisis. To wake up, we have to act like climate breakdown is actually happening.

One night after Circle, I realized the many benefits of sharing grief and unconditional presence together. Doing so:

1. Helps soften and renew our hearts, easing pain.
2. Connects us vulnerably, and thereby intimately, so we don't feel so alone.
3. Provides the "glue" of intimate community.
4. Connects us to compassion and empathy, beneath the level of discursive thought.
5. Creates space not only to voice, but to be with and to feel, what we don't make time for in everyday life.
6. Helps us realize and experience hitherto unknown parts of our wholeness via others' sharing.
7. Connects us with the Earth.
8. Allows us to share love in the midst of collapse and death, rather than distance ourselves and close off to what's painful.
9. Helps us regulate our emotions and relax and enjoy together.

## Extinction Rebellion

After completing thousands of hours of climate science research for the appendix of this book, I realized the best response to all I'd learned was to join Extinction Rebellion (XR). I felt called to act fast and directly at the level of government, to effect top-down change. After all, radical policy shifts have occurred when government gets involved, such as The New Deal under FDR and the retooling of factories during WWII to produce munitions. Extinction Rebellion and the youth strikes empower us to be at this forefront of change, entering the disenfranchised void between government and our personal lives—and to do it together, as community.

When I mentioned the idea of getting involved with XR to my good friend Benjamin, we decided to found Extinction Rebellion-Ojai. Benjamin changed his mind a few days later, but the seed was planted in me. Its germination moment would come. At Climate Circle a few weeks later, I suggested we watch and discuss a particular climate change video. At that moment my friend Jeff, who was seated next to me, turned and looked at me intently, put his hand on my knee, and said, "We need to do something." That something, he said, is rebellion. Thus was born Extinction Rebellion Ojai (XR-Ojai).

Extinction Rebellion is an action group founded on ten principles[197] and three demands (four in the US).[198] Due to its name, many don't realize XR is both a rebellion group *and* a regeneration movement. It's both Yin and Yang. On the one hand, XR fiercely stands up and demands a halt to fossil fuel emissions (to reach net-zero by 2025) via its second demand. This is a Yang function. On the other hand, it promotes regenerative culture via any methods appropriate to a given locale via its third principle. This is a Yin function.[199]

As mentioned in chapter 1, XR is informed by research showing that the participation of 3.5 percent of the population is needed to effect massive social change. Since it's now widely accepted that government involvement is necessary to make sweeping changes to both reduce carbon emissions and suck out surplus carbon from the atmosphere, I consider joining Extinction Rebellion, or other civil disobedience movements, to be the single most powerful action we can take to address climate crisis (Resource 2: Monbiot, "Only Rebllion," and Hedges, "Saving the Planet").

Working with XR is a rewarding experience, but it's not easy. We're volunteer strangers working together for the first time with a constantly evolving

---

197. "The Truth About Us," Extinction Rebellion, video.
198. "We Demand," Extinction Rebellion.
199. "The Truth About Us," Extinction Rebellion, video.

game plan, paying out-of-pocket, stressed-out from modern city life, and further stressed by climate crisis. Above all, XR is a lesson in putting a cause before personal grievances and ego. Even though XR is nonhierarchical, power struggles, shadow emotions, and hurt feelings occur regularly. Unaccountability and failure to follow through are also common. And there isn't really time or enough interest among all to work out these differences. Communication skills are challenged, and there are frequent opportunities to be more patient with others. On occasion I've needed to reach out to friends and other XR members for support in navigating disagreements with some members. We do the best we can, sometimes scrapping along. I boost my resolve, remembering this is how it could be when collapse hits harder. All the challenges of XR are therefore good training for even more chaotic times.

Like climate crisis itself, XR is a catalyst for personal and interpersonal growth. Its group dynamics are a crucible for quickly building emotional intelligence and critical-thinking skills. XR is a primo playground on which to practice many of the principles in this book. Previous inner work has prepared me well for XR, and I keep learning. I constantly remind myself of our greater purpose and goal: to help save humanity and the biosphere. The alternative—to quit and fail to mount a resistance against the forces that are killing us—is simply unacceptable, so I press on.

XR primarily challenges the first and third triangle of resilience relationships—relationship with self and with others. These challenges, skillfully navigated, help build these relationships. I've had to do some soul-searching and be with heightened states of sadness, fear, anger, helplessness, and hopelessness. I've sought solace and stress relief for this in the wilds. In total, I've been pushed to build all three of my triangle of resilience relationships in XR.

Shadow work (explored in depth in chapter 7) has also proven invaluable for navigating XR. I'm self-disciplined, self-motivated, and a high achiever, with high expectations of myself and others. My control issues and attachment to wanting things to go a certain way have been challenged in XR. I realize the motivation behind my passion is excellent, real-life results, so I back off some while keeping the vision of my heart alive. I've also received feedback that I am challenging to others. I listen to the criticism, try to sort out truth from others' projections, and adjust to be more malleable and thus efficient for the benefit of the whole.

A shadow emotion exacerbating my impatience is anxiety (and some anxiety is adaptive, as we explored in chapter 5). This makes sense, since launching XR grew out of learning horrific climate details and realizing we are all but too late to address this crisis. Attempting to facilitate meetings that maximize efficiency and productivity is an example of where my anxiety shows up as impatience and irritability. This anxiety also exacerbates my sense of urgency. Some of this urgency is helpful, and some is unhelpful. So I practice channeling some of my unhelpful, anxious urgency into helpful passion and perseverance, excitement and action. The rest I cope with by practicing surrender to the group process and employing the Twenty-Two Anxiety Tips in chapter 5. I also remind myself I am not saving the world single-handedly.

Others are also challenged by XR. Despite this, we work largely harmoniously together. Within just a couple months, we persuaded our city to declare climate emergency. We stormed every city council meeting and gave rousing, impassioned, fact-based testimony for the need to declare climate emergency, as well as the great opportunity before us to become a model, climate-progressive city. In one of these meetings, I testified, "Just as we community members have stuck our necks out to speak up and demand climate action, so must you council members rise to the occasion and do all you can to make Ojai a world leader for climate mobilization."[200] In January, 2020, several XR members and I directly contributed to the visioning of the Climate Mobilization Committee for how to drastically reduce emissions in Ojai. This committee was appointed by city council members in response to XR's working with the council to declare climate emergency.

In 2019, XR-Ojai: marched in the Fourth of July parade with banners and a "return the beaver to our watershed" float; contributed recommendations for a local government climate emergency mobilization committee; organized and marched in September with local youth activists in solidarity with the Global Climate Strike, and then accompanied them to city hall to speak their hearts and minds to local policy makers; led a nonviolent direct action

---

200. Ojai City Council, "2019 Meeting Videos," video.

protest workshop; contributed to moratorium declarations for new oil projects in Ventura County; demanded enforcement of gas-powered leaf blower bans; and raised climate awareness with our city council members and in our community generally.[201]

The most heartening of these endeavors for me was the youth climate strike, which I organized with a local chapter of Fridays for Future. Hundreds of young people showed up and found their voices and passion. Being with this many informed, inspired, courageous youth was the most inspiring group event I've ever participated in. While it breaks my heart that they are striking to save their lives, supporting youth to get boldly involved helps change the culture of apathy and denial that has delivered us where we are today.

Now, in 2020, we are in the phase of fleshing out the fossil fuel reduction ordinances we want the city to enact for climate emergency declaration. We are demanding that our local government embrace Extinction Rebellion's second demand to reduce greenhouse gas (GHG) emissions to net-zero by 2025, several years ahead of IPCC recommendations. This is wise because such massive mobilizations often take longer than expected and the IPCC's projections are conservative (a point discussed previously and also in the appendix). I've had a promising discussion of these two points with the climate scientist on the committee, and we are in complete agreement. So far, so good.

If you want to do good for the planet and humanity and become immersed in the transformative principles and practices offered in this book, while bolstering your sense of purpose at the cutting edge of evolution for all species, consider joining Extinction Rebellion. If you feel disenchanted about climate breakdown, there's nothing like mobilizing and taking action with your community to lift your spirits when feeling anxious, depressed, hopeless, and disempowered. XR might sometimes challenge these emotional states, but if you can view joining as an effort toward a higher goal, minimizing self-importance, and building resilience for harder times, it's a worthy way to spend your time.

In the end, rebellion is an act of dignity and moral courage. Chris Hedges conveys this notion well in his sobering essay, "The Last Act of the Human

---

201. Extinction Rebellion Ojai, Facebook.

Comedy": "Resistance grounded in action is its own raison d'être. It is catharsis. It brings us into a community with others who are coping with the darkness by naming it but refusing to submit to it. And in that act of resistance we find emotional wholeness, genuine hope and even euphoria, if not an ultimate victory."[202]

———

In earlier chapters, we explored the emotional intelligence skills needed to deeply transform ourselves and weather tough times, as well as how to employ difficult emotions to step more fully into climate warriorship. To this foundational skill set, we have added a thorough grounding in the holistic nature of climate crisis and, in these latter sections, the triangle of resilience relationships needed both to cope and to radically heal *through* climate initiation. We will now conclude the discussion by integrating all these domains for a regenerative climate cure vision, from the inside out and the ground up.

> ### • Exercise •
> ### Chapter 11 Journaling
>
> Please also refer to the additional in-text exercise for this chapter.
>
> Take out your journal or notepad, place it in front of you, and write out your responses to the following prompts.
>
> ### Journal/Activity
>
> List three friends, family members, or groups whom you can count on to an appreciable degree. In your own words, consider communicating to each how important they are to you and ask for feedback about your importance to them. Write down what you would say to them. Then consider presenting to them an "express agreement" or acknowledgment of accountability to show up for and to help each other. Examples might include agreeing to cook meals for one another, going for a walk in the woods once a week, being available by phone for support, checking in before going to the market to see if you can get anything for each

---

202. Hedges, "The Last Act of the Human Comedy."

other, and/or agreeing to have each other's back in preparation for, or during, a climate disaster.

## Journal

Please refer to the numbered list of community-building capacities at the beginning of the "New Guru" section of this chapter as context for each of the following categories. Reflect on and journal your responses to the following:

1. **Critical Thinking Skills:** Do you value the faculty of deductive reasoning and analyzing? What are your strengths in this regard and what are your challenges or weaknesses? Do you make an earnest attempt to get logistics straight and discern facts before making assumptions and indulging emotional reactions?

2. **Heart-Mind Union:** How well do your heart and mind operate in unison? List three ways they do; for example, are you able to remain empathic while also tracking logistics and what's true during conversations and in disagreements? Or, if you are angry, how well are you able to refrain from violent communication and return to relative neutrality while learning about and assessing the facts informing your upset to determine if your anger is justified and fairly and accurately delivered?

3. **Being with Difficulty:** How welcoming are you of difficulty and *being with* a challenging experience to mine its benefits? Choose three emotions and write about how each emotion both serves and injures you and your relationships. What can you do to mitigate this damage? Now list two other emotions you didn't choose and do the same.

4. **Past Wounding:** List three of your strongest emotional triggers (example: you get angry when you feel like you're being told what to do, when someone doesn't listen to you, or when someone isn't available to meet your needs). How does each interfere with intimacy in present time? How do you envision healing through these triggers to improve your relationships? If you don't know, are you willing to seek outside help?

5. **Joining with Others:** Are you satisfied with your level of community engagement? Is there a group, organization, or movement to address climate crisis you'd like to join? What commitments are you willing to make to join?

6. **Making Amends:** How easy and enjoyable is it for you to admit when you are wrong or have made a mistake, or to say "I'm sorry"? If it's challenging, why?

7. **Sacred Space:** Do you participate in a "sacred space" or "safe circle" to share with others about climate issues? If not, do you want to create or join such an existing group? If so, how and when will you do this?

# Conclusion
# REGENERATION

*Because we reject our own humanity, we reject what Jung calls the shadow side;*
*we've pushed that down into the unconscious, and the minute we do that,*
*we start projecting it out onto someone else so that someone else*
*has to carry our so-called darkness. What I'm suggesting*
*is that we have to now begin to own our own darkness.*[203]
~MARION WOODMAN

We can ignore our own and the world's pain. The misfortune of doing so is, in fact, the norm and has brought us where we are. Suffering pain is a hallmark of our humility, and of our capacity to be part of the whole and resist our desire to excessively dominate others and the natural world. Most of our dysfunctional relationship to the world is rooted in trying to escape emotional pain. We shove it down it, drug it, distract from it, pleasure over it, and project and displace it. Through denial, we secretly build the lethal mega-bomb of our shadow, which we then drop on the unwitting, including ourselves.

The year of 2020 will be remembered as the year of COVID-19. Like the pandemic, the darkness of climate crisis appears separate from our inner lives. Yet, what threatens from the outside has grown out of what we've killed inside us. This is especially obvious with climate change, as the external dynamic of ecocide is of our own making. Climate crisis is but one symptom of the many

---

203. Horváth, "Marion Woodman: Holding the Tension of the Opposites."

ways we have disavowed ourselves. In contrast, when we face and die through our pain, we come alive via our finer jewels of being human to heal the world.

Ecocide begins as a smarting, dark corner or an invisible, roiling storm of pain and disconnection inside us. At any moment, however, we can befriend our difficult emotions to reduce our pain and not discharge it onto one another and the Earth. If we have already displaced it, we can own our error, make amends, and adjust our actions. This is how we begin to withdraw the shadow we have asked others to "carry" by imposing our "so-called darkness" onto them. Marion Woodman calls it "so-called darkness" because our shadow is only malevolent when we disown and unconsciously act it out. When we own and work with our shadow, we allow it to birth our finer jewels and, at the least, keep our violence in check.

When we cease deranged activities and own our darkness, Yin and Yang begin to notice, converse, and cocreate once again. Thus begins the re-fertilization and blossoming of our world. This is a return to regenerative psyche: to a balance of rest and activity, to productivity and replenishment, to inner reflection, for wise action. It is a return to justice and integrity, to all that nourishes our relationships and our body-minds, rebuilds the soil, purifies the waters, and reinvigorates the air. We can and should press our governments, but we cannot wait for them to do this for us. We have to do it. And we have to show others the way, so more of us can muster the gumption to successfully degrow, resist, and renew.

## Our Many Forms of Exhaling

On the most practical level, we can resist the irremediable process of genetically engineering our food, which has contributed to the insect apocalypse and is escalating our deadly dependence on ever-more complex, untested pesticide cocktails. We can also reject the barrage of synthetic, toxic chemicals in the innumerable common products that fill our homes—such as artificially scented laundry detergents, air fresheners, colognes and perfumes—and are linked to allergies, depression and anxiety, sperm damage, autism, obesity, endocrine disruption, and cancer.[204] We must ban chemical products that outgas to the

---

204. Sigurdson, "Expert Panel Confirms Fragrance Ingredient Can Cause Cancer."; Nelson, "Fragrance Is the New Secondhand Smoke."

environment, and dismantle those that needlessly gas it, such as two- and four-stroke motors—especially leaf blowers. These *many forms of exhaling* share similar shadow poetics with our other $CO_2$ emissions, and the increasing methane releases from farming cattle and melting Arctic permafrost.

We must stop believing it's better to live in a synthetic, toxic slurry of "progress" than within moderate means that include a rational measure of technology. To stop burning up the planet we must reclaim our cool, or there will quickly be no life left to build upon. Maverick scientist and author Dr. Guy McPherson says, "If you think the economy is more important than the environment, try holding your breath while counting your money."[205] To breathe better, we must become integrated dark *and* light Earth citizens capable of living with more outer simplicity in exchange for a richer inner life. This includes breaking the many faces of the addiction cycle, which works squarely against the fertility cycle. Making the dark conscious, we become ripe for wisdom and more likely to choose heartfelt, common sense for the common good.

## Paradox for the Win

If we can't prevent nature from destroying us (because we have destroyed it), can we, as Carolyn Baker proposes, "collapse consciously"?[206] As a last gesture of dignity, can we work to save what is beautiful and sacred? Even if we despair, every desert poppy, needlessly scorched koala, or stranded orangutan that we can rescue or protect matters. Can we open our hearts to courageously face our folly and feel the ache of these times, especially the pain of the untold ecosystems we have injured along the way? When our hearts are heavy with unresolved grief, urban pollution and neurosis, frivolous distraction, and addiction to the unimportant, there's little room for the freedom to care for anything but ourselves. We can begin cleaning up our inner and outer acts at any moment.

Contrary to what the media and mega-corporations want us to believe, our difficult emotions are deeply liberating. They are the secret paths to sovereignty and freedom from mercenary maniacs' control over us—those who, for millennia, have tried to brainwash us into believing wholeness and freedom can't be found in heartbreak, outward simplicity, the beauty of the natural

205. McPherson, "Time for a Revolution."
206. Baker, *Sacred Demise: Walking the Spiritual Path of Industrial Civilization's Collapse.*

world, the dark earth beneath our feet, and the wisdom of our own bodies. This is the biggest lie and it's sold to us in every conceivable way. These dark domains are in fact what make us truly great, deeply humane, and able to care enough to live regeneratively on the planet. Like the phoenix they represent, our dark emotions harbor all the light we need to rise through the rubble of climate breakdown.

In the most absurd irony, our dark emotions gift us what we search for in trying to avoid them. "So without knowing it, your whole life is regulated by fear and pain that you're trying to escape from in various ways," says addiction expert Dr. Gabor Maté.[207] I invite us to step off this road to nowhere, break open, and live through the transformation of our core wounds into their obverse—our finer jewels of being human—faithful to the deep wisdom of Yin-Yang and the cycle of the seasons. When we revive this natural wheel of transformation inside us, we can join with and care more deeply for the natural world and one another, cleaving our love to the welfare of all. This is the embodied magic of living paradoxically, which is to live poetically and to feel the world come alive in us through our collective heartache and ensuing renewal.

## Vulnerable Strength

For the treasures we can't rescue in time, we can generate a quality of heart to expand and bend with the demise of the biosphere in passionate, broken-open witnessing. We may not be able to save ourselves or millions more species from extinction, but we can cherish and protect the good that remains, and what's beautiful inside and shared among us. To this end, reviving our triangle of resilience relationships—inner work, nature connection, human community—is an honest and genuinely hopeful way forward.

Revolution germinates in our own bodies, via inner activism and sacred permission. It puts down roots and grows through the building of sustainable Yin resources: spending quality time with one another, embracing our dark hearts, sharing embodied love, creating gardens and art, slowing down and minimizing, and sharing nurturing touch. It flowers through the embrac-

---

207. Caparrotta, "Dr. Gabor Maté on Childhood Trauma, the Real Cause of Anxiety and Our 'Insane' Culture."

ing of regenerative Yang: clear thinking, mobilizing and channeling healthy anger, courageously confronting unhealthy fears, resisting greed and addiction, protesting, and fighting for justice. Resiliency grows most robustly when we allow ourselves to be changed by our difficult emotions and the difficult news, by staying close enough to vital silence, one another, and the natural rhythms inside and outside us. This way, we can feel what is diseased and live close enough to reality to build a saner world.

## A Fear of Deaths

The paradox we fail to embrace returns to us as tragic irony. The metaphorical deaths we avoid return to us as literal death and destruction. Anthropologist and Pulitzer Prize-winning author Ernest Becker posits that our fear of death causes us to act so violently toward one another.[208] I wonder if it isn't our fear of *psychological* (metaphorical) death—of passing through death and rebirth while alive—that frightens us at least as much, and fuels our irrational cruelty.

American author and professor Norman Cousins proposed that dying with unlived lives inside us is more tragic than death itself. If so, we must seek to psychologically "die" while we're alive, so as not to accumulate too much infertile darkness and thereby suffer an infertile death with too much unlived life left inside us. When we live fully, I imagine we can face death with more equanimity, because we have not let too much infertile darkness accumulate inside and around us. This possibility is consistent with the epiphany many experience on their death beds, who wish they had dedicated themselves to what mattered more.

Some might argue that the urgency to live a full, meaningful life stems from a fear of death, or of dying a meaningless death. But, Holocaust survivor and hero Viktor Frankl says, "In some way, suffering ceases to be suffering at the moment it finds a meaning, such as the meaning of a sacrifice."[209] Since life is full of suffering, meaning in life is not dispensable and allows us to endure the worst. Facing literal death incites an urgency to live more fully, for *life is short* and *time is precious*. Climate crisis adds potency to this charge, presenting us with the ultimate death and rebirth initiation, and therefore the opportunity

---

208. Solomon, "Ernest Becker & The Denial of Death."
209. Frankl, *Man's Search for Meaning: Revised and Updated,* 117.

to most fully live. For myself, this includes Yang and Yin, respectively: I dedicate myself to the most heartfelt, passionate work I can on behalf of all, while making time to enjoy and be renewed by the simplest, and therefore most awesome, natural pleasures.

There is interplay among our capacities to care, to live well, to die while still alive, and finally to die fulfilled and less afraid. Becker says, "The irony of man's condition is that the deepest need is to be free of the anxiety of death and annihilation; but it is life itself which awakens it, and so we must shrink from being fully alive."[210] While I largely abide Becker's conclusions, I disagree that we *must* shrink from being fully alive. The key to unlock Becker's catch-22 is to die through our pain by grieving our hurts past and present. This way, we come more fully alive, thus uncoupling the cause (daily living) and effect (anxiety and shrinking from life) Becker describes, which I describe in the following poem:

### Common Ground

*So many fear the great death,*
*But dying a little each day*
*Deepens, decompresses*
*That same ground in us,*
*Molding our inevitable demise*
*Into an urn that drinks us*
*For eternity.*

## Withdrawing Our Shadow

Jung believed the most effective social, political, and spiritual work we can do is to withdraw from projecting our shadow onto another. In our discussion, *another* includes the Earth itself. If we are to heal our protracted self-loathing and our pervasive addiction to try to fill what must remain vitally (spiritually) empty inside us, as well as claim any politico-corporate victory, we must win the battle of reclaiming our emotional shadow and become capable of living without the specious power of junk things and toxic ideas that fail to fulfill us

---

210. Becker, *The Denial of Death*, 66.

and regenerate the biosphere. With this new freedom, we can rebirth a more sustainable summer from the depths of our present, infertile winter.

We withdraw our shadow by owning it and ceasing to project it. We embrace our ungrieved losses and unclaimed talents, our misplaced love and unrealized passions, our heartfelt dreams and pause-inducing nostalgias, as well as all that we cannot change. Outwardly, we remember, nurture, and spend time with animals and plants, mountains and bodies of water, lichens and soils—that are all unreasonably injured at our behest. We surrender to beauty by facing both the awe and suffering of our times, by trusting in the capacity of our hearts to be rebirthed from what brings us to our knees. This way, we might navigate the coming years of personal and collective crisis not only with more holy heartbreak and remunerative grief, but with more compassion, passion, and meaning than we thought possible.

Let us, then, find the courage to make our daily work that which honors our bodies, our entrusted chunks of Earth. We can take a vow of humility for the now-desperate hope to return richness and sanity to a world gone mad on external power and material fundamentalism—the symptoms of inner vacuity that spoil the party for those of us in love with outer simplicity and inner richness. Or, more practically, for the promise of tomorrow.

May we begin in earnest what we have neglected, which is not only to expose our hearts to ourselves, but to the natural world and each other. Whatever personal dark-night-of-the-soul work we have done prepares us for these times. Whatever more we have left should be commenced, as our disavowed inner lives increasingly close in on us from outside in the form of climate collapse, to which we can barely extend our trembling hands from our too-busy, overwhelmed lives.

There is yet much to celebrate, to be passionate about, and to engage. Let us enter our collective dark heart of healing together with the light of love we already have in hand to rebirth our care, so that "everything glows a little more from our presence here."[211] Through grief and shadow work, renewed intimacy with one another, and nature connection, we can fulfill the body of love as regeneration on every level.

---

211. Weber, "Thanksgiving: an Activist's Grace."

When we know that metaphorical death is truly the birth of our fuller selves, we can more confidently enter paradoxical healing and avoid lethal ironies. This is how we become more conscious of our unconscious, so we are *able* to choose a different fate, so we do not destroy ourselves further "through the might" of our "own technology and science."[212] May this path catalyze our cure, our hearts as one with the Earth and other humans, as medicine for our times.

## The Bottom Line

At the end of the day, we have to act differently—very differently. We must face, weather, and mitigate climate crisis by way of regenerative revolution. We must also rebel, because it's quite possible the corporate elite are well aware of the crisis at hand and deliberately allowing the world to burn (Resource 2: Plested, "How the Rich Plan," and Hedges, "Saving the Planet").

I have tried to expose the largely unseen factors that, unless recognized and worked with, prevent us from being the change we must. Changing our lifestyles is indeed "hitched to every other thing."[213] Curbing consumerism and fossil fuel use, as well as restoring enough of the natural world, are more difficult than they seem.

Ninety corporations create two-thirds of global emissions.[214] Please pause and just consider that for a moment. Our individual, bottom-up actions are no longer enough. We must make global, top-down changes. This is what brave young climate activists and Extinction Rebellion are pressing government to do, as we work to reach the critical 3.5 percent of the population threshold needed for massive social change. Make time for these efforts today by radically minimizing your life and dedicating yourself to inner work, to commune and enjoy time with others, and to engage in direct climate action.

If you can significantly reduce your carbon footprint and sustainably rebel without any of the healing offered in this book, fantastic. I believe some can do this and tolerate the sacrifices. Many, if not most of us, require more effort.

---

212. Jung, *The Undiscovered Self*, 110.

213. Muir, *My First Summer in the Sierra*, quoted in Laura Moncur's Motivational Quotations.

214. Goldenberg, "Just 90 Companies Caused Two-thirds of Man-made Global Warming Emissions."

Once we take a step outside the status quo of business as usual, invisible psycho-spiritual obstacles we didn't know existed come to light. Left unchallenged, these emotional wounds, unconscious biases, and irrational fears and anxieties neutralize our will to change and prevent us from sane progress. They are the same drivers that engendered and perpetuated our current chaos. Building triangle of resilience relationships helps us overcome these obstacles, to better cope and thrive through decline and any degree of renewal we can muster. Yet, because the climate bewitching hour is here, we must now make rebellion for top-down policy change our climate cure priority.

Renewable energy does not seem to be enough to save us from the worst of climate crisis. While they can help, renewables also require massive amounts of fossil fuels to produce and maintain. I don't think we are going to plant enough trees that can survive. I think we will spray the skies to reflect the sun's rays sooner than later and suffer its perils. I hope I'm wrong. Meanwhile, the most promising adjustment to our lifestyles we can now make is radical degrowth—cutting consumption, waste, and especially fossil fuel use—in essence, radically minimizing our impact and localizing our lives. We must walk away from empire.

———

Thankfully, the good word is out now about our bad situation. Climate crisis is real and rapidly descending upon us. Personal and planetary transformation are needed now, whether we like it or not. We've turned away from this challenge for too long, which is why we are in cataclysm. I hope the information I've shared with you has bolstered your mental, emotional, and spiritual preparation, and that it helps you mobilize outwardly, wholeheartedly, and effectively.

I imagine outer climate solutions are going to be coming faster and more furiously as conditions deteriorate. We must implement any of these fixes judiciously, even if they are only branch treatments for root problems. With some very good fortune, their exponential effects—be they any combination of renewables, geoengineering, artificial $CO_2$ sequestration methods, regenerative agriculture, degrowth, and planting billions of carbon-capturing trees—may help us prolong our lives and save the species that remain. They could buy us time to slow the locomotive of modern civilization. This wouldn't be regression, but a return to perennial values of decency, a lower *standard of living* in the name of survival, and leading more meaningful, compassionate lives. This could increase our *quality of living*. Ancient, Earth-centered wisdom is also invaluable for creating this new culture. Nature-ignorant despots and climate denialists must be swiftly dismissed; make sure you vote accordingly.

With your effort and resilience to expose yourself to reality, to better thrive and to care enough to be more directly engaged, we can change the tides—or at least some tides. Whether or not we can save ourselves and what's left of what we love is unknown. I sure hope you'll try with me. You are the answer. So am I. Yet, my effort is not enough without yours, and yours is not enough without mine. I encourage you to continue to embrace paradox: to embrace what's uncomfortable and to balance it with simple, wholesome pleasures. I will too. This is what's needed to save ourselves, so we and especially our children can enjoy a safer and saner world than we've ever known.

---

### • CONCLUSION EXERCISE •

Take out your journal or notepad, place it in front of you, and enjoy creating your responses to the following:

Now that you've completed this book, let's bring all the information together, beginning deep in your heart and manifesting out in the world. Below are three writing prompts and a final action prompt. Remember, there are no right or wrong answers, just honestly assessing where you are right now.

1. On a fresh sheet of paper, write down your responses to the following, even if there is some overlap from previous exercises. This is an overall, gut-level, final inventory:

    • Sit quietly, close your eyes, and feel deep into your essence. On a scale from zero to ten, rate how much you care for your life, the more-than-human world, and (y)our children.

    • Then, write down to what degree you feel it's worth mobilizing for climate action and how you see yourself engaging this.

    • After reading this book, how committed are you to your self-growth for the greater good?

- Which of the many recommendations and self-help tools from any of the chapters stand out as most important for you?

- Which unnecessary or unhelpful activities, distractions, or burdens are you willing to forego to take better care of yourself, others, and the natural world?

- Which emotions do you imagine will challenge you as you make any of the above changes in your life? What support can you garner to help you through these challenges?

2. Which unique gifts do you bring to addressing any aspect of climate crisis and how can you more fully exercise them?

3. On a fresh sheet of paper, write down the most empowered and fulfilling life you can imagine living as we all journey through climate crisis together.

4. Are you ready to live this life?

# Appendix I
# THE SCIENCE OF
# CLIMATE CRISIS

*Listen to the science.*[215]

~CLIMATE ACTIVIST GRETA THUNBERG ADDRESSING DONALD TRUMP

Climate science tells us just how dire our situation is, informing us how to respond, and to what degree. Comprehensive solutions must incorporate our emotional and spiritual responses as well as pragmatic actions. I therefore present a unique synthesis of climate science to provide poignant context for our climate healing journey.

The fourteen climate change-related themes presented here summarize the most compelling, surprising, and up-to-date (as of this writing) scientific evidence for our climate predicament. For the sake of concision, I have summarized these findings. You can find the full elaboration (including an additional theme) at my website (Resource 2: Weber, "The Science"), which I update as new studies emerge. In many cases, I cite popular articles that are more reader-friendly than posting lengthy and tedious scientific journal studies, though many of these studies are also linked in the articles provided. This will enable you to easily read more about any of the topics discussed.

The inner and outer climate cure measures I have proposed throughout this book would not be so urgent if our global crisis weren't so dire. So, be

---

215. Goodenough, "16-Year-Old Climate Activist Says Trump Obviously Doesn't 'Listen to the Science'."

forewarned, the following section does not paint a pretty picture, though there is some good news. As *New York Times* columnist and author David Wallace-Wells has written: "The number of 'good news' scientific papers … I could probably count on my two hands. The 'bad news' papers number probably in the thousands."[216] The difficult news apprises us of the extraordinarily daunting challenges if we want to save ourselves and the planet. It's imperative to have a comprehensive understanding of these issues to begin to truly grasp the scope of our problem and inform our responses.

Without a relatively in-depth understanding of the science, it's easy to make wrong, unconscious assumptions. For example, you might assume that just because you can hold the miracle of an iPhone in your hand—a gadget possessing more than 100,000 times the processing power of the Apollo 11 computer that landed us on the moon fifty years ago[217]—this implicitly means we have a cure for the climate problem. We don't. There are, however, many partial and possible solutions currently being contemplated, implemented to varying degrees, and researched. You also might also not know that massive climate damages are unfolding worldwide, right now, and that worse changes are in store. As environmental scientist James Conca writes in *Forbes*, "… There is no way to reduce carbon emissions in the next twenty years sufficient to mitigate the worst effects of climate change."[218]

If at any point you feel overwhelmed with the information presented in this section (or especially in the full text online), I invite you to pace yourself accordingly. To learn the basics of climate science, you can watch the short video by *National Geographic*, "Causes and Effects of Climate Change."[219]

None of the information you'll find ahead means we are doomed, at least not to extinction. It does describe our current condition and portends severe future challenges, especially if we do not do enough. No combination of readily implementable techno-fixes currently exists to save us from the worst of climate disruption. And, because retooling our entire economy and energy

---

216. Wallace-Wells, "Time to Panic: The Planet is Getting Warmer in Catastrophic Ways. And Fear May Be the Only Thing That Saves us."
217. Kendall, "Your Mobile Phone vs. Apollo 11's Guidance Computer."
218. Conca, "Why Solar Geoengineering May Be Our Only Hope to Reverse Global Warming."
219. National Geographic, "Causes and Effects of Climate Change," video.

infrastructure would take a massive toll on the already imperiled natural world (and humans too), I maintain that the optimal method for climate crisis mitigation is comprehensive degrowth.

Degrowth, or using less—a lot less—of everything that contributes to environmental and societal decline also means accepting a "lower" standard of living.[220] This is a radically sane, most wise form of climate action, especially because it (1) starves capitalism and undermines mercenary dishonesty, (2) directly decreases pollution and greenhouse gases (GHGs), and (3) immediately benefits the environment because we extract less from it. Unfortunately, minimizing consumption, "lowering" our standard of living, and drastically localizing commerce is not how many in developed nations (which produce the most GHGs) choose to exercise privilege, as political blogger Kevin Drum explains in his essay, "Why Climate Change Is So Hard."[221] Nor can the underprivileged afford to abdicate their meager livelihoods as they clear the Amazon rainforest for cattle raising, decimate the Indonesian jungle for palm oil plantations, and poison the land while mining rare metals like cobalt and lithium.[222] If wealthier nations could decrease demand, exploitation of the Earth would also decline. Instead, we protect immediate, excessive comforts at the expense of sowing the seeds for a disastrous future. We are addicted to more progress, which means more consumption and more desecration of the natural world.

As we accept this continued progress and consumption, then, we must work from many different angles to turn the downward spiral of climate crisis upward. Just as we do not know the exponential effects of current disrupting climate feedback loops, we cannot know the combined, exponential effects of mitigating solutions. This said, I present here a summary of our current predicament, which themes include: temperature rise, emissions, heat records, oceans, ice, the Gulf Stream, Bitcoin and big pharma, tipping points, wildfires and floods, methane and permafrost, species extinction, IPCC conservatism, reforestation and deforestation, and bullying and censorship of climate scientists.

---

220. Gauthier,"The Limits of Renewable Energy and the Case for Degrowth."
221. Drum, "Why Climate Change Is So Hard."
222. Conca, "Blood Batteries - Cobalt and the Congo."

# 1. Temperature Rise

Many scientists now report the likelihood of catastrophic climate breakdown occurring much sooner than the proverbial 2100 doomsday date cited in many scientific studies and popular climate change headlines. Highly respected Penn State climate scientist Michael Mann says, "We are seeing increases in extreme weather events that go well beyond what has been predicted or projected in the past. Increasingly, the science suggests that many of the impacts are occurring earlier and with greater amplitude than was predicted."[223] This view is pervasively echoed among climate scientists. Stanford researchers have warned that if we continue business as usual, "annual temperatures over North America, Europe and East Asia will increase 2–4 °C by 2046–2065."[224] These levels, which equate to a 3.6–7.2 degrees Fahrenheit rise, portend disaster.

# 2. Emissions

A 1.5 °C temperature rise above preindustrial levels is considered to be a catastrophic threshold beyond which significantly more severe climate disruption effects will likely result.[225] The IPCC says that to keep preindustrial temperature rise below +1.5°C, by 2030 we must reduce global carbon emissions by 45 percent.[226] But a little-known fact of the report is that to meet this goal, emissions must peak in 2020.[227] According to a landmark study by a group of top scientists from the World Meteorological Organization, not only are emissions *not* expected to peak in 2020, they are not expected to peak even by 2030.[228] We are therefore perilously behind in safeguarding our future.

Even if we were to have stopped all our emissions in 2017—which we did not, and instead have increased them through 2018 and 2019—another peer-reviewed study[229] shows that at least a +1.3°C temperature rise above

---

223. Berwyn, "Climate Change Is Happening Faster Than Expected, and It's More Extreme."

224. Carey, "Climate Change on Pace to Occur 10 Times Faster than any Change Recorded in Past 65 Million Years, Stanford Scientists Say."

225. IPCC, "Summary for Policymakers of IPCC Special Report on Global Warming of 1.5°C Approved by Governments."

226. Ibid.

227. M2020, "The Climate Turning Point."

228. WMO, "Landmark United in Science Report Informs Climate Action Summit."

229. Mauritsen and Pincus, "Committed Warming Inferred from Observations."

pre-industrial levels is already baked in to the climate equation for 2100. Scientists call this phenomenon "committed warming." This is because $CO_2$ emissions take many years (10.1 to be exact, explained shortly) to exert their full warming effect.[230] In other words, even if we stopped all emissions now, newly released $CO_2$ released prior to the stopping point would take another decade to exert its full effect.

The time lag for a molecule of $CO_2$ to exert its maximum warming effect was previously thought to be about forty years.[231] But a more recent, peer-reviewed study shows "it takes just ten years for a single emission of carbon dioxide ($CO_2$) to have its maximum warming effects on the Earth."[232] This means our emissions reach maximal effect during most of our lifetimes, not just in our children's, and not beginning in 2100. After this time, $CO_2$ remains in the atmosphere for thousands of years.[233]

Though it is theoretically feasible, we cannot in fact stop all emissions now, according to Myles Allen, a climate scientist contributing to the IPCC (Intergovernmental Panel on Climate Change) report. He says computer models show the soonest we can reach net-zero carbon—*and still keep the lights on*—is between the years 2040 to 2050; this means "we may well already be committed to a 1.5 degrees Celsius" global temperature rise.[234] Harvard atmospheric scientist James Anderson states that we must not only halt carbon pollution and remove it from the atmosphere, but also engage in a "new effort to reflect sunlight away from the earth's poles" to slow the melting ice caps. And this must be done ... by 2023.[235]

Culminating in 2050, the United States is set to unleash the world's largest influx of $CO_2$ emissions from new oil and gas development. "U.S. drilling

---

230. Ricke and Caldeira, "Maximum Warming Occurs about One Decade After a Carbon Dioxide Emission."

231. Marshall, "Climate Change: The 40 Year Delay Between Cause and Effect."

232. Ricke and Caldeira, "Maximum Warming Occurs about One Decade After a Carbon Dioxide Emission."

233. Archer and Brovkin, "The Millennial Atmospheric Lifetime of Anthropogenic $CO_2$ "

234. Allen, "The Green New Deal: One Climate Scientist's View, from the Other Side of the Atlantic."

235. McMahon, "We Have Five Years to Save Ourselves from Climate Change, Harvard Scientist Says."

into new oil and gas reserves—primarily shale—could unlock 120 billion metric tons of $CO_2$ emissions, which is equivalent to the lifetime $CO_2$ emissions of nearly 1,000 coal-fired power plants."[236] Despite urgent IPCC warnings, fossil fuel giants hope to invest trillions of dollars into new field exploration and development in the next decades.[237] Fearing that fossil fuel demand might decline, petrochemical companies like ExxonMobil, Shell, and Saudi Aramco are poised to increase plastic production (which utilizes oil, gas, and their byproducts) through 2050, driving half the world's oil demand and growth toward this aim and doubling the amount of plastic produced by 2040.[238]

Translating our energy consumption into more fathomable terms, Mark P. Mills writes in *Forbes*, "Roughly 85 percent of global energy comes from oil, coal and natural gas. For perspective, consider that if global hydrocarbons were all produced in the form of oil and stacked up in a row of barrels, that row would stretch from Washington D.C. to Los Angeles, and would grow in height by a Washington monument every single week."[239] Take that in for a moment.

Adding to the problem, energy requirements in developing countries, led by China and India, are projected to double by approximately 2040.[240] Massive wildfires and other natural disasters also contribute both to atmospheric and terrestrial pollution, as well as increased $CO_2$ levels.[241] These disasters accelerate warming, which precipitates further natural disasters, spiraling exponentially in a positive feedback loop.

---

236. "Drilling Toward Disaster: Why U.S. Oil and Gas Expansion is Incompatible with Climate Limits."

237. Galey, "$5-tn Fuel Exploration Plans 'Incompatible' with Climate Goals."

238. Gardiner, "A Surge of New Plastic Is About to Hit the Planet."

239. Mills, "'You Say You Want a Revolution' in the Physics of Energy: Good Luck Green New Deal."

240. Neuhauser, "Despite Climate Pledges, Global Energy Emissions on the Rise."

241. Berwyn, "How Wildfires Can Affect Climate Change (and Vice Versa)."

## 3. Heat Records

July, 2019, was the hottest month,[242] and 2019 the second-warmest year in recorded history.[243]

According to NASA, 2016 was Earth's warmest year on record, while 2017 had been the second-warmest prior to 2019.[244] 2016 surpassed 2015's heat record, which broke the 2014 record. This was the first time in recorded history the average global temperature broke records three years in a row.[245] 2018 has been declared the fourth hottest, "which means that the past five years have been the five warmest years in the modern record."[246] It also means that of the nineteen hottest years on record, eighteen will have occurred since 2001.[247] And there is now about a 75 percent chance 2020 will be the warmest year on record.[248] Moreover, these heat extremes are concentrating in the Arctic— where we need ice, not meltwater—with temperatures some twenty to thirty degrees, and as high as forty and fifty degrees Fahrenheit above average in 2016 and 2018.[249]

## 4. Oceans

The Earth's oceans absorb most of the carbon dioxide from our emissions. If it weren't for the oceans, our planet would be a broiling mess. Oceans have absorbed 93 percent of warming caused by our emissions, so only a small percentage of this increased heat shows up in the atmosphere and at the Earth's surface. How much heat is this? Fathom for yourself: "Research indicates that

---

242. National Oceanic and Atmospheric Association, "July 2019 Was Hottest Month on Record for the Planet."

243. Fountain and Popovich, "2019 Was the Second-Hottest Year Ever, Closing Out the Warmest Decade."

244. Yale School of Forestry & Environmental Studies, "It's Official: 2017 Was the Second Hottest Year on Record."

245. Gillis, "Earth Sets a Temperature Record for the Third Straight Year."

246. Miller, "Earth Just Experienced One of the Warmest Years on Record."

247. Ibid.

248. NOAA National Centers for Environmental Information, "Global Climate Report- March 2020."

249. Climate Nexus, "Temperatures Skyrocket in Arctic, Prompt Desperate 'Refreeze' Plan."; Samenow, "Red-hot Planet: All-time Heat Records Have Been Set All over the World During the Past Week."

since 1970, the world's oceans have absorbed 251 zettajoules of energy. But zettajoules are a pretty esoteric way of talking about heat. In more relatable terms, just one zettajoule would be enough to power twenty-five billion average American homes for a year." *Twenty-five billion homes.* This amount of energy is equivalent to forty-three times the amount of energy consumed in the United States in 2012.[250]

Oceans are warmed by all the heat they absorb, and acidified by their absorption of $CO_2$. While the oceans are protecting us from the worst effects of our excesses, rising ocean temperatures and increased acidification also mean incrementally less $CO_2$ can dissolve in the oceans.[251] The oceans will therefore progressively provide less and less of this buffering in the future. We won't be able to rely on the oceans' grace for much longer.

Hotter and more $CO_2$-laden oceans are causing the demise of coral reefs and other marine life. An exception is jellyfish, which are proliferating dangerously and choking life out of the seas.[252] These developments are in addition to the massive pollution problem of plastics that are further suffocating the oceans, with plastic microparticles finding their way into all forms of life there[253] and spreading into every nook and cranny of the globe.

All the world's coral reefs are in danger of disappearing by 2050 due to heat stress, acidification, and resultant bleaching.[254] The largest living structure on Earth, the majestic and once incredibly biodiverse Great Barrier Reef near Australia, is in steep decline.[255] [256]

Similar to Earth's surface temperatures, ocean temperatures have broken records for several straight years, while 2018 was the warmest year yet.[257] The oceans are not only warming more quickly but are also warmer than we

---

250. Kahn, "Looking for Global Warming? Check the Ocean."

251. Riebeck, "The Ocean's Carbon Balance;" Harnung and Johnson, *Chemistry and the Environment,* 186.

252. Jiang and Fegan, "Jellyfish are Causing Mayhem As Pollution, Climate Change See Numbers Boom."

253. Le Guern, "When the Mermaids Cry: The Great Plastic Tide."

254. Parker and Welch, "Coral Reefs Could Be Gone in 30 Years."

255. Woody, "Coral Cover on Great Barrier Reef Is in Steep Decline."

256. Hoegh-Guldberg, "The Decline of the Great Barrier Reef."

257. Pierre-Louis, "Ocean Warming Is Accelerating Faster than Thought, New Research Finds."

thought.[258] In fact, oceans are heating up 40 percent faster on average than a United Nations panel estimated five years ago.[259] Climate change is proceeding faster than previously expected and its effects are greater than those the IPCC factored into their climate models. The result is the IPCC modeling predictions are unrealistically favorable, despite already being dire; more on this just ahead.

## 5. Ice

In the Arctic, Greenland's enormous ice sheet is melting at an accelerated rate. "The only thing we can do is adapt and mitigate further global warming—it's too late for there to be no effect. We are watching the ice sheet hit a tipping point," says Ohio State University geophysicist Michael Bevis, the lead author of this new study.[260] A separate study by Eric Rignot, et al., shows Antarctica is also melting faster than previously anticipated and contributing more than expected to sea level rise.[261] In 2017, a one hundred square-mile chunk of ice broke off from Antarctica's Pine Island Glacier.[262] In 2018 an iceberg five times the size of Manhattan (115 square miles) calved from the same glacier and quickly broke apart.[263] Pine Island Glacier also seems to be calving more frequently in recent years.[264] In 2017, Antarctica's Larsen C ice shelf lost a massive iceberg roughly the size of Delaware.[265] Dr. Michael Mann says that melting in Antarctica and Greenland in the last few years has "literally doubled our projections of the sea level rise at the end of this century." [266]

A more recent development in Antarctica is the Florida-sized Thwaites Glacier, dubbed "the most dangerous glacier in the world." Scientists have discovered

---

258. Lijing Cheng et al., "How Fast Are the Oceans Warming?"

259. Ibid.

260. Meixler, "'A Tipping Point.' Greenland's Ice Is Melting Much Faster than Previously Thought, Scientists Say."

261. Eric Rignot et al., "Four Decades of Antarctic Ice Sheet Mass Balance from 1979–2017."

262. Mooney, "A Key Antarctic Glacier Just Lost a Huge Piece of Ice—the Latest Sign of its Worrying Retreat."

263. Geggel, "Antarctica's Pine Island Glacier Just Lost Enough Ice to Cover Manhattan 5 Times Over."

264. Ibid.

265. New Scientist staff and Press Association, "A Massive Iceberg Just Broke off Antarctica's Larsen C Ice Shelf."

266. Borenstein, "Climate Change Is More Extensive and Worse than Once Thought."

a giant cavity under the glacier roughly two-thirds the size of Manhattan and the height of a 100-story building (1000 feet tall).[267] Unfortunately, a figurative filling or root canal won't work to fix this erosion. Incredibly, most of the missing fourteen billion tons of ice has melted over the last three years, suggesting the exponential damage caused by recent record-setting temperature increases. If Thwaites melts, it's estimated to raise sea levels by two feet. This is what New York University geoscientist David Holland refers to as "almost the entire story" for sea level rise.[268] The most concerning aspect of Thwaites, however, is its function as the linchpin to keep neighboring glaciers in place. This is why it's called "the most dangerous glacier in the world."[269] "When Thwaites collapses it will take most of West Antarctica with it," contributing an additional ten to thirteen feet of sea level rise.[270]

## 6. The Gulf Stream and Thermohaline Weakening

Scientists are concerned that climate change could continue to weaken or even shut down the Gulf Stream, an ocean current that regulates temperature from the tropics to the Arctic. "A collapse could result in widespread cooling throughout the North Atlantic and Europe, increased sea ice in the North Atlantic, changes in tropical precipitation patterns, stronger North Atlantic storms, reduced precipitation and river flow, as well as reduced crop productivity in Europe. These effects would impact many regions around the globe."[271] While scientists believe a shutdown is unlikely, the risk is real and presents a major potential tipping point.

## 7. Bitcoin and Big Pharma

You might be surprised to learn that the mining of Bitcoin, if it stays on its current growth trajectory, can alone prevent us from meeting critical climate targets. This is due to the tremendous amount of electricity required to mine it

---

267. Dockrill, "Scientists Have Detected an Enormous Cavity Growing beneath Antarctica."
268. Geib, "Boaty McBoatface Is About to Investigate the 'Most Dangerous Glacier in The World'."
269. Ibid.
270. Pakalolo, "A Glacier the Size of Florida Is on Track to Change the Course of Human Civilization."
271. Cho, "Could Climate Change Shut Down the Gulf Stream?"

and the resultant creation of greenhouse gases. "A new study published in the peer-reviewed journal *Nature Climate Change* finds that if Bitcoin is implemented at similar rates at which other technologies have been incorporated, it alone could produce enough emissions to raise global temperatures by 2°C as soon as 2033."[272]

Big Pharma isn't much better. The pharmaceutical industry emits more $CO_2$ emissions than the automotive sector. "The total global emissions of the pharma sector amounts to about fifty-two megatonnes of $CO_2$ in 2015, more than the 46.4 megatonnes of $CO_2$ generated by the automotive sector in the same year."[273] Put them feathers in your hat.

## 8. Tipping Points

A topic frequently discussed in climate conversations is if we have passed the tipping point of no return. To this point, you've already learned about several "faster than expected" climate changes. An article from *The Guardian* titled, "Risks of 'Domino Effect' of Tipping Points Greater than Thought, Study Says" states: "Policymakers have severely underestimated the risks of ecological tipping points, according to a study that shows 45 percent of all potential environmental collapses are interrelated and could amplify one another ... Until recently, the study of tipping points was controversial, but it is increasingly accepted as an explanation for climate changes that are happening with more speed and ferocity than earlier computer models predicted. The loss of coral reefs and Arctic sea ice may already be past the point of no return. There are signs the Antarctic is heading the same way faster than thought."[274]

When changes continue faster than expected, they begin to grow exponentially due to positive feedback loops (which is what is meant by "environmental collapses are interrelated and could amplify one another"). Coauthor of the abovementioned study, Gary Peterson, says, "We're surprised at the rate of change in the Earth system. So much is happening at the same time and at a faster speed than we would have thought twenty years ago. That's a real concern.

---

272. University of Hawaii at Manoa, "Bitcoin Can Push Global Warming above 2 C in a Couple Decades."

273. Belkhir, "Big Pharma Emits More Greenhouse Gases than the Automotive Industry."

274. Watts, "Risks of 'Domino Effect' of Tipping Points Greater than Thought, Study Says."

We're heading ever faster toward the edge of a cliff."[275] What's more, the IPCC has inadequately accounted for these tipping points in its calculations, mentioning tipping points only a few times in its report. Founder of the Institute for Governance and Sustainable Development, Durwood Zaelke says, "The IPCC report fails to focus on the weakest link in the climate chain: the self-reinforcing feedbacks which, if allowed to continue, will accelerate warming and risk cascading climate tipping points and runaway warming."[276]

## 9. Wildfires and Floods

More ferocious, devastating wildfires fueled by climate change-driven drought, higher winds, and the deadwood of massive numbers of drought-stressed trees killed by insects have ravaged vast areas in California, Oregon, Washington, Canada, and Australia. Fires have burned across the Siberian taiga[277] and almost a dozen wildfires have reached above the Arctic Circle.[278] During the summer of 2019, more than 2.4 million acres burned in Canada and thirteen million acres burned in Siberia.[279] The most ferocious and extensive wildfires occurred across Australia in late 2019 into 2020, where thousands were forced onto the beaches and into the water for shelter against the encroaching blaze.[280] The tragic spectacle of millions of acres of burning Amazon rainforest flooded world headlines in late 2019. Scientists say that if approximately 20 percent of the Amazon burns it could reach a tipping point of no return, and as a result, that more than half the Amazon would become a savannah.[281]

In addition to fires ( a Yang force), their Yin counterpart, flooding, is also wreaking havoc. "Floods in inland areas are the most common type of natural disaster in the United States."[282] As sea levels rise, flooding will become

275. Ibid.

276. Harvey, "'Tipping Points' Could Exacerbate Climate Crisis, Scientists Fear."

277. Kahn, "Enormous Wildfires Are Spreading in Siberia."

278. Jonathon Watts, "Wildfires Rage in Arctic Circle as Sweden calls for help."

279. Fresco, "Huge Wildfires in the Arctic and Far North Send a Planetary Warning."

280. Yeung, Yee and McKenzie, "Thousands of Australian Residents Had to Take Refuge on a Beach as Wildfires Raged."

281. Montaigne, "Will Deforestation and Warming Push the Amazon to a Tipping Point?"

282. Union of Concerned Scientists, "Climate Change, Extreme Precipitation and Flooding: The Latest Science."

more of a problem, especially for the approximately 200 million people who live along coastlines fewer than fifteen feet (approximately three meters) above sea level.[283] Both fires and floods are slated to worsen in California and around the globe, bringing the "worst of both worlds."[284]

## 10. Methane and Permafrost

Because of warming temperatures, the melting of the Earth's permafrost in the Arctic is releasing more methane ($CH_4$), a greenhouse gas some eighty-four times more potent than $CO_2$ in the short term (approximately two decades).[285] While methane accounts for only 9 percent of total greenhouse gas emissions, it is a significant source of climate change exacerbation because of its powerful warming capacity.[286] More, while the peak heating effect of a $CO_2$ molecule occurs in about ten years, the peak effect of methane is reached in only months. Because methane warms much more quickly, it is currently responsible for about 25 percent of global warming.[287] One way to think about the relationship between $CO_2$ and $CH_4$ on global heating is: carbon dioxide controls how hot the planet ultimately gets, and methane controls how fast we get there.[288]

Dr. Natalia Shakhova at the University of Alaska, Fairbanks International Arctic Research Center[289] stated in 2008 that that a fifty-gigaton "burp" of methane (that's fifty billion tons) from the Eastern Siberian Arctic Shelf is "highly possible for abrupt release at any time,"[290] which could lead to catastrophic consequences for all life on the planet. More recently, in 2019, she reported this amount could potentially be more than 800 gigatons, which

283. World Ocean Review, "Living with the Oceans. A Report on the State of the World's Oceans."

284. Cowan, "Why 'The Worst of Both Worlds' Is in the Forecast."

285. Environmental Defense Fund, "Methane: The Other Important Greenhouse Gas."

286. Nyman, "Methane vs. Carbon Dioxide: A Greenhouse Gas Showdown."

287. Environmental Defense Fund, "Methane: The Other Important Greenhouse Gas."

288. Ocko, "UN Special Report Confirms Urgent Need to Reduce Methane Emissions."

289. "Methane Hydrates – Extended Interview Extracts with Natalia Shakhova."

290. N. Shakhova et al., "Anomalies of Methane in the Atmosphere Over the East Siberian Shelf: Is There any Sign of Methane Leakage from Shallow Shelf Hydrates?"

amount could have collected underground during one glacial period of approx-imately 100,000 years.[291]

A *Yale Climate Connections* column reports, "... It is likely a decent guess to speculate that the permafrost, and indeed the Arctic as a whole, is already at or very near a tipping point. The basis for such a claim is the simultaneous shift toward tipping points in a number of interconnected systems, many of which are positive reinforcing feedback mechanisms ... By acting now, and on a frantic global scale, we just might be able to delay the tipping and the climatic domino effect from taking hold."[292] But after tens of millions of acres of Siberian forest burned in 2018 and 2019, including massive burning of the Amazon, Africa, Indonesia, and Australia—our chances appear to be slimmer.

## 11. Species Extinction

We are currently losing species at 1,000 to 10,000 times the background rate, with 150 to 200 going extinct every day due to our many forms of exhaling.[293] In 2019, approximately 200 million animals burned in Bolivia's forest fires,[294] over one billion animals in the Australian bushfires,[295] and untold numbers of animals in the Amazon jungle. Koalas in Australia are near extinction, and orangutans are on the brink in Borneo and Sumatra due to habitat loss from human development.[296] Our current mass extinction event is the worst species die-off since the dinosaurs became extinct sixty-five million years ago.[297] Wild-life populations have diminished by an average of 60 percent over the last few decades.[298] Note, this is not 60 percent of individual animals but 60 percent of

---

291. Shakhova, Semiletov and Chuvilin, "Understanding the Permafrost–Hydrate System and Associated Methane Releases in the East Siberian Arctic Shelf."

292. Saha, "The Permafrost Bomb is Ticking."

293. Knight, "Biodiversity Loss: How Accurate Are the Numbers?"

294. Yale School of Forestry & Environmental Studies, "Wildfires in Bolivia Have Killed an Estimated 2 Million Animals So Far This Year."

295. Johnson, "More Than One Billion Animals Killed in Australia Wildfires Called a 'Very Conservative' Estimate."

296. "Why Are Orangutans in Danger of Becoming Extinct?," Orangutan Foundation International Australia.

297. "Halting the Extinction Crisis," Center for Biological Diversity.

298. Marshall, "Animal Populations Have Fallen 60 Percent and That's Bad Even if They Don't Go Extinct."

average population sizes. Unlike previous extinction events, however, humans are almost entirely responsible for the current mass die-off.

The most alarming extinctions, however, relate to insects. Entomologists know that insect loss is devastating to the biosphere, to which we also belong (surprise!). New Zealand bug expert Ruud Kleinpaste says of insects, "You go and take them out and all these things are falling over like a house of cards."[299] In a much-publicized study, the biomass of flying insects in a protected area in Germany—where we'd expect to find higher than average numbers— were down between 76 and 82 percent,[300] and according to a 2019 study, over 40 percent of insects worldwide are threatened with extinction.[301] The main cause is habitat lost to intensive, industrial-style agriculture. Synthetic fertilizers and pesticides, the introduction of invasive species, and climate change are additional causes. Climate change has especially affected tropical regions. The study's author Dr. Sanchez-Bayo concludes: "A rethinking of current agricultural practices, in particular a serious reduction in pesticide usage and its substitution with more sustainable, ecologically-based practices, is urgently needed to slow or reverse current trends, allow the recovery of declining insect populations and safeguard the vital ecosystem services they provide."[302] Thus, the problem with GMO crops, mentioned in chapter 9.

## 12. IPCC Conservatism

The IPCC (Intergovernmental Panel on Climate Change), a body of the United Nations (UN), is the world's authority on tracking climate change. It regularly interprets and disseminates a summary of climate change science, which governments use to help set policy, including that for greenhouse gas emissions.

It's noteworthy that the report-issuing branch of the IPCC is an assembly of government personnel, not scientists. Its reports are considered conservative for numerous reasons. One reason is that IPCC calculations, on the whole, do not

---

299. Palmer, "Insectageddon: New Zealanders Have 'Two Weeks of Life' after Insect Apocalypse – Expert."

300. Caspar A. Hallmann et al., "More than 75 Percent Decline over 27 Years in Total Flying Insect Biomass in Protected Areas."

301. Sanchez-Bayo and Wyckhuys, "Worldwide Decline of the Entomofauna: A Review of its Drivers."

302. Ibid.

account for tipping points, positive feedback loops, or methane releases. Carbon Capture and Sequestration/Storage—despite being included as a major mitigation method in many IPCC pathway projections to reduce emissions to stay below a 1.5°C rise—has not been widely implemented in the real world, and it in fact may be magical thinking to believe it can be.[303] Another reason is "there is no mention of the military sector's emissions in the fifth and latest IPCC assessment report."[304] Yet, the US Department of Defense "is the largest industrial consumer of fossil fuels in the world."[305] These statistics alone indicate significant underestimations by the IPCC.

Another cause for IPCC conservatism is that its contributing scientists need to be on board with any conclusion, so the information approved for publication is the least-common-denominator result. In other words, the IPCC makes a minimum set of recommendations that all scientists can agree on. This is both good and bad. It's good because we get more reliability. It's bad because largely conservative—and, apparently, underestimated—results make it through the review process. Another reason for conservatism is the IPCC editorial cutoff date, which precedes the publication of its reports by roughly two years. This means any new science released after the cutoff date is omitted because there isn't time for it to be properly reviewed and incorporated. The result is reports that are two years behind the cutting edge on the date they're issued. With the rapidly changing climate scene, IPCC data are essentially obsolete before official reports are released.[306]

Top climate scientists' conclusions also tend to be conservative.[307] Sir Robert Watson, a former NASA and British climate scientist who chaired the IPCC from 1997 to 2002, says, "Nonexperts who reject mainstream science often call scientists 'alarmists,' yet most researchers said they tend to shy away from worst-case scenarios. By nature, scientists said they are overly conservative. In

303. Heinberg, "The New IPCC Report Offers Climate Solutions that Depend on Magic."

304. Lorinez, "Demilitarization for Deep Decarbonization."

305. Ibid..

306. Farley, "Has the UN Climate Assessment Process Become Obsolete?"

307. Borenstein, "Climate Change Is More Extensive and Worse than Once Thought."; Holmes, "We Need to Accept We're Likely Underestimating the Climate Crisis."

nearly every case, when scientists were off the mark on something, it was by underestimating a problem, not overestimating."[308]

All this means we likely have much less time than the IPCC indicates.

## 13. Reforestation, Afforestation, and Deforestation

One of the more promising climate mitigation strategies is based on a study led by Dr. Thomas Crowther, who claims that planting 1.2 trillion new trees could absorb 200 gigatons of $CO_2$,[309] equivalent to about a decade of anthropogenic warming.[310] His method relies on the $CO_2$-sequestering power of trees. Considering a fleet of ten drones could plant up to 400,000 trees per day, planting a trillion new trees suddenly seems achievable.[311]

Spearheading efforts to plant a trillion trees is the "Trillion Trees" organization[312] led by Felix Finkbeiner, a twenty-one-year-old activist and PhD student in Crowther's lab who—with the help of 100,000 other youth between nine and twelve years old—planted his millionth tree when he was just twelve years old. "Forests are not only the livelihood of billions, but for us children forests are our future," he says.[313]

The journal *Science*, however, has published four highly critical comments of Crowther's work by other climate scientists. They claim that Crowther overestimated the amount of carbon trees could hold by a factor of five. They also highlighted other mistakes, such as that much of the land where these trees would be planted have other plants (already sequestering carbon) living there. Better than trees, therefore, might be to restore grasslands in drought- and wildfire-ravaged regions.[314]

---

308. Borenstein, "Climate Change Is More Extensive and Worse Than Once Thought."

309. Irwin, "The Ecologist Who Wants to Map Everything."

310. Gabbatiss, "Massive Restoration of World's Forests Would Cancel out a Decade of CO2 Emissions, Analysis Suggests."

311. Peters, "These Tree-planting Drones Are Firing Seed Missiles to Restore the World's Forests."

312. "One Trillion Trees Re-Grown, Saved from Loss and Better Protected Around the World by 2050," trilliontrees.org.

313. Large, "German 12-Year-old Boy Plants 1Million Trees, Takes Over UN Program to Plant a Trillion More."

314. Kerlin, "Grasslands More Reliable Carbon Sink Than Trees."

Trees, grasses, and other plants are arguably our best means to sequester carbon in the atmosphere.[315] While they offer a partial and potential short-term solution, reforestation and afforestation, along with other emission-reducing strategies, could buy us some time to become more truly sustainable.

We also must not forget that a cooperative effect from many innovations in combination—from renewables, tree planting, and soil regeneration, for example—could create exponential results to reduce climate crisis. It's important to think about the cumulative contribution of many different approaches, rather than only individual solutions. And while optimistic, these ambitious scenarios are still hypothetical. We have not planted anything close to 1.2 trillion trees, and every year we are losing an area of forest equal to the size of the United Kingdom, *not* including those lost to wildfires.[316] We do not know if such massive new tree plantings are feasible, and Dr. Crowther's assertions of their net effects on slowing climate change have been questioned. We also don't know how many trees would survive under worsening conditions such as inadequate rainfall, more prevalent and more powerful hurricanes, and flooding.[317]

Nonetheless, tree-planting efforts abound. Pakistan's prime minister announced plans to plant ten billion trees.[318] Scotland added more than twenty-two million trees to its forest in 2018.[319] Madagascar is planting sixty million trees.[320] Australia plans to plant one billion trees by 2050 to meet its Paris Climate Agreement pledge (may the bulk be planted before 2030!).[321] During the summer of 2019, Ethiopia broke a world record by alleging to have planted 350 million seedlings in twelve hours, with 2.6 billion planted throughout the country, and a final goal of four billion seedlings.[322] After decades of

---

315. Groot, "The Best Technology for Fighting Climate Change Isn't a Technology: It's Forests."

316. Fiona Harvey, "World Losing Area of Forest the Size of the UK Each Year, Report Finds."

317. Tutton, "Stronger Hurricanes Could Decimate Forests and Accelerate Climate Change, Warns Study."

318. Constable, "Pakistan Plans to Plant 10 Billion Trees to Combat Decades of Deforestation."

319. Good News Network, "Scotland Added 22 Million New Trees Last Year, Carrying the UK Goal on its Green Shoulders."

320. Mongabay, "Madagascar Is Planting 60 Million Trees in Ambitious Drive Inspired by Its President."

321. Sanchez and Keck, "Australia Will Plant 1 Billion Trees to Combat Climate Change."

322. O'Kane, "Ethiopia Plants 350 Million Trees in 12 Hours, Breaking World Record."

deforestation, Costa Rica has doubled its tree cover in the last thirty years.[323] Then, there is the radically sane "Forest Man of India," Jadav Payeng, who has single-handedly transformed a desiccated island into a thriving forest environment by planting tens of thousands of trees over forty years.[324] Imagine if even a fraction of us worked together to match one-tenth the efforts of this man who was at first considered crazy by locals.

## 14. Bullying & Censorship

Adding insult to climate injury, cutting-edge climate scientists conducting essential research are receiving threats to shut down their work. According to *Esquire* magazine, climate scientists "have been the targets of an unrelenting and well-organized attack that includes death threats, summonses from a hostile Congress, attempts to get them fired, legal harassment, and intrusive discovery demands so severe they had to start their own legal-defense fund, all amplified by a relentless propaganda campaign nakedly financed by the fossil-fuel companies."[325] Please do read the cited article!

Dishonest, aggressive tactics also have been deployed on other fronts. To protect corporate profits, scientists in the United Kingdom, Britain, United States, and other countries, were offered $10,000 a pop by fossil fuel lobbyist group American Enterprise Institute (AEI) to dishonestly weaken and debunk crucial climate science reports.[326] Defunding of the EPA (Environmental Protection Agency) and climate change research by our science-denying government has made matters even worse.

———

In summary, we are locked into committed warming for at least the next 10.1 years due to the lag time of warming from emissions we've already released into the atmosphere, unless we find a way to rapidly and efficiently reduce that amount by some massive means of carbon drawdown ($CO_2$

---

323. Dilonardo, "Costa Rica Has Doubled its Forest Cover in the Last 30 Years."

324. McCarthy, "A Lifetime of Planting Trees on a Remote River Island: Meet India's Forest Man."

325. Richardson, "When the End of Human Civilization Is Your Day Job."

326. Sample, "Scientists Offered to Dispute Climate Study."

sequestration). Warming limits and cautions made by the IPCC appear to be significantly underestimated for many reasons. Accelerating positive feedback loops are driving climate change exponentially, at which point existing predictions become even more unreliable and conservative. As conditions worsen, key environmental tipping points become more probable, which can then drive exponential deterioration. All support systems are currently in massive decline and we are in deep trouble.

Reducing our emissions will no longer suffice to sustain a habitable planet. We must also remove massive amounts of $CO_2$ from the atmosphere and safely store it, via Carbon Capture and Sequestration/Storage (CCS).[327] Since 1970, global carbon emissions from fossil fuels have steadily increased, save for a few years of temporary decline.[328] Even if we were to steadily and significantly reduce global emission levels each year for many consecutive years, there is still no immediate plan or collective solution for removing the astronomical amounts of excess atmospheric carbon. In fact, "We don't do anything on this planet on that scale," according to Dr. Hugh Hunt in the Department of Engineering at the University of Cambridge.[329] Factors such as increasing methane seeps, massive insect declines, loss of wildlife, climate refugee migrations, food and potable water shortages, wars, natural resource shortages, overpopulation, sea level rise, disease outbreaks, and our hastening unknown thresholds for precarious tipping points and the exponential changes that accompany them, leave us in a quandary.

Road signs on this apocalyptic journey include (1) the last time atmospheric $CO_2$ levels are known to have equaled the present levels was sixty-six million years ago when the dinosaurs went extinct[330], (2) similar major climate events to our present crisis occurred in the past when we lost this much Arctic ice, and (3) both heat and cold temperature records being shattered year after recent year are important, self-evident signals screaming "Stop!"

––––––

327. "What is Carbon Capture and Sequestration?," State of New York Department of Environmental Conservation.

328. U.S. Environmental Protection Agency, "Global Greenhouse Gas Emissions Data."

329. "Wadhams, Rees, Hunt – Climate Change and Carbon Dioxide Removal."

330. Nield, "Last Time Carbon Emissions Were This High, the Dinosaurs Went Extinct."

If everything you read in this book prior to reading the climate science did not move you to realize it's time to get involved, I hope you are now convinced. Amid all the bad news, the good news is there seems to be a small window in which we can still turn our ship around, "provided we muster an unprecedented level of cooperation, extraordinary speed and heroic scale of action," according to Nobel Prize-winning chemist Mario Molina.[331] The bad news is our predicament is even more critical than we know. We also are nowhere near the needed global cooperation and mobilization, evidenced by the disparate and lukewarm, nonbinding resolutions to reduce GHGs as a result of the Paris Agreement and subsequent global climate summits, such as those in Katowice, Poland and Madrid, Spain. Yet, we could still avoid extinction. Realistically, we won't escape without more serious harm.

Bear in mind, we have no plan for how to realistically respond to the IPCC's warnings. In fact, the warnings and predictions depend upon Carbon Capture and Sequestration / Storage technology we've not yet implemented, which has not been proven to work at scale, making any climate solutions more nebulous and the IPCC warnings even less dire than conditions warrant. My hunch is we will start spraying (geoengineering) the skies with sun-reflecting particles before too long, at least to buy time.

We can therefore simultaneously begin to cope in the short-term and prepare for the longer term by undoing the Faustian bargain of our addiction to the benefits of fossil fuels. This necessarily means living outside the paradigm of business as usual. So, it's time to get real: to feel deeply, think keenly, and act both radically and wisely. Thus this book.

331. Harvey, "'Tipping Points' Could Exacerbate Climate Crisis, Scientists Fear."

# Appendix II
# STEPS FOR GMO ERADICATION

## LEVEL I (Eliminate)

1. Learn which foods are GMO ("Genetically Modified Organism"): The current most common genetically modified foods are: corn (includes "sweet corn"), soy (includes lecithin), sugar (from beets), honey (via GMO crops' pollen), cotton (including cottonseed oil), canola (including canola oil), alfalfa, Hawaiian papaya, tobacco, yellow crookneck and zucchini squash, dairy (tainted with rBGH and from animals fed genetically modified foods), meat (all kinds, from animals fed genetically modified foods), salmon, and aspartame.

   HVP (Hydrolyzed Vegetable Protein), TVP (Textured Vegetable Protein), xanthan gum, vanillin, dextrose, lactic acid, maltodextrin, and vitamins A, B2, B6, B12, C, D, E, and K are most often GMO.

2. Print out the above list and carry it with you. Don't buy foods if they're not labeled "certified organic" or lack the "Non GMO Project Verified" certification.

3. Check food labels for GMO ingredients; if they are not listed as organic, they are likely GMO. Exceptions are products that bear the "Non-GMO Project Verified" label.

4. Buy as little commercially farmed processed food and as much local organic food as possible. Processed foods are more likely to have GMOs as well as hidden GMO ingredients.

5. Avoid commercial restaurants. Restaurants that are not specifically organic (few and far between) often use low-quality ingredients, which are often GMO and non-organic.

## LEVEL II (Outreach)

1. Share information about the dangers of GMO foods with everyone you can.

2. Ask grocery stores and restaurants, family and friends, not to deal in GMOs. Talk to your children's food director/organizer at school. Everywhere you go, let food-related organizations and people know: No GMOs.

3. Call or email food companies that do not specify suspect ingredients as GMO and ask if they are GMO.

4. Encourage anyone you know not to use Roundup; it is part and parcel of GMO food production, a probable carcinogen, and much more toxic than once suspected.

## LEVEL III (Community)

1. Organize rallies, protests, donate to and support organic groups, create and circulate petitions, set up information booths, and begin a public outreach to denounce GMOs and support sustainable, regenerative agriculture.

2. Additional actions: pass out GMO warning flyers, write articles, post notes at work, go to protests, read GMO articles and watch GMO videos. Host educational movie nights about GMOs. Plant that organic garden already! And get your family, neighbors, and greater community involved.

# RESOURCES

The seven categories below are composed of books, articles, videos, discussion and support groups, community support venues, nature connection opportunities, and mind-body practices to inform and cultivate diverse aspects of climate cure. Additional offerings by Jack Adam Weber can be found at: jackadamweber.com, his YouTube channel, and on his author pages at WakeUp-World.com and CollectiveEvolution.com.

## 1: Books

Baker, Carolyn. *Navigating the Coming Chaos: A Handbook for Inner Transition*. Indiana: iUniverse, 2011. Provides emotional and spiritual preparation for turbulent times. You might also enjoy Carolyn's other books on coping through climate chaos: *Collapsing Consciously, Dark Gold, Saving Animals from Ourselves*, and *Savage Grace* (the last two are written with Andrew Harvey).

Barrows, Anita and Joanna Macy. *Rilke's Book of Hours: Love Poems to God*. New York: Riverhead Books, 1996. A superb translation of some of Rilke's finest poems; includes a fascinating account of the great poet's life.

Climate Reality Project. Beginning the Conversation: A Family's Guide (free e-booklet). https://www.climaterealityproject.org/sites/default/files/kidsandclimatechangee-book.pdf. A clear, sensible guide for discussing climate change with children that includes simple facts and conversation starters.

Frankl, Viktor. *Man's Search for Meaning*. Boston: Beacon Press, 1959–2006. A classic and harrowing account of a psychiatrist's life through suffering and hope amid atrocious circumstances.

Harvey, Andrew. *The Hope: A Guide to Sacred Activism*. California: Hay House, 2009. From the passionately compassionate teacher and scholar, Harvey offers wise inner and outer guidance on activism as a soulful path.

Hawken, Paul. *Drawdown: The Most Comprehensive Plan Ever Proposed to Reverse Global Warming*. New York: Penguin Books, 2017. The encyclopedia for outer action (except rebellion) to reduce greenhouse gas emissions.

Jung, Carl. *The Basic Writings of C. G. Jung (Modern Library)*, New York: Random House, 1959. A good introduction to Jung's teachings and work in depth psychology.

Kelly, Brendan. *The Yin and Yang of Climate Crisis: Healing Personal, Cultural, and Ecological Imbalance with Chinese Medicine*. California: North Atlantic Books, 2015. Discusses climate change and outer action in the context of traditional Chinese medicine patterns of imbalance.

Korngold, Efrem and Harriet Beinfield. *Between Heaven and Earth: A Guide to Chinese Medicine*. New York: Random House, 1991. The best introduction to the basic principles and practice of Chinese medicine.

Krishnamurti, Jiddu. *Freedom from the Known*. New York: HarperCollins, 1969. My favorite book on Krishnamurti's radical teachings.

Leonard, David Bruce. *Medicine at Your Feet: Healing Plants of the Hawaiian Kingdom*. Hawaii: Roast Duck Productions, 1998-2019. An authoritative and exhaustive rendering of Hawaiian medicinal plants, including uses for food.

Levoy, Gregg. *Callings: Finding and Following an Authentic Life*. New York: Three Rivers Press, 1997. One of my favorite books of all time; exquisite, poetic prose and many astonishing, real-life accounts to help you awaken to your deepest callings and purpose.

Licata, Matt. *The Path Is Everywhere: Uncovering the Jewels Hidden Within You*. Colorado: Wandering Yogi Press, 2017. Heartfelt, wise counsel from a somatic therapist about our finer jewels of being human which emerge from transformative, body-centered emotional work.

May, Rollo. *The Courage to Create*. New York: W.W. Norton & Company, Inc., 1975. A key influence in my earlier years; I can't even remember what May said, but it changed me.

Mitchell, Stephen. *Letters to a Young Poet.* New York: Random House, 1984. Letters by favorite poet, Rilke, this is a compendium on fierce wisdom of the passion to write, think and feel deeply, and follow one's truth.

Oliver, Mary. *New and Selected Poems, Volume One.* Boston: Beacon Press, 1992. Just read her poems if you haven't … or if you haven't for a while, even if it was yesterday. My favorite of her poems, "No Voyage," was included in the Grief chapter but had to be removed for copyright reasons.

Pitchford, Paul. *Healing with Whole Foods: Asian Traditions and Modern Nutrition.* California: North Atlantic Books, 2002. I studied with Paul years ago, and his book is a classic on the holistic model for using herbs, food, and mind-body practices in a holistic context.

Richo, David. *Shadow Dance: Liberating the Power and Creativity of Your Dark Side.* Boston: Shambhala Publications, 1999. A helpful guide for befriending our positive and negative shadows and making them allies.

Richo, David. *When the Past is Present: Healing the Emotional Wounds that Sabotage Our Relationships.* Boston: Shambhala Publications, 2008. Crucial wisdom and excellent writing from one of my long-term mentors to supplement inner work, especially on grief and shadow work vis à vis "hurt people hurt others."

Rogers, Carl. *On Becoming a Person: A Therapist's View of Psychotherapy.* New York: Houghton Mifflin, 1961. From one of my heroes, this heartfelt classic guided me through my late teens and helped me learn the language and landscape of inner work. While staying at a mountain retreat deep in the Spanish Pyrenees, I wept deeply the winter I learned Dr. Rogers had passed away.

Tierra, Michal, C.A., N.D. *Planetary Herbology.* Wisconsin: Lotus Press, 1992. My favorite herbal handbook that categorizes many Western herbs within the Chinese system.

Walker, Dean Spillane. *The Impossible Conversation: Choosing Reconnection and Resilience at the End of Business as Usual.* Oregon: Dean Walker, 1997. A primer on facing climate crisis honestly with a broken-open heart and building meaningful relationships.

Weber, Jack Adam. *Rebearth: Poems for Personal and Planetary Transformation.* Please check www.jackadamweber.com for availability.

Weber, Jack Adam. *Nature of the Heart: Poems for Holistic Healing.* Hawaii: Earthbound Press, 2008. A collection of poems conveying the death-and-rebirth healing process through my core love wounds.

Welwood, John. *Journey of the Heart: The Path of Conscious Love.* New York: HarperCollins, 1991. A "bible" to me in my earlier years by one of my first teachers on how inner work and integrity develop from the path of authentic intimate relationships and deep love.

# 2: Articles

Bartz, Andrea. "How City Noise is Slowly Killing You." *Harper's Bazaar.* July 25, 2017. https://www.harpersbazaar.com/culture/features/a10295155/noise-detox/?f-bclid=IwAR0Ac8xI0m-HXPk5XNdmRErb-zu0lDtXiDr9me_k4XgmoZOmZy-DZsX-d8FE.

Gardner, Dan. "Why don't we care about climate change?" The Globe and Mail, December 21, 2018. https://www.theglobeandmail.com/opinion/article-why-dont-we-care-about-climate-change/.

Hedges, Chris. "The Last Act of the Human Comedy." Truthdig, September 2, 2019. https://www.truthdig.com/articles/the-last-act-of-the-human-comedy/.

Hedges, Chris. "Saving the Planet Means Overthrowing the Ruling Elites." Truthdig, September 23, 2019. https://www.truthdig.com/articles/saving-the-planet-means-overthrowing-the-ruling-elites/.

Hedges, Chris. "The World to Come." Truthdig, January 28, 2019. https://www.truthdig.com/articles/the-world-to-come/.

Jensen, Robert. "After the Harvest: Learning to Leave the Planet Gracefully." Common Dreams, June 14, 2014. https://www.commondreams.org/views/2014/06/14/after-harvest-learning-leave-planet-gracefully.

Leonard, David Bruce. "The Foundations of Nature Connection." Earth Medicine Institute, 2012. https://earthmedicineinstitute.com/more/articles/foundations-of-nature-connection/.

McDougall, Dan. "Life on Thin Ice: Mental Health at the Heart of Climate Crisis." The Guardian, August 12, 2019. https://www.theguardian.com/society/ng-interactive/2019/aug/12/life-on-thin-ice-mental-health-at-the-heart-of-the-climate-crisis.

McGrath, Matt. "Climate Change: 12 Years to Save the Planet? Make that 18 Months." BBC News, July 24, 2019. https://www.bbc.com/news/science-environment-48964736.

Masters, Robert Augustus. "Spiritual Bypassing: Avoidance in Holy Drag." https://
www.robertmasters.com/2013/04/29/spiritual-bypassing/#.

Monbiot, George. "Only Rebellion Will Prevent an Ecological Apocalypse." The
Guardian, April 15, 2019. https://www.theguardian.com/commentisfree/2019/
apr/15/rebellion-prevent-ecological-apocalypse-civil-disobedience.

Moss, Michael. "The Extraordinary Science of Addictive Junk Food." The New York
Times Magazine, February 20, 2013. https://www.nytimes.com/2013/02/24/
magazine/the-extraordinary-science-of-junk-food.html.

Nelson, Marilee. "Fragrance Is the New Secondhand Smoke." Branch Basics, January
4, 2015. https://branchbasics.com/blog/fragrance-is-the-new-secondhand-smoke/.

Pagett, Norman. "Humankind is on the road to nowhere." Medium, June 29, 2018.
https://medium.com/@End_of_More/an-infinity-of-futility-5fb525fc610c.

Plested, James. "How the Rich Plan to Rule a Burning Planet." Redflag, December 10,
2019. https://bit.ly/3853bye.

Real Simple. "Everything You Need to Know to Grow Your Own Vertical Garden."
Real Simple, September 6, 2019. https://www.realsimple.com/home-organizing/
gardening/how-to-make-a-vertical-garden.

Richardson, John H. "When the End of Civilization is Your Day Job." Esquire, July
20, 2018.https://www.esquire.com/news politics/a36228/ballad-of-the-sad-
climatologists-0815/.

Scher, Avichai. "Climate Grief: The Growing Emotional Toll of Climate Change."
NBC News, Dec. 24, 2018. https://www.nbcnews.com/health/mental-health/
climate-grief-growing-emotional-toll-climate-change-n946751.

Watts, Jonathan. "Human society under urgent threat from loss of Earth's
natural life." The Guardian, May 6, 2019. https://www.theguardian.com/
environment/2019/may/06/human-society-under-urgent-threat-loss-earth-
natural-life-un-report?fbclid=IwAR07WOwuUGM4SWumFlE_nv_cv5GV4TEPixI-
JOgDknuhABD5P4FNv32fkVcg.

Weber, Jack Adam. "Anxiety and Depression: What Sufferers & Those Who Love
Them Should Know." Collective Evolution, September 23, 2018. https://www
.collective-evolution.com/2018/09/23/anxiety-depression-what-sufferers-those-
who-love-them-should-know/.

Weber, Jack Adam. "Beyond Yoga: Stretching Into the Deep Heart." Wake Up World,
February 15, 2018. https://wakeup-world.com/2018/02/15/beyond-yoga-stretch-
ing-into-the-deep-heart/.

Weber, Jack Adam. "Coronation Unveiled: A Critique and Cure for Charles Eisenstein's Fairy Tale Pandemic Essay." Medium. May 7, 2020. https://medium.com

/@jackadamweber/coronation-unveiled-a-critique-and
-cure-for-charles-eisensteins-fairy-tale-pandemic-essay-c3446906a85b

Weber, Jack Adam. "Embodied Spirituality: The Truth Shall Set You Free." Collective
Evolution, April 6, 2019. https://www.collective-evolution.com/2019/04/06/
embodied-spirituality-the-truth-shall-set-you-free/?fbclid=IwAR3NkihmX55pybT-
niE0Mhz88kIWSRZPI30lR4E6AuL4Qi3Hjd4eUthuG20o.

Weber, Jack Adam. "Everyday Activism: Little Effort, Big Results." Collective
Evolution, June 1, 2019. https://www.collective-evolution.com/2019/06/01/
everyday-activism-little-effort-big-results/.

Weber, Jack Adam. "Grief Work: Love's Saviour." Collective Evolution, July 31, 2018.
https://www.collective-evolution.com/2018/07/31/grief-work-loves-saviour/

Weber, Jack Adam. "Healing Through Severe (Major) Depressive Disorder: Tips, Facts
& Insights." http://www.jackadamweber.com/wp-content/uploads/2019/04/
Depression-Tips-Insights.pdf.

Weber, Jack Adam. "Lockdown, with Benefits: A Model for Degrowth and a Surviv-
able Future." Medium. May 4, 2020. https://medium.com/@jackadamweber/
lockdown-with-benefits-a-model-for-degrowth-and-a-survivable-future-c93783b-
b455a.

Weber, Jack Adam. "Re-thinking Love: Why Our Hearts Must Also Be Minded." Wake
Up World, June 6, 2014. https://wakeup-world.com/2014/06/06/re-thinking-love-
why-our-hearts-must-also-be-minded/.

Weber, Jack Adam. "The Science of Climate Crisis." http://www.jackadam
weber.com/science-climate-crisis/.

Yalkin, Devin. "It's the End of the World as They Know It: The Distinct Burden of
Being a Climate Scientist." Mother Jones, July 8, 2019. https://www.motherjones.
com/environment/2019/07/weight-of-the-world-climate-change-scientist-grief/.

## 3: Video

60 Minutes. "Brain Hacking: Silicon Valley Is Engineering Your Phone, Apps and
Social Media to Get You Hooked, Says a Former Google Product Manager." January 10, 2018. 60 Minutes Overtime. YouTube video, 13:47,.https://www.youtube
.com/watch?v=awAMTQZmvPE.

Baker, Carolyn. "Placing Climate and Other Catastrophic Events Within a Larger
Story." March 10, 2019. Video, 1:21:08. https://www.youtube.com/watch?v=
hfNuIF668MQ&t=81s.

Extinction Rebellion (Jack Adam Weber). "Climate Crisis: How to Care Enough."
    August 14, 2019. Video, 17:13. https://www.youtube.com/watch?time_
    continue=97&v=bUDCFuyd71I&feature=emb_logo.

Harvey, Andrew and Carolyn Baker. "Saving Animals from Ourselves." May 20, 2019.
    Video, 23:37. https://www.youtube.com/watch?v=Js2mGBcbMIw&list=PL4Xrx-
    rM8jT7XVpXTgEIeQNWOOVKa-6LCv&index=10&t=296s.

Hippo Works. "Cool the Climate!" March 9, 2020. (Children's) Video: 28:42. https://
    cooltheclimate.com/.

Hynes, Jennifer with Dougie Hanson and Edoardo Ballerini; written by Bill McKibben.
    "Life on a Shrinking Planet." January 2, 2019. Video, 55:22. https://www.youtube
    .com/watch?v=Db6C0wKn440.

"Ice on Fire: Climate Change Documentary." June 28, 2019. Video, 1:37:43. https://
    www.youtube.com/watch?v=WgAflG6MW1c.

Jackson, Jeremy. "Ocean Apocalypse." Evening lecture filmed at Naval War College on
    January 9, 2013. Video, 1:28:11. https://www.youtube.com/watch?v=2zMN3dT-
    vrwY.

The Lightfoot Institute. "Nobody's Fuel: An Engineer's Guide to Saving the Planet."
    The Lightfoot Institute. August 29, 2019. YouTube video: 1:07:16. https://www
    .youtube.com/watch?v=EOeoXvRQPil&feature=youtu.be&fbclid=IwAR2en7Kb-
    zwD3n6NDVu-MxrZ93rfp4pHysKCR9tqXKpuh1sqARWq2OJ0QQ2E.

Moyers & Company. "The War on Climate Scientists." May 16, 2014. Video, 24:27.
    https://www.youtube.com/watch?v=mnSicq6Y1lY.

National Geographic. "Flight of the Starlings." November 15, 2016. Video, 2:00.
    https://www.youtube.com/watch?v=ZYvG-vEFz4c.

The Poetry of Predicament. "Healing Our Trauma Together In an Insane World."
    September 10, 2018. Video, 1:00:16. https://www.youtube.com/watch?v=-
    4S620OItCa8.

Rae, Kerwin. "Why It's Time To Think About Human Extinction / Dr. David
    Suzuki," Kerwin Rae. YouTube video, 1:00:24. December 16, 2018. https://www
    .youtube.com/watch?v=ktnAMTmgOX0&t=631s.

Read, Rupert. "Shed a Light: This Civilization is Finished, O What is to Be Done?."
    November 9, 2018. Video, 1:11:55. https://www.youtube.com/watch?v=uzCxF-
    PzdO0Y&t=1672s.

Solomon, Sheldon. "Ernest Becker and The Denial of Death." October 2, 2011. Video,
    1:00:36. https://www.youtube.com/watch?v=XpVkrIdz9-Y&t=1209s.

Stromsted, Tina. "On 'Marion Woodman and the Embodied Soul.'" March 3, 2015,
    Video, 13:59. https://www.youtube.com/watch?v=6Zja1jI01BU.

Thunberg, Greta. "The disarming case to act right now on climate change." February 13, 2019. Video, 11:12. https://www.youtube.com/watch?v=H2QxFM9y0tY.

UPFSI. "Scientists' Warning at Foresight Group, EU Commission." Filmed November 5, 2019 and delivered to EU Commission in Brussels, Belgium. Video, 39:53. https://www.youtube.com/watch?v=pMbeYJgH_6g.

Weber, Jack Adam. "The Monkers." February 8, 2020. Video, 0:15. https://www.youtube.com/watch?v=Oteao5RwtHA.

Weber, Jack Adam. "The Yin and Yang of Radical Transformation: Finding Sanity in Uncertain Times." September 22, 2018. Video, 2:19:53. https://www.youtube.com/watch?v=OgCG4QRGbs4&t=29s.

Weber, Jack Adam. "Wild Inside: Becoming Medicine for Our Times." August 11, 2013. Video, 2:36:09. https://www.youtube.com/watch?v=HQtOEBtAstA.

Woodman, Marion and Andrew Harvey."Dancing in the Flames." October 30, 2018. Video, 1:24:00. https://vimeo.com/ondemand/dancingintheflames.

Wyllie, Jan and Jennifer Hynes. "Mindbreaking: The Mental Health Effects of Environmental Change." May 29, 2019. Video, 26:38. https://www.youtube.com/watch?v=awAMTQZmvPE.

## 4: Facebook Discussion and Activist Groups

**Climate Change: Facts and Consequences:** A place to share and discuss the latest, breaking climate crisis developments. https://www.facebook.com/groups/1669506253318739/.

**Climate Cure:** An online community discussion and support group to meet and learn more about the dynamics discussed in this book. https://www.facebook.com/groups/486290622320989/.

**Ecopsychology:** A place to share and discuss the holistic benefits of connecting with the natural world vis-à-vis climate crisis: https://www.facebook.com/groups/ecopsychologygroup/.

**Ecosystem Restoration Camps:** A discussion and strategizing group for restoring degraded lands to sequester $CO_2$ and rehabilitate wilderness. https://www.facebook.com/groups/1206960359323785/.

**Everyday Activism:** A forum to network and share success stories for how to take sustainable action with "little effort for big results." https://www.facebook.com/Everyday-Activism-465603913777148/.

**Extinction Rebellion Ojai:** Our local XR page for Ojai, California; stay abreast of our progress and unique forms of rebellion to address climate emergency. https://www.facebook.com/Extinction-Rebellion-Ojai-606473273190095/.

**GMO Eradication Movement:** Learn more and network with others about GMOs and how to eliminate them from your diet. https://www.facebook.com/GMO-Eradication-Movement-GEM-317544958304228/.

**Nourish Practice:** Learn more and hear announcements here about this mind-body-heart rejuvenation and transformation practice. https://www.facebook.com/The-Nourish-Practice-237532323110454/.

**Sarah Baker Blogspot:** A passionate, deeply stirring environmentalist and nature lover's riveting posts: https://www.facebook.com/profile.php?id=100009907061612.

## 5: Community Support Venues

**Climate Change Café:** A support platform to help you create a climate change discussion and support group in your own community. http://climatechangecafe.org/.

**Death Café:** A community support group to discuss and be with the reality of death; go to the site to find or host a café in your area. https://deathcafe.com/.

**Ecovillages Directory:** A directory of ecovillages where you can live in community, live rurally, tend to the land, and grow food. https://www.ic.org/directory/ecovillages/.

**Good Grief Network:** Offers support for despair, inaction, and eco-anxiety while strengthening community ties. https://www.goodgriefnetwork.org/.

**Safe Circle Calls:** Climate author and activist Dean Spillane-Walker hosts online video support calls for those craving companionship through climate collapse. https://livingresilience.net/safecircle/.

## 6: Nature Connection (in person)

**Deep Nature Journeys:** Wilderness solo rite-of-passage retreats combined with awareness and Qi Gong training; led by Bud Wilson. http://www.deepnaturejourneys.com/.

**Earth Medicine Institute:** Acupuncturist and herbalist David Bruce Leonard offers certifications in global tropical plant medicines and nature skills; based in Hawaii. https://earthmedicineinstitute.com/.

**East-West Herbal Course:** Taught by elder herbalists Dr. Michael and Lesley Tierra. I took this course in my early twenties. A comprehensive introduction to Chinese, Ayurvedic, and Native American herbal medicine, with optional hands-on training. https://planetherbs.com/.

**Ecosystem Restoration Camps:** A community-based movement to restore degraded lands to sequester $CO_2$ and rehabilitate wilderness. *https://ecosystemrestorationcamps.org/*.

**Mahalo ʻAina Sanctuary:** A retreat center on the windward side of the Big Island of Hawaii for transformation in body, mind, and spirit, sustainable living, and authentic community building. https://www.facebook.com/mahaloainasanctuary/.

# 7: Mind-Body Practices

**Mindfulness Meditation:** An awareness and presence-based practice popularized by Dr. Jon Kabat-Zinn: https://www.mindful.org/meditation/mindfulness-getting-started/. Video here: https://www.youtube.com/watch?v=U70osw7R1A4.

**Nourish Practice, Series I:** The guided, somatic-based, rejuvenating, and deeply relaxing meditation-Qi Gong experience I developed: http://www.jackadamweber.com/downloadscds/.

**Nourish Practice, Series II:** Building on Series I, this is an in-depth guide to grief work and healing through core love wounds: http://www.jackadamweber.com/httpwww-jackadamweber-comrecordings/.

**Vipassana Meditation and Retreats:** A basic form of insight meditation that relaxes and focuses. Free 10-day retreats are offered: *https://www.dhamma.org/en-US/index*.

**Walking Meditation:** A form of mindfulness meditation especially for those who don't like to, or cannot, sit but prefer to move: https://jackkornfield.com/walking-meditation-2/.

# BIBLIOGRAPHY

60 Minutes. "Brain Hacking: Silicon Valley Is Engineering Your Phone, Apps and Social Media to Get You Hooked, Says a Former Google Product Manager." 60 Minutes Overtime. January 10, 2018. YouTube video, 13:47. https://www.youtube.com/watch?v=awAMTQZmvPE.

Abblett, Mitch. "Tame Reactive Emotions by Naming Them." *Mindful*, September 25, 2019. https://www.mindful.org/labels-help-tame-reactive-emotions-naming.

Acaroglu, Leyla. "Climate Change Is the Slowly Boiling Frog in the Pot of the Earth." *Quartz*. November 3, 2017. https://qz.com/1118052/climate-change-is-the-slowly-boiling frog-in-the-pot-of-the-earth/.

Alcock, Ian. Mathew P. White, Sabine Pahl, Raquel Duarte-Davidson, Lora E. Fleming. "Associations Between Pro-Environmental Behaviour and Neighbourhood Nature, Nature Visit Frequency and Nature Appreciation: Evidence From a Nationally Representative Survey in England." *Environment International* 136, (March 2020) https://doi.org/10.1016/j.envint.2019.105441.

Al Jazeera. "Thousands in New Zealand Kick-Start New Wave of Climate Protests," *Al Jazeera*. September 26, 2019. https://www.aljazeera.com/news/2019/09/thousands-zealand-kickstart-wave-climate-protests-190927033920880.html.

Allen, Myles. "The Green New Deal: One Climate Scientist's View, From the Other Side of the Atlantic." *Bulletin of the Atomic Scientists*. March 8, 2019. https://thebulletin.org/2019/03/the-green-new-deal-one-climate-scientists-view-from-the-other-side-of-the-atlantic/.

American Psychological Association. "Climate Change's Toll on Mental Health." American Psychological Association. March 29, 2017. https://www.apa.org/news/press/releases/2017/03/climate-mental-health.aspx.

Archer, David and Victor Brovkin. "The Millennial Atmospheric Lifetime of Anthropogenic $CO_2$, *Climatic Change* 90, no. 3, 283-297 (October 2008). https://link.springer.com/article/10.1007%2Fs10584-008-9413-1.

Arciga, Julie. "Climate Anxiety Groups Are the New Self-Care." *The Daily Beast*, September 17, 2019. https://www.thedailybeast.com/climate -anxiety-groups-are-the-new-self-care?ref=scroll.

Arora, Harbeen. "We Relate, Therefore We Are." *Creative Living: Discovering Your Beautiful Path & Lifestyle Toward Happiness & Well-Being*. Garden City, NY: Morgan James Publishing, 2010.

Association of Nature and Forest Therapy. "The Practice of Forest Therapy." Accessed January 29, 2020. https://www.natureandforesttherapy.org/about/the-practice-of -forest-therapy.

Associated Press. "UN Chief Calls Climate Change 'Most Important Issue We Face'." *New York Post,* December 3, 2018. https://nypost.com/2018/12/03 /un-chief-calls-climate-change-most-important-issue-we-face/.

Baker, Carolyn. *Sacred Demise: Walking the Spiritual Path of Industrial Civilization's Collapse*. Carolyn Baker, 2009.

Barbash, Elyssa. "Different Types of Trauma: Small 't' versus Large 'T'." *Psychology Today*, March 13, 2017. https://www.psychologytoday.com /us/blog/trauma-and-hope/201703/different-types-trauma-small-t-versus -large-t.

Bartlett, Al. "Arithmetic, Population and Energy - a Talk by Al Bartlett." Al Bartlett, Professor Emeritus, Physics. https://www.albartlett.org/presentations /arithmetic_population_energy.html.

Bartz, Andrea. "How City Noise is Slowly Killing You." *Harper's Bazaar*, July 25, 2017. https://www.harpersbazaar.com/culture/features/a10295155 /noise-detox/.

Becker, Ernest. *The Denial of Death*. New York: Free Press Paperbacks, 1973.

Belkhir, Lotfi. "Big Pharma Emits More Greenhouse Gases than the Automotive Industry." The Conversation. May 27, 2019. https://theconversation .com/big-pharma-emits-more-greenhouse-gases-than-the-automotive -industry-115285.

Berwyn, Bob. "Climate Change Is Happening Faster Than Expected, and It's More Extreme." Inside Climate News, December 6, 2017. https:// insideclimatenews.org/news/26122017/climate-change-science-2017-year -review-evidence-impact-faster-more-extreme.

———. "How Wildfires Can Affect Climate Change (and Vice Versa)." Inside Climate News. August 23, 2018. https://insideclimatenews.org/news/23082018/extreme -wildfires-climate-change-global-warming-air -pollution-fire-management-black-carbon-co2.

Betuel, Emma. "Scientists Discover a Major Lasting Benefit of Growing Up Outside the City." Inverse. May 21, 2019. https://www.inverse.com /article/56019-psychological-benefits-of-nature-mental-health?fbclid.

Borenstein, Seth. "Climate Change Is More Extensive and Worse than Once Thought." Phys.org. November 29, 2018. https://phys.org/news/2018-11 -climate-extensive-worse-thought.html?fbclid.

Bratman, Gregory N., J. Paul Hamilton, Kevin S. Hahn, Gretchen C. Daily, and James J. Gross. "Nature Experience Reduces Rumination and Subgenual Prefrontal Cortex Activation." *Proceedings of the National Academy of Sciences of the United States of America* 112, no. 28 (July 14, 2015). https://doi.org/10.1073/pnas.1510459112.

Breeze, Nick. "Methane Hydrates – Extended Interview Extracts with Natalia Shakhova." July 29, 2013. YouTube video, 8:36. https://www.youtube.com /watch?v=kx1Jxk6kjbQ.

———. "Peter Wadhams, Martin Rees, Hugh Hunt – Climate Change and Carbon Dioxide Removal." January 15, 2014. YouTube video, 5:05. https://www.youtube .com/watch?v=o-PITZo7qOY.

Byskov, Morten Fibieger. "Climate Change: Focusing on How Individuals Can Help Is Very Convenient for Corporations." Truth Theory. January 14, 2019. https://truth-theory.com/2019/01/14/climate-change-focusing-on-how-individuals-can help-is -very-convenient-for-corporations/?fbclid..

Cain, Áine. "The True Story Behind Thanksgiving Is a Bloody Struggle That Decimated the Population and Ended with a Head on a Stick." *Business Insider*. November 20, 2017. https://www.businessinsider.com/history-of-thanksgiving-2017-11.

Camp, Jim. "Decisions Are Largely Emotional, Not Logical: The Neuroscience Behind Decision-Making." Big Think. June 11, 2012. https://bigthink.com/experts -corner/decisions-are-emotional-not-logical-the-neuroscience- behind-decision-making.

Caparrotta, Martin. "Dr. Gabor Maté on Childhood Trauma, the Real Cause of Anxiety and our 'Insane' Culture." Human Window. November 23, 2019. https:// humanwindow.com/dr-gabor-mate-interview-childhood-trauma-anxiety-culture/.

Carey, Bjorn. "Climate Change on Pace to Occur 10 Times Faster Than Any Change Recorded in Past 65 Million Years, Stanford Scientists Say." Stanford News, August 1, 2013. https://news.stanford.edu/news/2013/august /climate-change-speed-080113.html.

Center for Biological Diversity. "Halting the Extinction Crisis." Center for Biological Diversity. Accessed December 2019. https://www.biologicaldiversity.org /programs/biodiversity/elements_of_biodiversity/extinction_crisis/.

Centers for Disease Control and Prevention. "About the CDC-Kaiser ACE Study." Centers for Disease Control and Prevention. Last updated April 13, 2020. https://www .cdc.gov/violenceprevention/childabuseandneglect /acestudy/about.html.

Cheng, Lijing, John Abraham, Zeke Hausfather, Kevin E. Trenberth. "How Fast Are the Oceans Warming?" Science 363, no. 6423, (January 11, 2019): 128-129. https:// doi.org/10.1126/science.aav7619.

Cho, Renee. "Could Climate Change Shut Down the Gulf Stream?." Columbia University Earth Institute. June 6, 2017. https://blogs.ei.columbia .edu/2017/06/06/could-climate-change-shut-down-the-gulf-stream/?fbclid.

Chödrön, Pema. *Comfortable with Uncertainty: 108 Teachings on Cultivating Fearlessness and Compassion.* Boston: Shambhala Publications, 2008.

Chu, Danial. "The Snake Rope: Essential Buddhist Teaching in a Simple Story." 1NetCentral.com Free Articles Directory. Accessed December 2019. http://www .1netcentral.com/articles/the-snake-rope-essential-buddhist-teaching/.

Clark, Carla. "The Science of Raising a Friendly Psychopath." Brainblogger. December 6, 2016. http://brainblogger.com/2016/12/06/the-science-of -raising-a-friendly-psychopath/.

Climate Nexus. "Temperatures Skyrocket in Arctic, Prompt Desperate 'Refreeze' Plan." EcoWatch. February 13, 2017. http://www.ecowatch .com/arctic-temps-refreeze-plan-2258889584.html.

Cole, K.C. "Why You Didn't See It Coming." Nautilus. October 15, 2015. http:// nautil.us/issue/29/scaling/why-you-didnt-see-it-coming.

Conca, James. "Blood Batteries - Cobalt And The Congo." *Forbes.* September 26, 2018. https://www.forbes.com/sites/jamesconca/2018/09/26 /blood-batteries-cobalt-and-the-congo/#773dc791cc6e.

———. "Why Solar Geoengineering May Be Our Only Hope to Reverse Global Warming." *Forbes.* September 10, 2019. https://www.forbes.com /sites/jamesconca/2019/09/10/solar-geoengineering-we-better-do-it-or-well -burn/#643fe07718ad.

Constable, Pamela. "Pakistan Plans to Plant 10 Billion Trees to Combat Decades of Deforestation." *Independent.* October 15, 2018. https://www.independent.co.uk /news/world/asia/pakistan-trees-planting-billions -forests-deforestation-imran-khan-environment-khyber -pakhtunkhwa-a8584241.html.

Corn, David. "It's the End of the World as They Know It." *Mother Jones.* July 8, 2019. https://www.motherjones.com/environment/2019/07/weight-of-the-world -climate-change-scientist-grief/.

Cowan, Jill. "Why 'The Worst of Both Worlds' Is in the Forecast," *The New York Times*. March 1, 2019. https://www.nytimes.com/2019/03/01/us/california-today -extreme-weather-forecast.html?fbclid.

Cummins, Ronnie. "Degeneration Nation 2018: The Darkest Hour." EcoWatch. January 31, 2018. https://www.ecowatch.com/degeneration-nation-2530287177.html.

Dilonardo, Mary Jo. "Costa Rica Has Doubled its Forest Cover in the Last 30 Years." Mother Nature Network. May 24, 2019. https://www.mnn.com/earth-matters /wilderness-resources/blogs/costa-rica-has-doubled-its-forest-cover-last-30 -years?fbclid.

Dockrill, Peter. "Scientists Have Detected an Enormous Cavity Growing beneath Antarctica." ScienceAlert. January 31, 2019. https://www.sciencealert.com/ giant-void-identified-under-antarctica-reveals-a-monumental-hidden-ice-retreat.

Drum, Kevin. "Why Climate Change Is So Hard." *Mother Jones*. August 25, 2019. https://www.motherjones.com/kevin-drum/2019/08/why-climate-change-is -so-hard/.

Dunne, Daisy. "Unregulated Solar Geoengineering Could Spark Droughts and Hurricanes, Study Warns." Carbon Brief. November 11, 2017. https://www.carbonbrief. org/unregulated-solar-geoengineering-could-spark -droughts-and-hurricanes study-warns.

Effiong, Utibe, and Richard L. Neitzel. "Assessing the Direct Occupational and Public Health Impacts of Solar Radiation Management with Stratospheric Aerosols." *Environmental Health* 15 (January 19, 2016). https://doi.org/10.1186/s12940-016-0089-0.

Ehrenreich, Ben. "To Those Who Think We Can Reform Our Way Out Of the Climate Crisis." *The Nation*. January 15, 2019. https://www.thenation.com/article /climate-change-fossil-fuel-capitalism-divorce/.

Eisenstein, Charles. "Amazon Forest Fires – Avoid This Trap." August 23, 2019. YouTube video, 13:35, https://www.youtube.com/watch?v=2mNboLb2Suc&feature=youtu.be&fbclid =IwAR3ZVrwZblowWsvOKVzeH9VhBBKgY9EpP8huvki-Wmi1NJ1T1u6fywbNr1aw.

———. "Grief and Carbon Reductionism." Charles Eisenstein. February 2016. https://charleseisenstein.org/essays/grief-and-carbon-reductionism/.

———. *The More Beautiful World Our Hearts Know Is Possible*. Berkeley, California: North Atlantic Books, 2013.

Elster, Naomi. "Lung Cancer Is Commonly Associated with Smoking. But Rates of the Disease among Non-Smokers—and Women—Are Rising." BBC Future. June 25, 2018. http://www.bbc.com/future/story/20180625-why-the-rate-of-women-getting-lung-cancer-is-rising.

Environmental Defense Fund. "Methane: The Other Important Greenhouse Gas." Environmental Defense Fund. Accessed December 2019. https://www.edf.org /climate/methane-other-important-greenhouse-gas.

Extinction Rebellion."The Truth About Us," Extinction Rebellion. Video, 7:50. https://rebellion.earth/the-truth/about-us/.

———."We Demand." Extinction Rebellion. Accessed January 29, 2020, https:// extinctionrebellion.us/demands.

———. "#Whereisyourplan," Extinction Rebellion. Video, 1:32. https://rebellion. earth/.

Extinction Rebellion Ojai. Facebook. https://www.facebook.com/Extinction -Rebellion-Ojai-606473273190095/.

Farley, Peter. "Has the UN Climate Assessment Process Become Obsolete?" InsideClimate News. September 8, 2017. https://insideclimatenews.org/news/08092017/ climate-change-ipcc-scientists-reports-overhaul-inefficient-hayhoe-stocker.

Fawbert, Dave. "'Eco-Anxiety': How to Spot It and What to Do About It." BBC Three. March 27, 2019. https://www.bbc.co.uk/bbcthree/article/ b2e7ee32-ad28-4ec4-89aa-a8b8c98f95a5?fbclid=IwAR3omhazDZeG-Zc3Mr0pgTKaw-7mX5no1Sx3Ve2tdYQnPnqMOjpQRIH63y1g.

Firman, Tehrene. "Why Does Anxiety Seem to Get Even Worse at Night?" Well + Good. November 8, 2018. https://www.wellandgood.com/good -advice/why-you-have-anxiety-at-night/.

Flavell, Christopher and Jeremy C.F. Lin. "U.S. Nuclear Plants Weren't Built for Climate Change." Bloomberg Businessweek. April 18, 2019. https://www.bloomberg. com/graphics/2019-nuclear-power-plants-climate-change/?fbclid=IwAR2CCH6d-CuQGvmzYn8tosAogX7J-Wxqg8PDQFZG38CbFFOvQSnmc9-OavWs.

Frankl, Viktor E. *Man's Search for Meaning: Revised and Updated.* Boston: Beacon Press, 1997.

———. *Man's Search for Meaning.* New York: Pocket Books, 1997.

French, Agatha. "Father Gregory Boyle, Author of New Book, to Pasadena Audience: Consider Radical Kinship and Compassion." *Los Angeles Times.* December 13, 2017. https://www.latimes.com/books/la-et-jc-gregory-boyle-20171213-story.html.

Fresco, Nancy. "Huge Wildfires in the Arctic and Far North Send a Planetary Warning." The Conversation. August 14, 2019. https://theconversation.com/huge -wildfires-in-the-arctic-and-far-north-send-a-planetary-warning-121167?fbclid.

Fogel, Alan. "Emotional and Physical Pain Activate Similar Brain Regions." *Psychology Today.* April 19, 2012. https://www.psychologytoday.com/us/blog/body-sense/201204/emotional-and-physical-pain-activate-similar-brain-regions.

Food and Agriculture Organization of the United Nations. "6 Ways Indigenous Peoples Are Helping the World Achieve #ZeroHunger." Food and Agriculture Organization of the United Nations. September 8, 2017. http://www.fao.org/indigenous-peoples/news-article/en/c/1029002/.

Fountain, Henry and Nadja Popovich. "2019 Was the Second-Hottest Year Ever, Closing Out the Warmest Decade." *New York Times*. January 15, 2020. https://www.nytimes.com/interactive/2020/01/15/climate/hottest year-2019.html.

Fox, Matthew. *Original Blessing: A Primer in Creation Spirituality Presented in Four Paths, Twenty-Six Themes, and Two Questions.* New York: Tarcher/Putnam, 2000.

Gabbatiss, John. "Massive Restoration of World's Forests Would Cancel Out a Decade of CO2 Emissions, Analysis Suggests." *Independent*. Video, 21:46. February 16, 2019. https://www.independent.co.uk/environment/forests-climate-change-co2-greenhouse-gases-trillion-trees-global-warming-a8782071.html?fbclid.

Galey, Patrick ."$5-tn Fuel Exploration Plans 'Incompatible' with Climate Goals." Phys.org. April 23, 2019. https://phys.org/news/2019-04-tn-fuel-exploration-incompatible-climate.html?fbclid.

Gardiner, Beth. "A Surge of New Plastic Is About to Hit the Planet." *Wired*. January 20, 2020, https://www.wired.com/story/a-surge-of-new-plastic-is-about-to-hit-the-planet/.

Gardner, C.J. and C.F.R. Wordley. "Scientists Must Act on Our Own Warnings to Humanity." *Nature Ecology and Evolution 3* 1271–1272, (September 2019), https://www.nature.com/articles/s41559-019-0979-y.

Gauthier, Philippe. "The Limits of Renewable Energy and the Case for Degrowth." Resilience. November 21, 2018. https://www.resilience.org/stories/2018-11-21/the-limits-of-renewable-energy-and-the-case-for-degrowth/?fbclid=IwAR3sC5-H1R_K_qT66-5R7n0-.

Garza, Eric. "Awakening to the Traumacene." Medium. May 29, 2019. https://medium.com/age-of-awareness/awakening-to-the-traumacene-8d5dcb92ea7f.

Geggel, Laura. "Antarctica's Pine Island Glacier Just Lost Enough Ice to Cover Manhattan 5 Times Over." LiveScience. October 30, 2018. https://www.livescience.com/63974-pine-island-iceberg-calves-2018.html.

Geib, Claudia. "Boaty McBoatface Is About to Investigate The 'Most Dangerous Glacier in The World'." ScienceAlert. May 1, 2018. https://www.sciencealert.com/the-most-dangerous-glacier-in-the-world-sea-rise-thwaites-glacier-antarctic.

Gandhi, Mahatma. *The Collected Works of Mahatma Gandhi*, Vol. 13. New Delhi, India: Ministry of Information and Broadcasting, 1964. https://www.gandhiashramsevagram.org/gandhi-literature/mahatma-gandhi collected-works-volume-13.pdf.

Gillis, Justin. "Earth Sets a Temperature Record for the Third Straight Year." *The New York Times*. January 18, 2017. https://www.nytimes.com/2017/01/18/science/earth-highest-temperature-record.html.

Goodenough, Patrick. "16-Year-Old Climate Activist Says Trump Obviously Doesn't 'Listen to the Science'." CNSNews. August 29, 2019. https://www.cnsnews.com/news/article/patrick-goodenough/16-year-old-climate-activist-says-trump-obviously-doesnt-listen.

GMO Eradication Movement. "11 Steps for GMO Eradication." Facebook, November 8, 2012. https://www.facebook.com/317544958304228/photos/?tab=album&album_id=438358489556207.

———. "60 Minutes Australia: Roundup and Cancer." Sustainable Pulse. September 13, 2019. Video, 10:41. https://sustainablepulse.com/2019/09/13/watch-here-worlds-most-popular-weed-killer-probably-causes-cancer-60-minutes-australia/#.XjSN2iMkqUk.

Goldenberg, Suzanne. "Just 90 Companies Caused Two-Thirds of Man-Made Global Warming Emissions." *The Guardian*. November 20, 2013. https://www.theguardian.com/environment/2013/nov/20/90-companies-man-made-global-warming-emissions-climate-change.

Good News Network. "Scotland Added 22 Million New Trees Last Year, Carrying the UK Goal on its Green Shoulders." Good News Network. June 14, 2019. https://www.goodnewsnetwork.org/scotland-added-22-million-new-trees-last-year/?fbclid.

Green, Matthew. "Extinction Rebellion: Inside the New Resistance." Financial Times. April 10, 2019. https://www.ft.com/content/9bcb1bf8-5b20-11e9-9dde-7aed-ca0a081a?fbclid.

Grist staff. "To Fear Or Not to Fear." Grist. March 2, 2019. https://grist.org/article/to-fear-or-not-to-fear-a-conversation-between-david-wallace-wells-and-eric-holthaus/.

Grohol, John M. "What is Catastrophizing?" Psych Central. October 8, 2018. https://psychcentral.com/lib/what-is-catastrophizing/.

Grohol, John M. "What's the Difference Between CBT and DBT?" Psych Central. October 8, 2018. https://psychcentral.com/lib/whats-the-difference-between-cbt-and-dbt/.

Groot, Han de. "The Best Technology for Fighting Climate Change Isn't a Technology: It's Forests." *Scientific American*. December 5, 2018. https://blogs.scientificamerican.com/observations/the-best-technology-for-fighting-climate-change-isnt-a-technology/.

Hagedorn, Gregor, Peter Kalmus, Michael Mann, Sara Vicca, Joke Van den Berge, Jean-Pascal van Vpersele, Dominique Bourg, et. al. "Concerns of Young Protestors Are Justified." *Science* 364, issue 6436 (April 12, 2019). https://science.sciencemag.org/content/364/6436/139.2.

Hallmann, Caspar A. Martin Sorg, Eelke Jongejans, Henk Siepel, Nick Hofland, Heinz Schwan, Werner Stenmans, et. al. "More than 75 Percent Decline Over 27 Years in Total Flying Insect Biomass in Protected Areas." *PLOS ONE* 12, no. 10 (October 18, 2017). https://doi.org/10.1371/journal.pone.0185809.

Hänninen, Otto, Anne B. Knol, Matti Jantunen, Tek-Ang Lim, André Conrad, Marianne Rappolder, Paolo Carrer, et. al. "Environmental Burden of Disease in Europe: Assessing Nine Risk Factors in Six Countries," *Environmental Health Perspectives* 122, no. 5 (May 1, 2014). https://doi.org/10.1289/ehp.1206154.

Hansen, Ellie. "Our Climate Change Inaction: Is 'Climate Trauma' the Missing Link?" Columbia Political Review. May 27, 2019. http://www.cpreview.org/blog/2019/5/our-climate-change-inaction-is-climate-trauma-the-missing-link?fbclid=IwAR2Jg-mgD27PDx2F42HL84rf9bMAalBUObdc474-LO_-nO4Sq9EisFbc5b3g.

Harnung, Sven E. and Matthew S. Johnson. *Chemistry and the Environment.* Cambridge: Cambridge University Press, 2012.

Haque, Umair. "What Kind of People Are We Becoming?" Eudaimonia. June 14, 2019. https://eand.co/what-kind-of-people-are-we-becoming-1982068e1f45?fbclid.

Harari, Yuval Noah. *Sapiens: A Brief History of Humankind.* New York: HarperCollins Publishers, 2015.

Harvey, Fiona. "'Tipping Points' Could Exacerbate Climate Crisis, Scientists Fear." *The Guardian.* October 9, 2018. https://www.theguardian.com/environment/2018/oct/09/tipping-points-could-exacerbate-climate-crisis-scientists-fear.

———. "World Losing Area Of Forest the Size Of the UK Each Year, Report Finds." *The Guardian.* September 12, 2019. https://www.theguardian.com/environment/2019/sep/12/deforestation-world-losing-area-forest-size-of-uk-each-year-report-finds.

Hedges, Chris. "The Last Act of the Human Comedy." Truthdig. September 2, 2019. https://www-truthdig-com.cdn.ampproject.org/v/s/www.truthdig.com/articles/the-last-act-of-the-human-comedy/?amp&usqp=mq331AQEKAFwAQ==&amp_js_v=0.1&fbclid.

———. "The Messiahs of Hope Assure Us Everything Will Be OK in the End. But It Won't." Common Dreams. September 2, 2019. https://www.commondreams.org/views/2019/09/02/messiahs-hope-assure-us-everything-will-be-ok-end-it-wont.

Heinberg, Richard. "The New IPCC Report Offers Climate Solutions that Depend on Magic." *Pacific Standard.* October 8, 2018. https://psmag.com/environment/2018-ipcc-report-includes-magical-thinking.

Henn, Jamie. "This Is the Scariest Thing about the IPCC Report – It's the Watered Down, Consensus Version. The Latest Science Is Much, Much, Much More Terrifying." Twitter, October 9, 2018, https://twitter.com/Agent350/status/1049717120697753601.

Herrando-Pérez, Salvador, Corey J. A. Bradshaw, Stephan Lewandowsky, David R. Vieites. "Statistical Language Backs Conservatism in Climate-Change Assessments." *BioScience* 69, no. 3 (March 2019). https://academic.oup.com/bioscience/article/69/3/209/5382637?fbclid.

Heshmat, Shahram. "Anxiety vs. Fear: What is the Difference?" *Psychology Today.* December 3, 2018. https://www.psychologytoday.com/us/blog/science-choice/201812/anxiety-vs-fear.

Hickman, Caroline. "What Psychotherapy Can Do for the Climate and Biodiversity Crises." The Conversation. June 7, 2019, https://theconversation.com/what-psychotherapy-can-do-for-the-climate-and-biodiversity-crises-116977?utm_medium=ampfacebook&utm_source=facebook&fbclid=IwAR0mI21wrLKaimfgk1tc7_KGYqRcio7zbw2x-TNloqWX_QNVAeW64cw_f2E.

Hoegh-Guldberg, Ove. "The Decline of the Great Barrier Reef." Skeptical Science. July 2015. https://www.skepticalscience.com/great-barrier-reef-decline.htm.

Holmes, Jack. "We Need to Accept We're Likely Underestimating the Climate Crisis." *Esquire.* January 22, 2019. https://www.esquire.com/news-politics/a25990174/greenland-ice-melt-antarctica-climate-change-crisis/?fbclid.

Holthaus, Eric. "The Climate Crisis is Racist. The Answer is Anti-Racism." The Correspondent. May 28, 2020. https://thecorrespondent.com/496/the-climate-crisis-is-racist-the-answer-is-anti-racism/65663772944-cc6110b0?fbclid.

———. "U.N. Climate Report Shows Civilization Is at Stake If We Don't Act Now." Grist. October 8, 2018. https://grist.org/article/scientists-calmly-explain-that-civilization-is-at-stake-if-we-dont-act-now/.

Housman, Justin. "Scottish Doctors Are Now Issuing Prescriptions to Go Hiking." *Adventure Journal.* October 22, 2018. https://www.adventure-journal.com/2018/10/scottish-doctors-are-now-issuing-prescriptions-to-gohiking/?fbclid.

Intergovernmental Panel on Climate Change. "Summary for Policymakers of IPCC Special Report on Global Warming of 1.5°C approved by governments." Intergovernmental Panel on Climate Change. October 8, 2018. https://www.ipcc.ch/2018/10/08/summary-for-policymakers-of-ipcc-special-report-on-global-warming-of-1-5c-approved-by-governments/.

IRENA. "Global Energy Transformation: A Roadmap to 2050 (2019 Edition)." IRENA. April 2019. https://irena.org/publications/2019/Apr/Global-energy-transformation-A-roadmap-to-2050-2019Edition?fbclid=IwAR0qNIivmzdMeRyNVOsPPAXM-2Muih8C09q9mUNKnG7yGhzLf9pDOz_PBwuU.

Irwin, Aisling. "The Ecologist Who Wants to Map Everything." *Nature*. September 20, 2019. https://www.nature.com/articles/d41586-019-02846-4.

Jiang, Hong and Sasha Fegan. "Jellyfish are Causing Mayhem As Pollution, Climate Change See Numbers Boom." ABC Radio National Late Night Live. January 6, 2019. https://www.abc.net.au/news/2019-01-06/the-magic-and-mayhem-of-jellyfish/10377112.

Johnson, Jake. "More Than One Billion Animals Killed in Australia Wildfires Called a 'Very Conservative' Estimate." Common Dreams. January 7, 2020. https://www.commondreams.org/news/2020/01/07/more-one-billion-animals-killed-australia-wildfires-called-very-conservative.

———. "'Ominous' UN Report Warns Human Activity Has Pushed One Million Plant and Animal Species to Brink of Extinction.'" Common Dreams. May 6, 2019. https://www.commondreams.org/news/2019/05/06/ominous-un-report-warns-human-activity-has-pushed-one-million-plant-and-animal.

Jordan, Rob. "Stanford Researchers Find Mental Health Prescription: Nature." *Stanford News*. June 30, 2015. https://news.stanford.edu/2015/06/30/hiking-mental-health-063015/.

Ju, Anne. "Courage Is the Most Important Virtue, Says Writer and Civil Rights Activist Maya Angelou at Convocation." *Cornell Chronicle*. May 24, 2008. https://news.cornell.edu/stories/2008/05/courage-most-important-virtue-maya-angelou-tells-seniors.

Jung, Carl. "Good and Evil in Analytical Psychology." *The Collected Works of C. G. Jung, Vol. 10, Civilization in Transition*. Princeton, NJ: Princeton University Press, 1959.

———. *The Undiscovered Self.* New York: Signet, 1956.

———. "When a situation is not made conscious, it happens outside, as fate.'" *Collected Works 9ii: Christ, A Symbol of the Self.* http://jungcurrents.com/fate.

Kahn, Brian. "Enormous Wildfires Are Spreading in Siberia." Gizmodo. May 15, 2018. https://earther.gizmodo.com/enormous-wildfires-are-spreading-in-siberia-1826040230.

———. "Looking for Global Warming? Check the Ocean." Climate Central. April 21, 2015. https://www.climatecentral.org/news/global-warming-ocean-heat-18905.

Kaufman, Carolyn. "Three-Dimensional Villains – Finding Your Character's Shadow." Ezine Articles. January 24, 2007. https://ezinearticles.com/?Three-Dimensional-Villains---Finding-Your-Characters-Shadow&id=428279.

Kendall, Graham ."Your Mobile Phone vs. Apollo 11's Guidance Computer."
RealClear Science. July 2, 2019. https://www.realclearscience.com/arti-
cles/2019/07/02/your_mobile_phone_vs_apollo_11s_guidance_com-
puter_111026.html.

Kerlin, Kat. "Grasslands More Reliable Carbon Sink Than Trees." UC Davis Science &
Climate. July 9, 2018. https://climatechange.ucdavis.edu/news/grasslands-more-
reliable-carbon-sink-than-trees/.

Kidner, David W. "Depression and the Natural World: Toward a Critical Ecology of
Psychological Distress." Critical Psychology. May 5, 2007. https://www.academia
.edu/35580523/Depression_and_the_natural_world_toward_a_critical_ecology_
of_psychological_distress?auto=download.

Kirste, Imke, Zeina Nicola, Golo Kronenberg, Tara L. Walker, Robert C. Liu, Gerd
Kempermann. "Is Silence Golden? Effects of Auditory Stimuli and Their Absence
on Adult Hippocampal Neurogenesis." *Brain Structure & Function* 220, no.2 (March
2015): 1221–1228. https://pubmed.ncbi.nlm.nih.gov/24292324/.

Knight, Richard. "Biodiversity Loss: How Accurate Are the Numbers?" *BBC News*.
April 25, 2012. https://www.bbc.com/news/magazine-17826898.

Kogevinas, Manolis. "Probable Carcinogenicity of Glyphosate." *BMJ* 365, l161 (April 8,
2019). https://doi.org/10.1136/bmj.l1613.

Kolbert, Elizabeth. "Why Facts Don't Change Our Minds." *The New Yorker*.
February 17, 2017. https://www.newyorker.com/magazine/2017/02/27/
why-facts-dont-change-our-minds?utm_campaign=falcon&utm_source=face-
book&utm_brand=tny&utm_medium=social&utm_social-type=owned&m-
bid=social_facebook&fbclid.

Large, John. "German 12-Year-old Boy Plants 1Million Trees, Takes Over UN Program
to Plant a Trillion More." Good News Network. July 1, 2018. https://www.good-
newsnetwork.org/german-12-year-old-boy-plants-1million-trees-takes-over-un-pro-
gram-to-plant-a-trillion-more/?fbclid.

Lawton, Graham. "If We Label Eco-Anxiety as an Illness, Climate Denialists Have
Won." New Scientist. October 9, 2019. https://www.newscientist.com/article/
mg24432512-900-if-we-label-eco-anxiety-as-an-illness-climate-denialists-have-
won/#ixzz6AhS6CRKp.

Lear, Linda. *Rachel Carson: Witness for Nature*. New York: Mariner Books, 1997.

Le Guern, Claire. "When the Mermaids Cry: The Great Plastic Tide." Coastal Care.
November 2019. http://plastic-pollution.org/.

Levin, Kelly. "New Global CO2 Emissions Numbers Are In. They're Not Good."
World Resources Institute. December 5, 2018. https://www.wri.org/
blog/2018/12/new-global-co2-emissions-numbers-are-they-re-not-good.

Linaman, Todd. "Is It Anger or Unresolved Grief?" Relational Advantage. October 1, 2015. https://www.relationaladvantage.com/blog/is-it-anger-or-unresolved-grief.

Llosa, Patty de. "The Neurobiology of 'We'." https://www.drdansiegel.com/uploads/The Neurobiology of We - Patty de Llosa.pdf.

Lorinez, Tamara. "Demilitarization for Deep Decarbonization." International Peace Bureau. September 2014. http://www.ipb.org/wpcontent/uploads/2017/03/Green_Booklet_working_paper_17.09.2014.pdf

Loudenbeck, Tanza, and Abby Jackson. "The 10 Most Critical Problems in the World, According to Millennials." *Business Insider.* February 26, 2018. https://www.businessinsider.com/world-economic-forum-world-biggest-problems-concerning-millennials-2016-8.

MacGillivray, Greg. "The Camping Trip that Changed the Nation." MacGillivray Freeman's National Parks Adventure. Video, 1:50. https://nationalparksadventure.com/the-camping-trip-that-changed-the-nation/.

MacMillan, Amanda. "The Simple Habit That Can Help You Fight Depression." Health. March 14, 2018. https://www.health.com/depression/mindfulness-meditation-depression.

Macy, Joanna., and Chris Johnstone. *Active Hope: How to Face the Mess We're in without Going Crazy.* Novato, CA: New World Library, 2012.

Macy, Joanna., and Peter Reason and Melanie Newman, eds. *Stories of the Great Turning.* London and Philadelphia: Jessica Kingsley Publishers, 2016.

———. *Greening of the Self.* Berkeley, Ca.: Parallax Press, 2013.

———. "The Greening of the Self." *Engaged Buddhist Reader: Ten Years of Engaged Buddhist Publishing.* Berkeley, California: Parallax Press, 1996.

Horváth, Hacsi. "Marion Woodman: Holding the Tension of the Opposites." Recorded in 1991, posted June 18, 2018. YouTube video, 14:10. https://www.youtube.com/watch?v=ITQ7C8ibDFY&t=17shttps://www.youtube.com/watch?v=ITQ7C8ibDFY&t=17s.

Marlow, Kellee and Véronica Duport Deliz, dir. *Art of Courage.* 2015. http://artofcouragemovie.com/.

Marshall, Alan. "Climate Change: The 40 Year Delay Between Cause and Effect." Skeptical Science. September 22, 2010. https://skepticalscience.com/Climate-Change-The-40-Year-Delay-Between-Cause-and-Effect.html.

Marshall, Michael. "Animal Populations Have Fallen 60 Percent and That's Bad Even if They Don't Go Extinct." *Forbes.* October 30, 2018. https://www.forbes.com/sites/michaelmarshalleurope/2018/10/30/animal-populations-have-fallen-60-per-cent-and-thats-bad-even-if-they-dont-go-extinct/ - 1613bd4c4cf1.

Mauritsen, Thorsten and Robert Pincus. "Committed Warming Inferred from Observations." *Nature Climate Change* 7, 652–655 (2017), http://doi.org/10.1038/nclimate3357.

Mazur, Laurie. "Despairing about the Climate Crisis? Read This: A Conversation with Scientist Susanne Moser about Climate Communication, the Benefits of Functional Denial, and the Varied Flavors of Hope." *Earth Island Journal* (Winter 2020). http://www.earthisland.org/journal/index.php/articles/entry/despairing-about-climate-crisis?fbclid=IwAR3wFUMun1gC-bzUxVpxz2m-UygJ_jBEuw1-3bD71lmq-2li-j2O-mvdbFQk.

McBride, Karyl. "The Long-Term Impact of Neglectful Parents." *Psychology Today*. August 21, 2017. https://www.psychologytoday.com/us/blog/the-legacy-distorted-love/201708/the-long-term-impact-neglectful-parents.

McCarthy, Julie. "A Lifetime of Planting Trees on a Remote River Island: Meet India's Forest Man." *National Public Radio's Morning Edition*. December 26, 2017. https://www.npr.org/sections/parallels/2017/12/26/572421590/hed-take-his-own-life-before-killing-a-tree-meet-india-s-forest-man.

McDougall, Dan. "'Ecological Grief': Greenland Residents Traumatized By Climate Emergency." *The Guardian*. August 12, 2019. https://www.theguardian.com/society/ng-interactive/2019/aug/12/life-on-thin-ice-mental-health-at-the-heart-of-the-climate-crisis?fbclidI.

McMahon, Jeff. "We Have Five Years to Save Ourselves from Climate Change, Harvard Scientist Says." *Forbes*. January 15, 2018. https://www.forbes.com/sites/jeffmcmahon/2018/01/15/carbon-pollution-has-shoved-the-climate-backward-at-least-12-million-years-harvard-scientist-says/?fbclid.

McPherson, Guy. "Time For a Revolution." Nature Bats Last. May 28, 2009. https://guymcpherson.com/2009/05/time-for-a-revolution/.

Meixler, Eli. "'A Tipping Point' Greenland's Ice Is Melting Much Faster than Previously Thought, Scientists Say." *Time*. January 22, 2019. http://time.com/5509148/greenland-ice-melting-four-times-faster/?fbclid.

Miller, Brandon. "Earth Just Experienced One of the Warmest Years on Record." *CNN*. February 6, 2019. https://www.cnn.com/2019/02/06/world/2018-global-temp-hottest-year-noaa-nasa/index.html.

Mills, Mark P. "'You Say You Want a Revolution' in the Physics of Energy: Good Luck Green New Deal." *Forbes*. February 28, 2019. https://www.forbes.com/sites/markpmills/2019/02/28/you-say-you-want-a-revolution-in-the-physics-of-energy-good-luck-green-new-deal/?fbclid.

Minthorn, Robin Starr, and Alicia Fedelina Chávez, eds. *Indigenous Leadership in Higher Education*. New York: Routledge, 2015.

Monbiot, George. "For the Sake of Life on Earth, We Must Put a Limit on Wealth." *The Guardian.* September 19, 2019. https://www.theguardian.com/commentis-free/2019/sep/19/life-earth-wealth-megarich-spending-power-environmental-damage?fbclid.

Montaigne, Fen. "Will Deforestation and Warming Push the Amazon to a Tipping Point?" Yale Environment 360. September 4, 2019. https://e360.yale.edu/features/will-deforestation-and-warming-push-the-amazon-to-a-tipping-point.

Mooney, Chris. "A Key Antarctic Glacier Just Lost a Huge Piece of Ice—the Latest Sign of its Worrying Retreat." *The Washington Post.* September 25, 2017. https://www.washingtonpost.com/news/energy-environment/wp/2017/09/25/a-key-antarctic-glacier-just-lost-a-piece-of-ice-four-times-the-size-of-manhattan/?utm_term=.b732c8b67918.

———. "The Radical Political Implications of Spending Time Outdoors." *The Washington Post.* March 6, 2015. https://www.washingtonpost.com/news/energy-environment/wp/2015/03/06/the-radical-political-implications-of-spending-time-outdoors/?utm_term=.595d431a9df7.

Mui, Chunka. "3 Reasons There Might Be No Path to Success on Climate Change." *Forbes.* October 1, 2019. https://www.forbes.com/sites/chunk-amui/2019/10/01/3-reasons-there-might-be-no-path-to-success-on-climate change/?fbclid.

Muir, John. *My First Summer in the Sierra.* Boston and New York: Houghton Mifflin Co., 1911. Quoted in Laura Moncur's *Motivational Quotations.* http://www.quotation-spage.com/quote/41720.html.

M2020. "The Climate Turning Point." Mission2020. April 2017. https://mission2020.global/climate-turning-point/.

Nakazawa, Donna Jackson. "7 Ways Childhood Adversity Changes a Child's Brain." ACES Too High News. September 8, 2016. https://acestoohigh.com/2016/09/08/7-ways-childhood-adversity-changes-a-childs-brain/.

The National Academies Press. *Understanding Child Abuse and Neglect.* Washington, DC: The National Academies Press, 1993. https://www.nap.edu/read/2117/chapter/8.

National Geographic. "Causes and Effects of Climate Change." Video, 2:49. https://video.nationalgeographic.com/video/101-videos/0000015d-3cb1-d1cb-a7fd-fcfd49980000.

National History Museum. "Scientists Say We Will Face Worse Pandemics Than COVID-19 Unless We Protect Nature." National History Museum. April 29, 2020. https://www.nhm.ac.uk/discover/news/2020/april/we-will-face-worse-than-covid-19-unless-we-protect-nature.html?utm_source=fb-link-post-20200514-kp&utm_medium=social&utm_campaign=news&fbclid.

National Oceanic and Atmospheric Association. "July 2019 Was Hottest Month on Record for the Planet," National Oceanic and Atmospheric Assocation. August 15, 2019. https://www.noaa.gov/news/july-2019-was-hottest-month-on-record-for-planet.

The Nature Conservancy. "Poll Suggests Kids Need to Get Outdoors and Play!" Nancy Stewart Books. October 23, 2011. https://nancystewartbooks.blogspot.com/2011/10/poll-sugests-kids-need-to-get-outdoors.html.

Nelson, Marilee. "Fragrance Is the New Secondhand Smoke." Branch Basics. January 4, 2015. https://branchbasics.com/blog/fragrance-is-the-new-secondhand-smoke/.

Neuhauser, Alan. "Despite Climate Pledges, Global Energy Emissions on the Rise." U.S. News & World Report. November 12, 2018. https://www.usnews.com/national-issues/energy-environment/articles/2018-11-12/despite-climate-pledges-global-energy-emissions-on-the-rise?fbclid.

New York State Writers Institute. "Neuroscientist Joseph LeDoux on Anxiety and Fear." New York State Writers Institute. September 28, 2016. Youtube video, 14:12. https://www.youtube.com/watch?v=87xF-wB9LEs.

*New York Times* Archives. "Atomic Education Urged by Einstein; Scientist in Plea for $200,000 to Promote New Type of Essential Thinking." *The New York Times.* May 25, 1946. https://www.nytimes.com/1946/05/25/archives/atomic-education-urged-by-einstein-scientist-in-plea-for-200000-to.html.

Nield, David. "Last Time Carbon Emissions Were This High, the Dinosaurs Went Extinct." Science Alert. March 23, 2016. https://www.sciencealert.com/carbon-emissions-now-higher-than-they-ve-been-since-the-dinosaurs-went-extinct.

*New Scientist* Staff and Press Association. "A Massive Iceberg Just Broke off Antarctica's Larsen C Ice Shelf." *New Scientist.* July 12, 2017. https://www.newscientist.com/article/2140457-a-massive-iceberg-just-broke-off-antarcticas-larsen-c-ice-shelf/.

NOAA National Centers for Environmental Information. "Global Climate Report-March 2020." NOAA National Centers for Environmental Information. April 2020. https://www.ncdc.noaa.gov/sotc/global/202003/supplemental/page-2.

Nuñez, Christina, and Leticia Pfeffer. "13 Amazing Coming of Age Traditions From Around the World." Global Citizen. July 21, 2016. https://www.globalcitizen.org/en/content/13-amazing-coming-of-age-traditions-from-around-th/.

Nyman, Patti. "Methane vs. Carbon Dioxide: A Greenhouse Gas Showdown." OneGreenPlanet.org. http://www.onegreenplanet.org/animalsandnature/methane-vs-carbon-dioxide-a-greenhouse-gas-showdown/.

Ocko, Ilissa. "UN Special Report Confirms Urgent Need to Reduce Methane Emissions." Environmental Defense Fund. October 11, 2018. http://blogs.edf.org/

energyexchange/2018/10/11/un-special-report-confirms-urgent-need-to-reduce-methane-emissions/.

O'Kane, Caitlin. "Ethiopia Plants 350 Million Trees in 12 Hours, Breaking World Record." *CBS News.* July 30, 2019. https://www.cbsnews.com/news/ethiopia-plants-350-million-trees-12-hours-breaking-world-record-2019-07-30/.

Oliver, Tom. "The Age of the Individual Must End – Our World Depends on It." *The Guardian.* January 16, 2020. https://www.theguardian.com/books/2020/jan/16/the-age-of-the-individual-must-end-tom-oliver-the-self-delusion?fbclid.

Orangutan Foundation International Australia. "Why Are Orangutans in Danger of Becoming Extinct?," Orangutan Foundation International Australia. Accessed December 2019. https://orangutanfoundation.org.au/why-are-orangutans-in-danger-of-becoming-extinct/.

Oppenheimer, Michel. "Avoiding Two Degrees of Warming 'Is Now Totally Unrealistic'." *The Atlantic.* June 3, 2017. https://www.theatlantic.com/science/archive/2017/06/oppenheimer-interview/529083/.

Orban, Ester, Kelsey McDonald, Robynne Sutcliffe, Barbara Hoffmann, Kateryna B. Fulks, Nico Dragano, Anja Viehmann, et al. "Residential Road Traffic Noise and High Depressive Symptoms after Five Years of Follow-up: Results from the Heinz Nixdorf Recall Study." *Environmental Health Perspectives* 124 no. 5 (May 1, 2016). https://doi.org/10.1289/ehp.1409400.

OXFAM International. "World's Richest 10% Produce Half of Carbon Emissions While Poorest 3.5 Billion Account for Just a Tenth." OXFAM International. Last modified December 2, 2015. https://www.oxfam.org/en/press-releases/worlds-richest-10-produce-half-carbon-emissions-while-poorest-35-billion-account.

Paddon, Christopher. "The Earth Wisdom of Male Initiation." Titanic Lifeboat Academy. July 19, 2016. https://titaniclifeboatacademy.org/index.php/home-port/big-picture/19-articles/techno-socio-milieu/46-the-earth-wisdom-of-male-initiation.html.

Pagett, Norman. "Humankind Is on the Road to Nowhere." Medium. June 29, 2018. https://medium.com/@End_of_More/an-infinity-of-futility-5fb525fc610c.

Pakalolo. "A Glacier the Size of Florida Is on Track to Change the Course of Human Civilization." Daily Kos. April 1, 2019. https://www.dailykos.com/stories/2019/4/1/1841208/-A-glacier-the-size-of-Florida-is-on-track-to-change-the-course-of-human-civilization.

Palmer, Scott. "Insectageddon: New Zealanders Have 'Two Weeks of Life' after Insect Apocalypse – Expert." Newshub. December 2, 2019. https://www.newshub.co.nz/home/new-zealand/2019/02/insectageddon-new-zealanders-have-two-weeks-of-life-after-insect-apocalypse-expert.html?fbclid.

Parker, Laura and Craig Welch. "Coral Reefs Could Be Gone in 30 Years." *National Geographic*. June 23, 2017. https://news.nationalgeographic.com/2017/06/coral-reef-bleaching-global-warming-unesco-sites/.

"The Persona." http://psikoloji.fisek.com.tr/jung/persona.htm.

Pesticide Action Network North America. "Farmworkers Represent the Backbone And Marrow of Our Agricultural Economy. Yet This Group Is One of the Least Protected from on-the-Job Harms—Including Exposure to Pesticides." Pesticide Action Network North America. https://www.panna.org/frontline-communities/farmworkers.

Peters, Adele. "These Tree-Planting Drones Are Firing Seed Missiles to Restore the World's Forests." FastCompany. April 10, 2019. https://www.fastcompany.com/90329982/these-tree-planting-drones-are-firing-seed-missiles-to-restore-the-worlds-forests.

Peterson, Jordan B. Quoted on Instagram. Posted September 18, 2019. https://www.instagram.com/p/B2kEdVql0EY/?hl=en.

Pierre-Louis, Kendra. "Ocean Warming Is Accelerating Faster than Thought, New Research Finds." *The New York Times*. January 10, 2019. https://www.nytimes.com/2019/01/10/climate/ocean-warming-climate-change.html.

Plumer, Brad. "Carbon Dioxide Emissions Hit a Record in 2019, Even as Coal Fades." New York Times. December 3, 2019. https://www.nytimes.com/2019/12/03/climate/carbon-dioxide-emissions.html.

Popescu, Adam. "This Scientist Thinks She Has the Key to Curb Climate Change: Super Plants." *The Guardian*. April 16, 2019. https://www.theguardian.com/environment/2019/apr/16/super-plants-climate-change-joanne-chory-carbon-dioxide.

Purves, D., G.J. Augustine, D. Fitzpatrick, et al., eds., "The Interplay of Emotion and Reason," in *Neuroscience*, 2nd ed., Sunderland, MA: Sinauer Associates, 2001.

Queally, Jon. "What's Not in the Latest Terrifying IPCC Report? The 'Much, Much, Much More Terrifying' New Research on Climate Tipping Points." Common Dreams. October 19, 2018. https://www.commondreams.org/news/2018/10/09/whats-not-latest-terrifying-ipcc-report-much-much-much-more-terrifying-new-research.

Rae, Kerwin. "Why It's Time To Think About Human Extinction / Dr. David Suzuki." YouTube video, 1:00:24. December 16, 2018. https://www.youtube.com/watch?v=ktnAMTmgOX0&t=631s.

Reese, Hope. "Naomi Klein: We Are Sleepwalking toward Apocalypse." JSTOR Daily. September 18, 2019. https://daily.jstor.org/naomi-klein-we-are-sleepwalking-toward-apocalypse/?fbclid.

Reid, Adam Greydon. "'The Addicted World' Clip from 'Marion Woodman: Dancing in the Flames.'" July 6, 2010. YouTube video, 2:30. https://www.youtube.com/watch?v=z3h4n-_NEgU.

Richardson, John H. "When the End of Human Civilization Is Your Day Job." *Esquire.* July 20, 2018. https://www.esquire.com/news-politics/a36228/ballad-of-the-sad-climatologists-0815/.

Richo, David. *How to Be an Adult in Relationships: The Five Keys to Mindful Relationships.* Boston: Shambhala, 2002. Quoted at The Daily Om, https://www.dailyom.com/cgi-bin/display/librarydisplay.cgi?lid=1707.

———. *When the Past Is Present: Healing the Emotional Wounds that Sabotage our Relationships* Boston: Shambhala Publications, 2008.

Ricke, Katharine L. and Ken Caldeira. "Maximum Warming Occurs About One Decade After a Carbon Dioxide Emission." *Environmental Research Letters* 9, no. 12 (December 2, 2014). https://iopscience.iop.org/article/10.1088/1748-9326/9/12/124002.

Riebeck, Holly. "The Ocean's Carbon Balance." NASA Earth Observatory. July 1, 2008. https://earthobservatory.nasa.gov/features/OceanCarbon.

Rignot, Eric, Jérémie Mouginot, Bernd Scheuchl, Michiel van den Broeke, Melchior J. van Wessem and Mathieu Morlighem. "Four Decades of Antarctic Ice Sheet Mass Balance from 1979–2017." *Proceedings of the National Academy of Sciences of the United States of America* 116, no. 4 (January 22, 2019): 1095-1103. https://doi.org/10.1073/pnas.1812883116.

Robson, David. "The '3.5% Rule': How a Small Minority Can Change the World." BBC Future. May 13, 2019. https://www.bbc.com/future/article/20190513-it-only-takes-35-of-people-to-change-the-world.

Roosevelt, Franklin D. "Inaugural Address, March 4, 1933." in *The Public Papers of Franklin D. Roosevelt, Volume Two: The Year of Crisis, 1933.* Samuel Rosenman, ed. New York: Random House, 1938.

Rosenthal, Neil. "Relationships: Hurt People Hurt Others." *The Denver Post.* August 25, 2016. https://www.denverpost.com/2016/08/25/relationships-hurt-people-hurt-others/.

Rosin, Hanna. "The End Of Empathy." *National Public Radio.* April 15, 2019. https://www.npr.org/2019/04/15/712249664/the-end-of-empathy?utm_source=facebook.com&utm_medium=social&utm_campaign=npr&utm_term=nprnews&utm_content=20190415&fbclid.

Saha, Raj. "The Permafrost bomb is Ticking." Yale Climate Communications. February 2018. https://www.yaleclimateconnections.org/2018/02/the-permafrost-bomb-is-ticking/.

Samenow, Jason. "Red-hot Planet: All-Time Heat Records Have Been Set All Over the World During the Past Week." *The Washington Post*. July 5, 2018. https://www.washingtonpost.com/news/capital-weather-gang/wp/2018/07/03/hot-planet-all-time-heat-records-have-been-set-all-over-the-world-in-last-week/?noredirect=on&utm_term=.a9b031299ea3.

Sample, Ian. "Scientists Offered to Dispute Climate Study." *The Guardian*. February 2, 2007. https://www.theguardian.com/environment/2007/feb/02/frontpagenews.climatechange.

Sanders, U.S. Senator Bernie. Facebook. March 31, 2019. https://m.facebook.com/story.php?story_fbid=10157792158047908&id=9124187907&ref=m_notif.

Sanchez-Bayo, Francisco and Kris A.G. Wyckhuys. "Worldwide Decline Of the Entomofauna: A Review Of Its Drivers." *Biological Conservation* 232 (April 2019): 8-27. https://doi.org/10.1016/j.biocon.2019.01.020.

Sanchez, Erica and Madeleine Keck. "Australia Will Plant 1 Billion Trees to Combat Climate Change." Global Citizen. February 20, 2019. https://www.globalcitizen.org/en/content/australia-will-plant-1-billion-trees/?fbclid.

Schalk, Cloete. "An Independent Global Energy Forecast to Compare with the IEA's WEO 2019." Energypost.eu. September 5, 2019. https://energypost.eu/an-independent-global-energy-forecast-to-2050-to-compare-with-the-ieas-weo-2018/?fbclid=IwAR3UYEFBhvRX0Q2464YTFsy06RztnDAOVvRXgsjmk8NrZOmgmwF-DAshh_IM.

Schwartz, Tony. "I Wrote 'The Art of the Deal' with Trump. His Self-Sabotage Is Rooted In His Past." *The Washington Post*. May 16, 2017. https://www.washingtonpost.com/posteverything/wp/2017/05/16/i-wrote-the-art-of-the-deal-with-trump-his-self-sabotage-is-rooted-in-his-past/?utm_term=.80790d02bf9f.

Shakhova, Natalia, I. Semiletov, A. Salyuk, D. Kosmach. "Anomalies of Methane In the Atmosphere Over the East Siberian Shelf: Is There Any Sign Of Methane Leakage from Shallow Shelf Hydrates?" *Geophysical Research Abstracts* 10, EGU2008-A-01526, (2008). https://meetings.copernicus.org/www.cosis.net/abstracts/EGU2008/01526/EGU2008-A-01526.pdf.

Shakhova, Natalia, Igor Semiletov, and Evgeny Chuvilin. "Understanding the Permafrost–Hydrate System and Associated Methane Releases In the East Siberian Arctic Shelf." *Geosciences* 9, no.6 (2019): 251. https://doi.org/10.3390/geosciences9060251.

Siegel, Daniel J. *Pocket Guide to Interpersonal Neurobiology: an Integrative Handbook of the Mind*. New York: W.W. Norton & Company, 2012.

———. "The Neurological Basis of Behavior, the Mind, the Brain and Human Relationships." The Garrison Institute. March 9, 2011. Video, 54:48. https://www.youtube.com/watch?v=B7kBgaZLHaA&t=1449s).

Sigurdson, Tina. "Expert Panel Confirms Fragrance Ingredient Can Cause Cancer." EWG News and Analysis. August 2014. https://www.ewg.org/enviroblog/2014/08/expert-panel-confirms-fragrance-ingredient-can-cause-cancer-.W4jL25NKjOQ.

Sliwa, Jim. "Climate Change's Toll on Mental Health." American Psychological Association. March 29, 201. https://www.apa.org/news/press/releases/2017/03/climate-mental-health.aspx.

Smith, Phoenix. "We all must strengthen ourselves" Facebook, September, 2019.

Sneed, Annie. "Get Ready for More Volcanic Eruptions As the Planet Warms." *Scientific American*. Last modified December 21, 2017. https://www.scientificamerican.com/article/get-ready for-more-volcanic-eruptions-as-the-planet-warms/.

The Soil Association. "The Impact of Glyphosate on Soil Health: the Evidence to Date." The Soil Association. https://www.soilassociation.org/media/7202/glyphosate-and-soil-health-full-report.pdf.

Solomon, Andrew. "Depression, the Secret We Share." TEDxMet. October 2013. Video, 29:14. https://www.ted.com/talks/andrew_solomon_depression_the_secret_we_share?language=en.

Solomon, Sheldon. "Ernest Becker & The Denial of Death." PangeaProgressRedux. October 2, 2011. Video, 1:00:36. https://www.youtube.com/watch?v=X-pVkrIdz9-Y.

Somé, Sobonfu. "Embracing Grief: Surrendering to Your Sorrow Has the Power to Heal the Deepest of Wounds." Sobonfu Somé. http://www.sobonfu.com/articles/writings-by-sobonfu-2/embracing-grief/.

State of New York Department of Environmental Conservation. "What Is Carbon Capture and Sequestration?" State of New York Department of Environmental Conservation. https://www.dec.ny.gov/docs/lands_forests_pdf/ccspamphlet.pdf.

Stevens, Jane Ellen. "Nearly 35 Million U.S. Children Have Experienced One Or More Types of Childhood Trauma." ACES Too High News. May 13, 2013. https://acestoohigh.com/2013/05/13/nearly-35-million-u-s-children-have-experienced-one-or-more-types-of-childhood-trauma/.

Stone, Maddie. "Climate Change Fueled the Australia Fires. Now Those Fires Are Fueling Climate Change." Grist. January 10, 2020. https://grist.org/climate/climate-change-fueled-the-australia-fires-now-those-fires-are-fueling-climate-change/?fbclid.

Survival International. "Survival Condemns Steven Pinker's 'Brutal Savage' Myth." Fair Planet. July 13, 2013. https://www.fairplanet.org/story/survival-condemns-steven-pinkers-brutal-savage-myth/.

Suttie, Jill. "How Does Valuing Money Affect Your Happiness?." *Greater Good Magazine*. October 30, 2017. https://greatergood.berkeley.edu/article/item/how_does_valuing_money_affect_your_happiness.

Suttie, Jill. "How to Raise an Environmentalist." *Greater Goods Magazine*. September 14, 2016. https://greatergood.berkeley.edu/article/item/how_to_raise_an_environmentalist.

Taft, Victoria. "Treasury Secretary Just Stated Obvious About Teen Environmental Oracle Greta Thunberg and the Left Is Melting Down." PJ Media. January 23, 2020. https://pjmedia.com/trending/treasury-secretary-just-stated-obvious-about-teen-environmental-oracle-greta-thunberg-the-left-is-melting-down/.

Taylor, Jim. "Technology: Virtual vs. Real Life: You Choose." *Psychology Today*. May 31, 2011. https://www.psychologytoday.com/us/blog/the-power-prime/201105/technology-virtual-vs-real-life-you-choose.

Than, Ker. "Depressed? Go Play in the Dirt." LiveScience. April 11, 2007. https://www.livescience.com/7270-depressed-play-dirt.html.

Timsit, Annabelle. "These Millennials Are Going on 'Birth Strike' Because of Climate Change." Quartz. April 14, 2019. https://qz.com/1590642/these-millennials-are-going-on-birth-strike-due-to-climate-change/.

Tollefson, Jeff. "First Sun-Dimming Experiment Will Test a Way to Cool Earth." *Nature 563* (November 27, 2018): 613-615. https://www.nature.com/articles/d41586-018-07533-4.

Trillion Trees. "One Trillion Trees Re-Grown, Saved from Loss and Better Protected Around the World by 2050." Trillion Trees. https://www.trilliontrees.org/.

Trisos, Christopher H., Giuseppe Amatulli, Jessica Gurevitch, Alan Robock, Lili Xia, Brian Zambri. "Potentially Dangerous Consequences For Biodiversity of Solar Geoengineering Implementation and Termination." *Nature Ecology & Evolution* 2 (January 22, 2018): 475–482. https://www.nature.com/articles/s41559-017-0431-0.

Trout, Kelly and Lorne Stockman. "Drilling Toward Disaster: Why U.S. Oil and Gas Expansion Is Incompatible With Climate Limits." Oil Change International. January 2019. http://priceofoil.org/content/uploads/2019/01/Drilling-Toward-Disaster-Web-v3.pdf?fbclid=IwAR3-v5td_d6sjfIeaFzRRz8aXMquS35X-F0B-2aXZtbQGwyQRwyWUTAHxGrI.

Tutton, Mark. "Stronger Hurricanes Could Decimate Forests and Accelerate Climate Change, Warns Study." *CNN*. March 25, 2019. https://edition.cnn.com/2019/03/25/health/hurricane-maria-forest-climate/index.html.

Union of Concerned Scientists. "Climate Change, Extreme Precipitation and Flooding: The Latest Science." Union of Concerned Scientists. July 2, 2018. https://

www.ucsusa.org/global-warming/global-warming-impacts/floods - .XFTfX-89KjOQ.

United Nations Environment Programme. "Cut Global Emissions By 7.6 Percent Every Year For Next Decade to Meet 1.5°C Paris Target - UN Report." United Nations Environment Programme. November 26, 2019. https://www.unenvironment.org/news-and-stories/press-release/cut-global-emissions-76-percent-every-year-next-decade-meet-15degc.

University of Colorado at Boulder. "Healthy, Stress-Busting Fat Found Hidden in Dirt." ScienceDaily. Accessed January 13, 2020. www.sciencedaily.com/releases/2019/05/190529094003.htm.

University of Hawaii at Manoa. "Bitcoin Can Push Global Warming above 2 C in a Couple Decades." Phys.org. October 29, 2018. https://phys.org/news/2018-10-bitcoin-global-couple-decades.html.

U.S. Environmental Protection Agency. "Global Greenhouse Gas Emissions Data," U.S. Environmental Protection Agency. January 19, 2017. https://www.epa.gov/ghgemissions/global-greenhouse-gas-emissions-data.

Vyawahare, Malavika, and Valisoa Rasolofomboahangy. "Madagascar Is Planting 60 Million Trees in Ambitious Drive Inspired by Its President." EcoWatch. January 21, 2020. https://www.ecowatch.com/madagascar-tree-planting-2644879937.html?xrs=RebelMouse_fb&ts=1579616572&fbclid.

Wallace-Wells, David. "The Uninhabitable Earth: Famine, Economic Collapse, a Sun That Cooks Us: What Climate Change Could Wreak—Sooner Than You Think." New York Intelligencer. July 2017. http://nymag.com/intelligencer/2017/07/climate-change-earth-too-hot-for humans.html?fbclid=IwAR1L-HxCSZY_9Q717mNx6HA6EVKh-DN9OK6rt3ON0JvNfdMKpqbQvmzS8x_c.

———. "Time to Panic: The Planet is Getting Warmer in Catastrophic Ways. And Fear May Be the Only Thing That Saves us," *The New York Times*. February 16, 2019. https://www.nytimes.com/2019/02/16/opinion/sunday/fear-panic-climate-change-warming.html.

Walker, Pete. "13 Steps for Managing Flashbacks." Pete Walker, M.A., MFT. Accessed December 2019. http://pete-walker.com/13StepsManageFlashbacks.htm.

Wamsley, Laurel. "New Zealand Commits to Being Carbon Neutral by 2050—With a Big Loophole." *National Public Radio*. November 7, 2019. https://www.npr.org/2019/11/07/777259573/new-zealand-commits-to-being-carbon-neutral-by-2050-with-a-big-loophole.

Watson, Johanna. *Child Neglect: Literature Review.* Ashfield, NSW: NSW Department of Community Services, 2005. http://www.community.nsw.gov.au/__data/assets/pdf_file/0003/321636/research_child_neglect.pdf.

Watts, Jonathan. "Greta Thunberg, Schoolgirl Climate Change Warrior: 'Some People Can Let Things Go. I Can't'." *The Guardian*. March 11, 2019. https://www.theguardian.com/world/2019/mar/11/greta-thunberg-schoolgirl-climate-change-warrior-some-people-can-let-things-go-i-cant.

———. "Risks of 'Domino Effect' of Tipping Points Greater Than Thought, Study Says." *The Guardian*. December 20, 2018. https://www.theguardian.com/environment/2018/dec/20/risks-of-domino-effect-of-tipping-points-greater-than-thought-study-says?fbclid.

———. "Wildfires Rage In Arctic Circle As Sweden Calls For Help." *The Guardian*. July 18, 2018. https://www.theguardian.com/world/2018/jul/18/sweden-calls-for-help-as-arctic-circle-hit-by-wildfires.

Weber, Jack Adam. "Thanksgiving: An Activist's Grace." Wake Up World. November 27, 2011. https://wakeup-world.com/2011/11/27/thanksgiving-an-activists-grace/.

Weston, Phoebe. "'They Should Be Allowed to Cry': Ecological Disaster Taking Toll On Scientists' Mental Health." *The Independent*. October 10, 2019. https://www.independent.co.uk/environment/ecological-disaster-mental-health-awareness-day-scientists-climate-change-grief-a9150266.html?fbclid=IwAR08a-I4j-jnTeWAQ-qUJPv4hb65T4r_8KuXEYVZXNBO3xj1oVp1aggY4afk.

White, Benjamin. "States of Emergency: Trauma and Climate Change." *Ecopsychology* 7, no. 4 (December 30, 2015). https://www.liebertpub.com/doi/abs/10.1089/eco.2015.0024.

Whitmore-Williams, Susan Clayton,; Christie Manning, Kirra Krygsman, Meighen Speiser. "Mental Health and Our Changing Climate: Impacts, Implications, and Guidance." American Psychological Association, Climate for Health, EcoAmerica. March 2017. https://www.apa.org/news/press/releases/2017/03/mental-health-climate.pdf.

Wolchover, Natalie. "A World Without Clouds." Quantamagazine. February 25, 2019. https://www.quantamagazine.org/cloud-loss-could-add-8-degrees-to-global-warming-20190225/?fbclid=IwAR3_NzHGAbpnKDbQV6hzO5YWbEu81F0g-ZB3sqXL8tPWlZM402YT7FWhJ_K4.

Wolpert, Stuart. "UCLA Neuroscientist's Book Explains Why Social Connection Is As Important As Food and Shelter." *UCLA Newsroom*. October 10, 2013. http://newsroom.ucla.edu/releases/we-are-hard-wired-to-be-social-248746.

Wood, Harold. "Quotations from John Muir." The John Muir Exhibit. Accessed December 2019. https://vault.sierraclub.org/john_muir_exhibit/writings/favorite_quotations.aspx.

Woodman, Marion. "Essay: Why is True Equality Taking so Long?" New Thought Evolutionary. Accessed January 2020. https://newthoughtevolutionary.wordpress.com/tag/marion-woodman/.

———. "Holding the Tension of the Opposites." Hacsi Horváth. Posted June 18, 2018, originally filmed in 1991. YouTube video, 49:10. https://www.youtube.com/watch?v=ITQ7C8ibDFY&t=17s.

Woody, Todd. "Coral Cover on Great Barrier Reef Is in Steep Decline," News Deeply. July 5, 2018. https://www.newsdeeply.com/oceans/articles/2018/07/05/no-cover-corals-on-great-barrier-reef-hit-record-low.

World Meteorological Organization. "Landmark United in Science Report Informs Climate Action Summit." World Meteorological Organization. September 22, 2109. https://public.wmo.int/en/media/press-release/landmark-united-science-report-informs-climate-action-summit.

World Ocean Review. "Living with the Oceans. A Report On the State Of the World's Oceans." World Ocean Review. 2010. https://worldoceanreview.com/en/wor-1/coasts/living-in-coastal-areas/.

Yale School of Forestry & Environmental Studies. "It's Official: 2017 Was the Second Hottest Year on Record." YaleEnvironment360. January 4, 2018. https://e360.yale.edu/digest/its-official-2017-was-the-second-hottest-year-on-record.

Yale School of Forestry & Environmental Studies. "Wildfires in Bolivia Have Killed an Estimated 2 Million Animals So Far This Year." YaleEnvironment360. October 1, 2019. https://e360.yale.edu/digest/wildfires-in-bolivia-have-killed-an-estimated-2-million-animals-so-far-this-year.

Yeung, Jessie, Isaac Yee and Sheena McKenzie. "Thousands of Australian Residents Had to Take Refuge On a Beach as Wildfires Raged." CNN. December 31, 2019. https://www.cnn.com/2019/12/30/australia/australia-mallacoota-beach-fire-intl-hnk-scli/index.html.

Zuckerman, Jocelyn C. "As the Global Demand for Palm Oil Surges, Indonesia's Rainforests are Being Destroyed." Audubon. Fall 2016. https://www.audubon.org/magazine/fall-2016/as-global-demand-palm-oil-surges-indonesias.

#FridaysforFuture. "What We Do." #FridaysforFuture. Accessed December 2019. https://www.fridaysforfuture.org/about.

## To Write to the Author

If you wish to contact the author or would like more information about this book, please write to the author in care of Llewellyn Worldwide Ltd. and we will forward your request. Both the author and publisher appreciate hearing from you and learning of your enjoyment of this book and how it has helped you. Llewellyn Worldwide Ltd. cannot guarantee that every letter written to the author can be answered, but all will be forwarded. Please write to:

Jack Adam Weber
% Llewellyn Worldwide
2143 Wooddale Drive
Woodbury, MN 55125-2989
Please enclose a self-addressed stamped envelope for reply,
or $1.00 to cover costs. If outside the U.S.A., enclose
an international postal reply coupon.

Many of Llewellyn's authors have websites with additional
information and resources. For more information,
please visit our website at http://www.llewellyn.com